Germany's Role in the Euro Crisis

Franz-Josef Meiers

Germany's Role in the Euro Crisis

Berlin's Quest for a More Perfect Monetary Union

Springer

Franz-Josef Meiers
Institute of Political Science
Friedrich-Alexander University Erlangen-Nuremberg
Erlangen, Germany

ISBN 978-3-319-20513-7 ISBN 978-3-319-20514-4 (eBook)
DOI 10.1007/978-3-319-20514-4

Library of Congress Control Number: 2015949244

Springer Cham Heidelberg New York Dordrecht London

Printed on acid-free paper

Springer International Publishing AG Switzerland is part of Springer Science+Business Media (www.springer.com)

Preface

This book is a study of Germany's role in the euro crisis since 2009. It shows how the German economic model of ordoliberalism has shaped the perception of German decision makers and their response to the gathering storm within the currency union over the last 6 years. The peculiar concept of postwar Germany's stability culture has become the compass for German decision makers to pave their way through the brush of the crisis. West Germany's postwar economic success ("Wirtschaftswunder") under the ordoliberal economic doctrine made the maintenance of order in a social market economy and price stability enforced by an independent central bank and fiscal probity the Alpha and Omega of German economic policy. But the ordoliberal concept developed to meet the postwar challenges of the German economy lays open some structural limits and deficiencies of Germany's preferred strategy of expansionary fiscal contraction and internal devaluation, the distressed euro member countries where asked to adopt to reach the promised land.

For many observers, the euro crisis revealed another uncomfortable reality: Berlin's primacy. Germany as the continent's biggest economy has emerged from the crisis as the Union's undisputed economic and political powerhouse. Germany's preeminent role in the euro crisis management is again the subject of often deep and bitter contention in and outside of Europe. This book explicitly rejects the realist/pessimistic assessment that the Berlin Republic today behaves in a nineteenth and twentieth century fashion where it shows no qualms to pull the levers of power to push the European institutions and partners into preferred German interests and policy outcomes even if it meant a worsening of an already dire economic situation in the euro area's misery belt and a weakening of European institution. Reviving the German question in a new form not only reinforces old stereotypes, prejudices, and misconceptions about the role of Germany within the context of the euro-Atlantic institutions, but also leads to highly dubious and misleading conclusions that the Berlin Republic is drifting away from the "long road west" and that the German

Überpower can only be balanced by countervailing coalitions. These unfounded fears actually conceal the real challenges the Berlin Republic faces in putting the currency union on a lasting and stable foundation. I hope that my analysis will provide some useful insights of the paradoxes of German power for policy decision makers, experts in international organizations and think tanks, and students in and outside of Europe. The book has been written with the aim to provide a better understanding of the sources of German conduct and to draw appropriate conclusions for Germany's indispensable role within its principal institutional context.

Special mention must be made of the superb proofreading of Ms. Jane Ralph, B.A., M.A., Chartered Librarian at the Library of Political Science of the University Erlangen-Nürnberg. She has greatly improved the readability of my sometimes teutonic English. I am most grateful to the University Erlangen-Nürnberg which provided me an extremely stimulating academic environment that allowed me to write this book. I am deeply indebted to the Financial Times of its very informative coverage of and balanced commentaries, particularly of Martin Wolf, of the euro crisis. I also want to thank my editor Dr. Johannes Glaeser and his assistant Judith Kripp who have been supportive, competent, and patient in shepherding my manuscript through the labyrinth of the editorial process. Lastly, I recognize gratefully two anonymous reviewers for their highly valuable advice to make my analysis more concise. Any remaining errors and omissions are, of course, my own.

This book is dedicated to my wonderful wife Gisela and our two delightful children Friederike and Jean-Pascal.

Erlangen, Germany Franz-Josef Meiers

Contents

Chapter 1
Introduction: Europe's Powerhouse

What is good for Germany is also good for Europe.
Angela Merkel, September 11, 2014

Whatever is good for the eurozone economy is good for Germany.
Benoît Cœuré, January 16, 2015

When faith meets evidence, evidence doesn't stand a chance.
Mario Draghi, quoting Paul Krugman, January 15, 2015

There is nothing He (God) does not wish to be investigated and understood by reason.
Tertullian, quoted by Commissario Guido Brunetti in Donna Leon, By Its Cover, London: William Heinemann 2014, p. 151

Five years after the start of the crisis, there is a consensus that with the pledge of Mario Draghi, the head of the European Central Bank (ECB) "to do whatever it takes", the immediate threat of a breakup of the European Monetary Union (EMU) has receded. Not a single member, even Greece the worst pupil in the euro class, has been forced out. A sense of cautious optimism has returned to the euro area. Better than expected economic data and declining sovereign bond yields in crisis-hit countries of the eurozone since late 2013, have revived confidence that the nascent recovery is gaining momentum. The European Commission, the European Central Bank (ECB), the International Monetary Fund (IMF), and the Organization for Economic Cooperation and Development (OECD) foresee the annual real GDP increases by up to 1.2 % in 2014, compared with a decline of 0.4 % last year. Growth in 2015 and 2016 is seen at 1.5 % and close to 2 % respectively.[1] The eurozone governments reduced their budget deficits for 2013 to 3 % of Gross Domestic Product (GDP), in line with their target for the first time since 2008.[2] The eurozone is no longer under siege in financial markets. Borrowing costs for the economies of the euro misery belt—Portugal, Ireland, Italy, Greece and Spain

[1] European Commission (2014, pp. 1, 7), European Central Bank (2014a), International Monetary Fund (2014, p. 26), Organization for Economic Cooperation and Development (2014), Eurostat (2014a).

[2] Eurostat (2014b).

F.-J. Meiers, *Germany's Role in the Euro Crisis*,
DOI 10.1007/978-3-319-20514-4_1

(PIIGS)—have fallen to levels since the debt crisis erupted in early 2010. The high demand for eurozone periphery debt reflected rising confidence in the creditworthiness of euro area economies. Ireland, Spain and Portugal have exited their bailout programs and can now finance themselves in the bond markets. This leaves Greece and Cyprus as the only Eurozone countries now under assistance.

In a major change from his first year in office, French President François Hollande began to embrace the "German path" of fiscal austerity and business-friendly structural reforms.[3] He announced a "responsibility pact", that signalled a need to go "faster, further and deeper" by reducing labor costs, tackling onerous labor regulation, and cutting government spending by at least 50 billion euros between 2015 and 2017. "We need to produce more, and better. Action is therefore needed on supply. Yes, supply! This is not contradictory with demand. Supply even creates demand."[4] The new Italian Prime Minister Matteo Renzi also pledged an economic reform package including a 10 billion euros tax cut for low earners and a 10 % cut in labor costs paid by the private sector to boost stagnant growth and to stimulate depressed levels of private consumption. Most of the tax cuts, he pledged, would be funded by public spending cuts, higher taxes on capital income and increased VAT revenues.[5]

The German government in particular, feels vindicated that the medicine of rigorous and painful austerity—deep spending cuts and rising taxes, i.e. value-added tax, property taxes, business taxes—and a strengthening of competitiveness through wage cuts, sweeping reforms of the social security system and more flexible labour markets were essential to address the root cause of the sovereign debt crisis—fiscal profligacy—and to lay the foundation for steady and sustainable growth.[6] Chancellor Merkel praised Ireland and Spain as examples of how crisis countries could turn the corner from recession to recovery. "The successes of Ireland and Spain are just two examples what resolute action of individual countries and joint European backing could produce together." Hence, the principle that solidarity and individual responsibility belong together had turned out to be right.[7] "Efforts which were so painful, and for such a long time, are producing now some positive outcomes," declared Mario Draghi.[8] The eurozone crisis, though temporarily stabilized, is far from over. The shoots of recovery are still "very green", as Mario Draghi put it. When asked if the Eurozone's financial and economic crisis was over, he gave a guarded response. It was "premature to declare

[3] Frankenberger (2014), Evans-Pritchard (2014), Krugman (2014), Münchau (2014).

[4] Ouverture de la conférence de presse du président de la République au Palais de l'Élysée le 14 janvier 2014, Élysée, Paris, January 14, 2015. http://www.elysee.fr/declarations/article/ouverture-de-la-conference-de-presse-du-president-de-la-republique-au-palais-de-l-elysee-le-14-janvier-201/.

[5] Dinmore (2014), Yardley and Pianigiani (2014), Dinmore and Sanderson (2014).

[6] Schäuble (2013, 2015), Peel et al. (2013).

[7] Deutscher Bundestag (2013, p. 240), Deutscher Bundestag (2015, p. 8882).

[8] European Central Bank (2014b).

any victory". The region's gradual recovery was "still weak, still fragile, still uneven", "meaning that there are several risks."[9]

For many observers, the euro crisis revealed another uncomfortable reality: Berlin's primacy. Germany as the continent's biggest economy has emerged from the crisis as the Union's undisputed economic and political powerhouse. The perception of Berlin as the emerging capital of the European Union has raised three interrelated accusations. Firstly, Berlin's economics critics like Lawrence Summers, Paul Krugman, Martin Wolf or Joseph Stiglitz repeatedly warned that a fixation on debt and deficits would lead to a disturbing "Japanese" future of "secular stagnation" characterized by a prolonged period of slow growth, chronically weak demand, and high joblessness.[10] Imposing austerity programs on countries in the middle of a deep recession would be a fundamentally flawed response which like medieval blood-letting would effectively be a "suicide pact" for these economies, Stiglitz observed. Germany's deficit target fetishism would not only unnecessarily prolong and exacerbate the downturn; it would also undermine the long-run growth prospects, Krugman added.[11] Against the better judgment of the IMF, the OECD and informed economic opinion, Berlin refuses to recognize that the adjustment within the Eurozone has to be symmetrical. As Christine Lagarde, then French Finance Minister, said in May 2010: "It takes two to tango."[12] Instead, Germany's attitude is beggar-your-neighbour, protecting its own well-being at the expense of other countries' imbalances. This selfish behaviour also contributed to the "persistent shortage of demand" of the depressed world economy.[13]

Secondly, Berlin's political critics see Germany, like Japan in the late 1980s, as an unstoppable "juggernaut" or "hyperpuissance" using its unabated economic and monetary might to assert its role of a heartless, self-righteous, Calvinist austerity task-master who is prepared to risk a bitter conflict with its closest partners, notably France.[14] Chancellor Merkel has emerged as a particular lightening rod. She is perceived as the exclusive decision maker in Europe at the expense of Germany's EU partners being downgraded to decision takers. Her unrelenting determination to force upon the European partners the German Diktat of strict fiscal austerity has transmogrified the Eurozone into "an economic prison", with Germany as "the jailer" and the German inspired and enforced monetary stability rules as "the bars".[15] With the rising stature of the EU's pre-eminent member, the "benign

---

[9] European Central Bank (2013a, b, 2014c, d), World Economic Forum (2014).

[10] Summers (2012, 2013a, b, c, 2014, pp. 27–38), Krugman (2013a), Wolf (2013a, b), Lew (2013), Roubini (2012).

[11] Moore (2012), Krugman (2011, 2012a, b), Briancon (2012).

[12] Lagarde (2010). See also Wolf (2014, pp. 339, 341).

[13] Krugman (2013b, c), Tilford (2010, 2012), Wolf (2010a, b, 2012), Monti (2013).

[14] Kundnani (2011, pp. 39–43), Kundnani (2014, pp. 6, 96, 99, 102–105, 108, 110–114), Evans-Pritchard (2012), Moravcsik (2012, p. 60), Feldstein (1997).

[15] Chaffin (2013), Douthat (2013), Moore (2013). See also Kundnani (2012), Vinocur (2012), Soros (2012), Traynor (2011).

hegemon" has yielded to the temptation of an "imperial power" determined to take control of Europe for the third time in less than 100 years.

Third, a "Germany unbound"[16] marks a tectonic shift from the "reflexive"[17] commitment of a "Europeanized Germany"[18] to a "Germanized Europe"[19] in which the socialising effects of cooperation and multilateral action within the institutional structures of the Euro-Atlantic community have been superseded by a "go-it-alone", power-conscious and power-capable foreign policy[20] that is only looking for Germany's national interest and shows no interest in Europe anymore.[21] Is the stubborn insistence on rigid fiscal adjustment another ominous sign of the Berlin Republic moving away from the "long road west"?[22]

Both Ulrich Beck and Hans Kundnani argue that behind the mask of the problem-solving "Merkel method" where decisions "appear to be borne at the back of her [Merkel's] brain"[23] hides an adroit calculation and execution of power. The European integration project conceived largely to constrain German power, actually served to increase it,[24] as the unraveling of euro crisis since 2009 vividly demonstrates. In Beck's view, Chancellor Merkel has seized the euro crisis as "her occasione, 'the propitious moment'" "to restructure power relations in Europe." The "key lever" of "the new German power in Europe" is its "economic power", not, as in former times, force as the ultima ratio." The "Merkiavelli method" rests on the art of "deliberate hesitation. . .as a means of coercion". The policy of procrastination leaves the debtor euro-states no choice but to succumb to the demands of "the strongest and wealthiest economy in the EU" and "to satisfy the

[16] Szabo (2004a, pp. 115–116, 151).

[17] Katzenstein (1997, p. 19), Anderson and Goodman (1993, pp. 55, 60–62).

[18] Bulmer and Paterson (1996, p. 17). See also Anderson (1997, pp. 80–107), Anderson (1999), Bulmer (1997, pp. 49–79).

[19] Harnisch and Schieder (2006, pp. 95–108), Crawford (2007, pp. 15, 19, 34, 42–43, 53, 104, 106, 113, 115, 120, 123–124, 140, 175, 176, 186), Paterson (2010, pp. 41–52), Paterson (2011, pp. 72–74), Bulmer and Paterson (2010, pp. 1051–1073), Morisse-Schilbach (2011, pp. 28–41).

[20] The Kohl government's decision in late December 1991 to grant diplomatic recognition to Croatia and Slovenia, Chancellor Schröder's public clash with U.S. President George W. Bush over U.S. policy in Iraq and the Merkel government's abstention from the NATO's military intervention in Libya in spring 2011 are cited as examples of a more assertive unilateral foreign policy of the Berlin Republic. Binder (1992), Horsley (1992, pp. 239–240), Libal (1997, pp. 100, 105, 106, 162, 163, 164), Maull (2003, p. 17), Maull (2011, pp. 93–117), Szabo (2004a, pp. 77, 116, 151, 152).

[21] Vinocur (2010a, b, 2011), Tooze (2010), Stephens (2010, 2011), Cohen (2011), Errera (2012), Heilbrunn (2012).

[22] Winkler (2007).

[23] The Economist (2006).

[24] The Swiss journalist René Fritz Alleman concluded some 60 years ago that Chancellor Adenauer played the European game because he better understood than most Germans that Germany would not only regain its unrestricted equal status but also a leading role even if the outline of Europe had been designed by French architekts in French hegemonic style. Alleman (1956, p. 174). See also Simms (2013).

conditions of Germany's stability policies". Merkel's siren call is: "better a German euro than no euro at all." The "truths" of the Protestant work ethic are applied to the crisis-ridden Europe: "Suffering purifies." Attempts to enmesh the Berlin Republic into an ever deeper web of European integration actually produced a "German Europe". The European Union since the Maastricht treaty has developed into a "hierarchical dependency (hegemony)" instead of "equal participation (reciprocity)" with Germany as the would-be "good hegemon" at the top and Merkel as "the uncrowned queen of Europe."[25] Kundnani argues that the driving force of German behaviour in the euro crisis is a return to classical German great power politics, a lust for an "assertive, nationalistic, adversarial, zero-sum, semi-hegemony" that reflects the geo-economic pre-eminence of the Berlin Republic in Europe. The emergence of German "hegemony" has turned "the network structure" within the EU into a "hub-and-spoke relational structure." The "geo-economic power uses economic means in a way that seems more Clausewitzian than Kantian." The "new German nationalism" which increasingly questions the foreign-policy parameters of the Federal Republic, namely Westbindung, raises doubts whether the geo-economic power remains "committed to the West". In other words, "German history is not yet at an end."[26]

The "Merkiavelli method" poses the central question of concern: does the Berlin Republic today behave in a nineteenth and twentieth century fashion where it shows no qualms to pull the levers of power to push the European institutions and partners into preferred German interests and policy outcomes even if it means a worsening of an already dire economic situation in the euro area's misery belt and a weakening of European institutions? Has the "German question re-emerged in geo-economic form" as Kundnani argues. "Is the danger in Europe now of a geo-economic version of the conflicts within Europe between 1871 and 1945"? In short: "Has history returned to Europe"?[27]

The book's main argument is that the different responses to the euro crisis can best be explained by different conceptions of self, historical memory, and institutional practices. The euro crisis is like a strong beam of light. The light gets filtered by national lenses that create distinctive national responses. The lens through which German decision makers have perceived the euro crisis is the culture of stability. It is the economic concept of 'Ordoliberalismus' which gives German attitudes to economic policy special characteristics. West Germany's post-war economic success ("Wirtschaftswunder") under the ordoliberal economic doctrine, made the maintenance of order in a social market economy and price stability enforced by an independent central bank the Alpha and Omega of German economic policy. This specific German economic concept has shaped, to a high degree, the

[25] Beck (2013, pp. 46, 47, 49, 50, 51, 52, 54, 59, 61, 64).

[26] Kundnani (2014, pp. 92, 103, 104, 108, 112, 114).

[27] Kundnani (2014, pp. 108, 110, 111, 112). See also Feldstein (1997, pp. 69, 72), Szabo (2004a, pp. 149–153), Szabo (2004b, pp. 50–52).

perception and response of German decision makers to the gathering storm in the euro area.[28]

The book proceeds as follows: I begin with a brief review of the central tenets of the economic concept of ordoliberalism. The second part deals with the Merkel government's euro crisis management since late 2009. Four phases can be identified: a laissez-faire policy from late 2009 until March 2010, to be followed by a reactive step-by-step engagement marked by Berlin's insistence of a quid pro quo of solidity in return for solidarity, Merkel's acquiescence to the ECB's OMT program and the German design of a more perfect monetary union. The third part deals with the shift of the euro crisis in 2014 from the acute to the chronic, from the periphery to the centre with Berlin still stubbornly saying Nein to a policy of fiscal and monetary easing and debt forgiveness in response to persistent stagnation of the euro area economy, particularly in France and Italy, the rising deflationary pressure as a result of prolonged weakness of aggregate demand within the currency zone, and the re-emergence of the Greek debt crisis which brought back the spectre of the country's default. The forth part will evaluate Germany's role in the euro crisis management. First, does Germany's policy prescription of expansionary fiscal contraction and internal devaluation successfully address the root causes of the euro crisis? Second, does Germany as Europe's undisputed economic and political powerhouse extend its sway over its European partners by forcing them to surrender to the German Diktat of fiscal Disziplin and economic efficiency? Lastly, does the euro crisis signify a fundamental change from Germany's traditional European vocation to "Germanized" Europe"? I end with the central political challenges "Merkelism"[29] faces in the near future to resolve the euro crisis and to put the monetary union on a sound and sustainable footing.

References

Alleman, R. F. (1956). *Bonn ist nicht Weimer*. Cologne: Kiepenheuer & Witsch.

Anderson, J. (1997). Hard interests, soft power, and Germany's changing role in Europe. In P. J. Katzenstein (Ed.), *Tamed power. Germany in Europe* (pp. 80–107). Ithaca, NY: Cornell University Press.

Anderson, J. (1999). *German unification and the union of Europe*. Cambridge: Cambridge University Press.

Anderson, J. J., & Goodman, J. B. (1993). Mars or minerva? A United Germany, in a post-cold war Europe. In R. O. Keohane, J. S. Nye, & S. Hoffmann (Eds.), *After the Cold War. International institutions and state strategies in Europe, 1989–1991*. Cambridge, MA: Harvard University Press.

Beck, U. (2013). *German Europe*. Cambridge: Polity Press.

The Economist. (2006, January 12). The Merkel method. *The Economist*. http://www.economist.com/node/5389782

[28] Katzenstein (2003, pp. 732, 733), Wolf (2014, p. 54).

[29] Legrain (2015).

Binder, D. (1992, January 7). By Bonn's assertiveness, policymakers see evidence of unilateral approaches. *International Herald Tribune*.

Briancon, P. (2012, March 5). Will Spain be sacrificed to a cult of austerity? *International Herald Tribune*.

Bulmer, S. (1997). Shaping the rules? The constitutive politics of the European Union and German power. In P. J. Katzenstein (Ed.), *Tamed power. Germany in Europe*. Ithaca, NY: Cornell University Press.

Bulmer, S., & Paterson, W. E. (1996). Germany in the European Union: Gentle giant or emergent leader? *International Affairs, 72*(1), 9–32.

Bulmer, S., & Paterson, W. E. (2010). Germany and the EU: From "tamed power" to normalized power? *International Affairs, 86*(5), 1051–1073.

Chaffin, J. (2013, June 24). Berlin's dominant role raises hackles. *Financial Times*.

Cohen, R. (2011, April 18). Merkel in miniature. *New York Times*.

Crawford, B. (2007). *Power and German policy*. Basingstoke: Palgrave Macmillan.

Deutscher Bundestag. (2013, December 18). *Plenarprotokoll 18/5*. Berlin. http://dipbt.bundestag.de/doc/btp/18/18005.pdf

Deutscher Bundestag. (2015, March 19). *Plenarprotokoll, 18/94*. Berlin. http://dipbt.bundestag.de/doc/btp/18/18094.pdf

Dinmore, G. (2014, March 14). Italy's Matteo Renzi pledges tax cuts and labour reforms. *Financial Times*.

Dinmore, G., & Sanderson, R. (2014, April 7). Renzi takes his time to tackle deeper labour woes. *Financial Times*.

Douthat, R. (2013, July 1). Prisoners of the euro. *International Herald Tribune*.

Errera, G. (2012, November 6). France is running out of time to restrain Germany. *Financial Times*.

European Central Bank. (2013a, September 5). *Introductory statement to the press conference (with Q&A) by Mario Draghi, President of the ECB*. Frankfurt am Main. http://www.ecb.europa.eu/press/pressconf/2013/html/is130905.en.html

European Central Bank. (2013b, January 23). *Interview with Neue Zürcher Zeitung*. http://www.ecb.europa.eu/press/key/date/2014/html/sp140123.en.html

European Central Bank. (2014a, March 6). *Introductory statement by Mario Draghi to the press*. Frankfurt am Main. http://www.ecb.europa.eu/press/pressconf/2014/html/is140306.en.html

European Central Bank. (2014b, May 8). *Introductory statement by Mario Draghi to the press conference (with Q&A)*. Frankfurt am Main. http://www.ecb.europa.eu/press/pressconf/2014/html/is140508.en.html

European Central Bank. (2014c, January 9). *Introductory statement to the press conference (with Q&A) by Mario Draghi*. http://www.ecb.europa.eu/press/pressconf/2014/html/is140109.en.html

European Central Bank. (2014d, August 7). *Introductory statement to the press conference (with Q&A) by Mario Draghi*. Frankfurt am Main. http://www.ecb.europa.eu/press/pressconf/2014/html/is140807.en.html

European Commission, Directorate-General for Economic and Financial Affairs. (2014, May 5). *European economic forecast spring 2014*. Brussels. http://ec.europa.eu/economy_finance/publications/european_economy/2014/pdf/ee3_en.pdf

Eurostat. (2014a, December 12). *Real GDP growth rate-volume*. Luxembourg. http://ec.europa.eu/eurostat/tgm/table.do?tab=table&init=1&language=en&pcode=tec00115&plugin=1

Eurostat. (2014b, April 23). *Euro area and EU28 government deficit at 3.0% and 3.3% of GDP respectively*. News Release 64/2014, Luxembourg. http://epp.eurostat.ec.europa.eu/cache/ITY_PUBLIC/2-23042014-AP/EN/2-23042014-AP-EN.PDF

Evans-Pritchard, A. (2012, April 1). Germany's reluctant hegemony and misguided Calvinism. *The Telegraph*. http://www.telegraph.co.uk/finance/comment/ambroseevans_pritchard/9179236/Germanys-reluctant-hegemony-and-misguided-Calvinism.html

Evans-Pritchard, A. (2014, January 14). Francois Hollande vows 'supply-side' assault on French state, doubles down on EMU austerity agenda. *The Telegraph.* http://www.telegraph.co.uk/finance/comment/ambroseevans_pritchard/10572654/Francois-Hollande-vows-supply-side-assault-on-French-state-doubles-down-on-EMU-austerity-agenda.html
Feldstein, M. (1997). EMU and international conflict. *Foreign Affairs, 76*(6), 60–76.
Frankenberger, K.-D. (2014, January 16). Auf deutschen Wegen zu neuen Kräften. *Frankfurter Allgemeine Zeitung.*
Harnisch, S., & Schieder, S. (2006). Germany's new European policy: Weaker, leaner, meaner. In H. W. Maull (Ed.), *Germany's uncertain power. Foreign policy of the Berlin Republic.* Basingstoke: Palgrave Macmillan.
Heilbrunn, J. (2012, October 24). All roads lead to Berlin. *The National Interest.* http://nationalinterest.org/article/all-roads-lead-berlin-7622
Horsley, W. (1992). United Germany's seven cardinal sins. *Millenium, 21*(2), 225–242.
International Monetary Fund. (2014, June 25). *Euro area policies.* IMF Country Report No. 14/198, Washington, DC. http://www.imf.org/external/pubs/ft/scr/2014/cr14198.pdf
Katzenstein, P. J. (1997). United Germany in an integrating Europe. In P. J. Katzenstein (Ed.), *Tamed power. Germany in Europe.* Ithaca, NY: Cornell University Press.
Katzenstein, P. J. (2003). Same war – different views: Germany, Japan and counterterrorism. *International Organization, 57*(4), 731–760.
Krugman, P. (2011, September 19). The bleeding cure. *New York Times.*
Krugman, P. (2012a, April 15). Europe's economic suicide. *New York Times.*
Krugman, P. (2012b, May 18). Apocalypse fairly soon. *New York Times.*
Krugman, P. (2013a, November 16). Secular stagnation, coal mines, bubbles, and Larry Summers. *New York Times.* http://krugman.blogs.nytimes.com/2013/11/16/secular-stagnation-coalmines-bubbles-and-larry-summers/?_php=true&_type=blogs&_r=0
Krugman, P. (2013b, November 4). Those depressing Germans. *New York Times.*
Krugman, P. (2013c, November 1). The harm Germany does. http://krugman.blogs.nytimes.com/2013/11/01/the-harm-germany-does/
Krugman, P. (2014, January 17). Scandal in France. *New York Times.*
Kundnani, H. (2011). Germany as a geo-economic power. *Washington Quarterly, 34*(3), 31–45.
Kundnani, H. (2012, January 6). The eurozone will pay a high prize for Germany's economic narcissm. *The Guardian.* http://www.theguardian.com/commentisfree/2012/jan/06/eurozone-germany-ordoliberalism
Kundnani, H. (2014). *The paradox of German power.* London: C. Hurst.
Lagarde, C. (2010, March 15). Transcript of Interview with Christine Lagarde. *Financial Times.* http://www.ft.com/cms/s/0/78648e1a-3019-11df-8734-00144feabdc0,s01=1.html
Legrain, P. (2015, February 19). Greece should not give in to Germany's bullying. *Foreign Policy.* http://foreignpolicy.com/2015/02/19/greece-should-not-give-in-to-germanys-bullying-euro-syriza-merkel-varoufakis/
Lew, L. (2013, July 18). Put job growth at the heart of global recovery. *Financial Times.*
Libal, M. (1997). *Limits of persuasion. Germany and the Yugoslav crisis, 1991–1992.* Westport, CT: Praeger.
Maull, H. W. (2003). Deutschland auf Abwegen? In H. W. Maull, S. Harnisch, & C. Grund (Eds.), *Deutschland im Abseits? Rot grüne Außenpolitik* (pp. 1998–2003). Baden-Baden: Nomos.
Maull, H. W. (2011). Deutsche Außenpolitik: Orientierungslos. *Zeitschrift für Politikwissenschaft, 21*(1), 93–117.
Monti, M. (2013, December 17). Europe's north and south must reform together. *Financial Times.*
Moore, M. (2012, January 17). Stiglitz says European austerity plans are a 'suicide Pact'. *The Telegraph.* http://www.telegraph.co.uk/finance/financialcrisis/9019819/Stiglitz-says-European-austerity-plans-are-a-suicide-pact.html
Moore, C. (2013, March 22). Southern Europe lies prostrate before the German imperium. *The Telegraph.* http://www.telegraph.co.uk/news/worldnews/europe/cyprus/9948545/Southern-Europe-lies-prostrate-before-the-German-imperium.html

Moravcsik, A. (2012). Europe after the crisis. How to sustain a common currency. *Foreign Affairs, 91*(3), 60.

Morisse-Schilbach, M. (2011). Ach Deutschland: Greece, the eurocrisis and the costs and benefits of being a benign hegemon. *Internationale Politik und Gesellschaft, 14*(1), 28–41.

Münchau, W. (2014, January 20).The real scandal is France's stagnant economic thinking. *Financial Times.*

Organization for Economic Cooperation and Development. (2014, May 6). *OECD economic outlook* (Vol. 2014, Issue 1, pp. 94–98). Paris. http://www.oecd-ilibrary.org/economics/oecd-economic-outlook-volume-2014-issue-1_eco_outlook-v2014-1-en

Paterson, W. E. (2010). Does Germany still have a European vocation? *German Politics, 19*(1), 41–52.

Paterson, W. E. (2011). The reluctant hegemon. *Journal of Common Market Studies, 49*, 57–75.

Peel, Q., Thomson, A., & Fontanella-Khan, J. (2013, August 15). Berlin and Brussels credit fiscal discipline and reform for Eurozone recovery. *Financial Times.*

Roubini, N. (2012, April 13). Europe's short vacation. *Project Syndicate.* http://www.project-syndicate.org/commentary/europe-s-short-vacation

Schäuble, W. (2013, September 17). Ignore the doomsayers. *Financial Times.*

Schäuble, W. (2015, April 16). German priorities and eurozone myths. *International New York Times.*

Simms, B. (2013, March 14). Cracked heart of the new world. *New Statesman.* http://www.newstatesman.com/world-affairs/europe/2013/03/cracked-heart-old-world

Soros, G. (2012, June 26). A tragic, historical mistake by the Germans. *Spiegel Online.* http://www.spiegel.de/international/europe/george-soros-says-germany-must-change-course-on-euro-crisis-a-841061.html

Stephens, P. (2010, March 26). Merkel's myopia reopens Europe's German question. *Financial Times.*

Stephens, P. (2011, June 10). Why Berlin is resetting its compass. *Financial Times.*

Summers, L. (2012, April 29). Growth not austerity is best remedy for Europe. *Financial Times.*

Summers, L. (2013a, November 8). *Speech at IMF 14 annual research conference in honour of Stanley Fisher.* Washington, DC. http://larrysummers.com/imf-fourteenth-annual-research-conference-in-honor-of-stanley-fischer/

Summers, L. (2013b, March 18). Europe cannot allow unfinished business to fester. *Financial Times.*

Summers, L. (2013c, December 16). Why stagnation might prove to be the new normal. *Financial Times.*

Summers, L. (2014). Reflections on the "New secular stagnation hypothesis". In C. Teulings & R. Baldwin (Eds.), *Secular stagnations: Facts, causes, and cures.* London: Centre for European Policy Research. http://www.voxeu.org/sites/default/files/Vox_secular_stagnation.pdf

Szabo, S. F. (2004a). *Partying ways. The crisis in German-American relations.* Washington, DC: The Brookings Institution.

Szabo, S. F. (2004b). Germany and the United States after Iraq: From alliance to alignment. *Internationale Politik und Gesellschaft, 7*(1), 41–52.

Tilford, S. (2010, July 14). Germany's euro advantage. *International Herald Tribune.*

Tilford, S. (2012, June 25). *Berlin's dangerous sense of invulnerability.* http://www.realclearworld.com/articles/2012/06/25/berlins_dangerous_sense_of_invulnerability_100100.html

Tooze, A. (2010, May 5). The message from Berlin that Europe failed to grasp. *Financial Times.*

Traynor, I. (2011, December 9). As the dust settles, a cold new Europe with Germany in charge will emerge. *The Guardian.* http://www.theguardian.com/business/2011/dec/09/dust-settles-cold-europe-germany

Vinocur, J. (2010a, March 23). Germany suffers a fit of willfulness. *International Herald Tribune.*

Vinocur, J. (2010b, May 4). Pondering the German question. *International Herald Tribune.*

Vinocur, J. (2011, July 5). Questioning Berlin's lead in Europe. *International Herald Tribune.*
Vinocur, J. (2012, May 28). Merkel's stubborn march of folly. *International Herald Tribune.*
Winkler, H. A. (2007). *Germany: The long road west. Volume II: 1933–1990.* Oxford: Oxford University Press.
Wolf, M. (2010a, March 23). Excessive virtue can be a vice for the world economy. *Financial Times.*
Wolf, M. (2010b, May 19). The Eurozone stumbles into a beggar-my neighbour policy. *Financial Times.*
Wolf, M. (2012, April 10). Why the Bundesbank is wrong. *Financial Times.*
Wolf, M. (2013a, November 20). Why the future looks sluggish. *Financial Times.*
Wolf, M. (2013b, July 11). How Austerity has failed. *The New York Review of Books.* [http://www.nybooks.com/articles/archives/2013/jul/11/how-austerity-has-failed/
Wolf, M. (2014). *The shifts and the shocks. What have we Learned – and have still to learn – from the financial crisis.* London: Allen Lane.
World Economic Forum. (2014, January 24). *Global economic outlook 2014.* Davos. http://www.weforum.org/sessions/summary/global-economic-outlook-2014
Yardley, J., & Pianigiani, G. (2014, March 13). Italian leader offers plan to fix economy. *New York Times.*

Chapter 2
"Made in Germany": Categorical Imperatives of Ordoliberalism

As the culture of reticence (Kultur der Zurückhaltung) explains best the path dependency of Germany's foreign and security policy to ideational factors—norms, beliefs, values—of a liberal world order,[1] then the culture of stability (Stabilitätskultur) best describes the German approach to economic, monetary and fiscal policy since the founding of the Bonn Republic in May 1949. Germany's post-war social market economy (Soziale Marktwirtschaft) premises on the economic theory of ordoliberalism. The central feature of ordoliberal thinking is a political authority which consciously shapes the economic system. The strong state is the guardian both of a free economy that assures undistorted market competition among self-interested entrepreneurs and robust social-ethical frameworks which protect individual freedom from the fallacies of unbridled market competition. Entrepreneurial and personal freedom can only flourish on the basis of order. Freedom is effective only as ordered, rule-based freedom. The free economy and the enlightened state are thus "two sides of the same coin."[2]

The culture of stability wedded to the norms and principles of a liberal social market economy developed to meet the post-war challenges of the German economy is the driving force of Germany's economic, monetary and fiscal policy to date. The core elements[3] of the German socio-economic model are:

- Individual responsibility. The German economic model rests on the principle of individual responsibility. It reflects an almost religious belief that countries have to live with the consequences of their decisions. Fiscal rectitude is an expression of a frugal, debt avoiding national government. Trade surplus is viewed as confirmation of the country's economic sobriety as reflected in the country's competitive edge in world markets. Contrary, deficits are the inevitable result of

[1] Longhurst (2004, pp. 2, 137, 140, 142–144, 147, 151–152); Dalgaard-Nielson (2006, pp. 10–11, 143–147).

[2] Bonefeld (2012).

[3] Dullien and Guérot (2012, pp. 2–5), Bonatti and Fracasso (2013), Kundnani (2012).

F.-J. Meiers, *Germany's Role in the Euro Crisis*,
DOI 10.1007/978-3-319-20514-4_2

a profligate government living beyond its means. Current account imbalances are the consequence of a loss of competitiveness which is rooted in a misalignment of wages and productivity and a weak export performance particularly in the manufacturing sector. Imposing fiscal discipline through deep government spending cuts and higher taxes are the default means against fiscal thrift. Competitive gains through sweeping labour market reforms and drastic wage cuts enable countries with current account deficits to cut back their labour costs and to increase their exports. The implementation of the Agenda 2010 adopted 10 years ago by the Schröder government proved that the country's pronounced erosion of global competitiveness could be restored through internal devaluation, namely the reduction of labour unit costs and a relaxation of labour market rules. The German case vindicated the ordoliberal narrative that structural repair works: the "sick man of Europe" transformed into "Modell Deutschland über alles".[4]

- Financial markets' constructive disciplinary force. Financial markets reward prudent and productive economic and fiscal behaviour and punish sinful deficit spending. The readiness of sinner countries to adopt fiscal and structural repair measures accelerate the economic outlook and strengthen the confidence in financial markets that strict fiscal and current account targets will be reached; this in turn stimulates more investment which provides a sound basis for robust and sustainable growth The imposition of higher risk premiums in the form of higher bond yields is the logical consequence to overspending and overborrowing. Profligate national economies have to bear the burden of misbehaviour (higher cost of debt financing) and adjustment (expansionary fiscal contraction and internal devaluation). Bailouts are seen as moral hazard: they rescue governments in profligate countries by the back door and take off the pressure to make the necessary fiscal and structural adjustment. Virtuous countries would ultimately be made liable for bad decisions made by others while sinner countries would be awarded with no disciplinary measures left to punish their misbehaviour.
- Neo-mercantilist orientation. The German socio-economic model is strongly connected with an export-oriented structure on which the country's post-war economic miracle had been founded. The protection of the country's market shares in the world requires unrelenting efforts by both state and non-state actors (entrepreneurs and labour unions) to sustain the competitive edge of the German industrial base. Supply factors—prices, wages and the welfare system—have to be constantly adjusted to maintain the competitiveness of German economy. Export strength demonstrates the high efficiency of the German economy in an increasingly globalized world economy. Germany's neo-mercantilist orientation implies a high dependence on exports and foreign markets for economic growth.

[4] The Economist (1999, 2011). For a critical assessment of Chancellor Schröder's comprehensive reform program see Dullien (2013, 2014, pp. 146–160), Posen (2013).

It sees the German economy not as the Continent's "consumer of last resort" but as its "main factory".[5]

- Anti-inflationary rectitude. With a historical aversion to inflation, the German political and economic elite, particularly the Bundesbank, define price stability as the pre-condition for steady growth. Price stability defined as inflation rates below, but close to 2 % over the medium-term is the pre-condition for both the quantity and quality of economic growth, real disposable income and strong consumer demand, which in turn underpins social and political stability.[6] A Keynesian policy of unconstrained deficit spending and loose monetary policy to promote growth and employment would lead to profligacy, ballooning inflation and eventually the erosion of the economic and financial system. Never deserting the cause of safeguarding the currency became the Bundesbank's central mission. Erich Keller, rector of the Bundesbank's University of Applied Sciences, summed up the central bank's creed succinctly, "We have a mantra, only one goal—price stability."[7]
- Fiscal probity. Sound fiscal policy is based on the dictum: one can only spend the money one has. The Swabian saying *Schaffe, schaffe, Häusle baue* ("work, work to build a house") implies that one can only purchase as much as one earns through honest work. Private and public debt-fuelled spending contradicts the central tenet of frugal housekeeping and balanced budgeting. Economies have to be rebalanced away from debt-fueled consumption after the maxim: you cannot cure debt with more debt. Promoting growth by increasing fiscal deficits is like Adam eating the apple: it is an eternal sin. A national government living beyond its means has only one option to return to the virtuous path of fiscal frugality: it has to go through the purgatory of strict fiscal and structural adjustment to reach the promised land of sound monetary policy, fiscal balance and stable economic growth.
- Independence of the central bank. Article 12 of the Bundesbank Law of July 26, 1957 states: "In exercising the powers conferred on it by this Act, it is independent of instructions from the federal government."[8] The central bank's independent status is the best way to assure price stability, lasting growth, employment, and prosperity. As the custodian of a stable currency, the Bundesbank became "modern Germany's Knights of the Holy Grail"[9] whose primacy of a stability-oriented monetary policy was conceived as a shining model for other countries.

---

[5] Bonatti and Fracasso (2013, p. 1031).

[6] Marsh (1992a, pp. 36, 37, 226–227), Stark (2014).

[7] Kulish (2012).

[8] Gesetz über die Deutsche Bundesbank in der Fassung der Bekanntmachung vom 22. Oktober 1992 (BGBl. I S. 1782), das zuletzt durch Artikel 23 des Gesetzes vom 4. Juli 2013 (BGBl. I S. 1981) geändert worden ist. http://www.iuscomp.org/gla/statutes/BBankG.htm.

[9] Marsh (1992a, p. 48).

- Germany's economic creed. The German social market economy model is seen as the beacon to the world. In response to the global financial crisis, Chancellor Angela Merkel stated in her New Eve's speech 2009 that the social market economy is the shining example whose virtuous principles should be transferred abroad. "Only if we identify the causes, can we lead the world out of the crisis. To this end, we need clear principles: the state is the guardian of economic and social order. Competition needs a sense of proportion and social responsibility. These are the principles of the social market economy. They apply to us, but that is not sufficient. These principles must be followed worldwide."[10] Helmut Schlesinger, the President of the German Central Bank, put the German creed in a nutshell when he said in mid-January 1992, "There is a Kultur of stability in Germany that is what we need in Europe as well."[11] The central ingredients of Germany's Kultur of stability are price stability, fiscal probity, flexibility to ensure that each national economy can function effectively, and an enduring commitment to monetary and fiscal rules for which national governments bear primary responsibility.

The question whether Germany should give up the Deutschmark in favour of the euro sparked an intense debate within the country. The Deutschmark symbolized the post-war Wirtschaftswunder, a stable currency and the country's re-emergence as a respected European and global player. In order to reassure domestic veto players like the Bundesbank the Kohl government made the abandonment of the Deutschmark contingent upon the take-over of cardinal principles of Germany's ordoliberal model, particularly German-style fiscal discipline, price stability and central bank independence as the necessary condition for low inflation. Chancellor Kohls's grand bargain was safeguarded by three pillars: the Maastricht Treaty making each member state liable for its own national finances, the Stability and Growth Pact mandating fiscal prudence, and an independent ECB maintaining price stability. Germany's emphasis on the principle of law implied three things. Firstly, the legal Maginot Line established by the Maastricht Treaty and the Stability and Growth Pact ensures that the euro area member countries are willing and able to adjust their economic and fiscal policies to the norms of a stability-oriented monetary policy. Secondly, in a democratic European monetary union, states remain liable for their own debts. Fiscal arrangement involving systematic and substantial transfers of financial resources across countries, i.e. bailouts, mutualization of debt, common Eurozone bonds, contradict the fundamental principle on which a union of countries rests: they share a common currency but remain sovereign when it comes to public finances. Thirdly, member countries in chronic non-compliance with the rules on fiscal and monetary stability would have to pay a maximum fine of 0.5 % of GDP deposited in non-interest bearing accounts of the ECB.[12]

[10] Bundesregierung (2008), Marsh (1992a, pp. 226, 228).

[11] von Weizsäcker (1992), Marsh (1992b, p. 252).

[12] Marsh (1992a, pp. 35, 206–207, 214, 228), Dyson (1994, pp. 237–238, 255), Kirchhof (2012, 2014), Issing (2012, 2014), Sinn (2012, 2014, pp. 18, 62, 115, 174).

The German creed coalesced into a single policy: what is good for Germany and the D-Mark would be good for Europe. The Kohl government signed the monetary union with the broad expectation that the euro would become the old Deutschmark in European clothes with member state emulating the "Modell Deutschland über alles" and a central bank fiercely defending a rigorous monetary Stabilitätspolitik.[13] As former President German President Richard von Weizsäcker wrote, "It is no exaggeration to say that our monetary concept becomes part of the European constitution and our social market economy the basic law of European economic policy."[14] Ever since the conclusion of the Maastricht Treaty, German governments have pursued a rules-based approach to the governance of the euro area based on nominal targets and sanctioning mechanisms ("Excessive Deficit Procedures") to prevent unsound fiscal policies from undermining monetary stability and the credibility of the euro project. The sovereign debt crisis within the euro area twisted the German ordoliberal premises of sound monetary and fiscal policies and independence of the central bank like a tornado.

References

Bonatti, L., & Fracasso, A. (2013). The German model and the European crisis. *Journal of Common Market Studies, 51*(6), 1028–1032.

Bonefeld, W. (2012). Freedom, crisis and the strong state. On German ordoliberalism. *New Political Economy, 17*(5), 638. 642.

Bulmer, S., Jeffery, C., & Paterson, W. (2000). *Germany's European diplomacy: Shaping the regional milieu.* Manchester: Manchester University Press.

Bundesregierung. (2008). *Neujahrsansprache 2009 von Bundeskanzlerin Dr. Angela Merkel am 31. Dezember 2008*, Berlin, December 31, 2008. http://www.bundesregierung.de/Content/DE/Bulletin/2009/01/01-1-bk-neujahr.html

Crawford, B. (2007). *Power and German foreign policy: Embedded hegemony in Europe.* Basingstoke: Palgrave Macmillan.

Dalgaard-Nielson, A. (2006). *Germany pacifism and peace enforcement.* Manchester: Manchester University Press.

Dullien, S., & Guérot, U. (2012, February). *The long shadow of ordoliberalism: Germany's approach to the Euro crisis.* London: European Council on Foreign Relations. http://ecfr.eu/page-/ECFR49_GERMANY_BRIEF.pdf

Dullien, S. (2013, July). *A German model for Europe?* London: European Council on Foreign Relations. http://www.ecfr.eu/page/-/ECFR83_GERMANY_BRIEF_AW.pdf

Dullien, S. (2014). German reforms as a blueprint for Europe. In S. Collignon & P. Esposito (Eds.), *Competiveness in the European economy.* London: Routledge.

Dyson, K. (1994). *Elusive union: The process of economic and monetary union in Europe.* Harrow: Longman.

Issing, O. (2012, July 30). Europe's political union is an idea worthy of satire. *Financial Times.*

[13] The Economist (2012), Marsh (1992a, pp. 217, 218), Marsh (1992b, p. 249), Bulmer et al. (2000, pp. 94, 100), Dyson (1994, pp. 154–159), Crawford (2007, pp. 120–124, 142).

[14] von Weizsäcker (1992).

Issing, O. (2014, March 26). Get your finances in order and stop blaming Germany. *Financial Times*.

Kirchhof, P. (2012, July 12). Wir spielen mit dem Feuer. *Frankfurter Allgemeine Zeitung*.

Kirchhof, P. (2014, January 13). Geldeigentum und Geldpolitik. *Frankfurter Allgemeine Zeitung*.

Kulish, N. (2012, December 14). With European Bank in spotlight, Bundesbank is left in Shadows. *New York Times*.

Kundnani, H. (2012, May 8). *Germany: What hegemon?* London: European Council on Foreign Relations. http://ecfr.eu/content/entry/commentary_germany_what_hegemon

Longhurst, K. (2004). *Germany and the use of force: The evolution of German security policy 1990–2003*. Manchester: Manchester University Press.

Marsh, D. (1992a). *The most powerful bank. Inside Germany's Bundesbank*. New York: Times Books.

Marsh, D. (1992b). *The Bundesbank. The bank that rules Europe*. London: Heinemann.

Posen, A. S. (2013, June 14). Getting Germany past internal devaluation. *Die Welt*. http://www.iie.com/publications/opeds/oped.cfm?ResearchID=2424

Sinn, H.-W. (2012, August 27). Judgment day for the Eurozone. *Project Syndicate*. http://www.project-syndicate.org/commentary/judgment-day-for-the-eurozone-by-hans-werner-sinn/german

Sinn, H.-W. (2014). *Gefangen im Euro*. München: Redline Verlag.

Stark, J. (2014, April 14). Doom-mongers risk a self-fulfilling prophecy. *Financial Times*.

The Economist. (1999, June 3). The sick man of the euro. *The Economist*. http://www.economist.com/node/209559/

The Economist. (2011, April 14). Modell Deutschland über alles. *The Economist*. http://www.economist.com/node/21552579

The Economist. (2012, April 14). Modell Deutschland über alles. *The Economist*. http://www.economist.com/node/21552579

von Weizsäcker, R. (1992, April 13). Meilenstein Maastricht. *Frankfurter Allgemeine Zeitung*.

Chapter 3
Teetering at the Edge of the Precipice: Merkel's Politics of Small Steps, 2009–2013

The euro crisis began in October 2009 when the new Greek government admitted that its predecessors had vastly understated the country's fiscal deficit. All euro area countries with large external imbalances suffered severe financial pressure. The euro crisis is a mix of three crises: a government debt crisis where some member countries, notably Greece, had accumulated excessively high public debt that questioned its ability to finance further budget deficits and to service its debt in full; a banking crisis where banks in Spain and Ireland suffered severe losses because of their significant exposure to a property bubble that busted in 2009; and a macroeconomic crisis where declining competitiveness and slow growth compounded the burden of some indebted countries, especially Italy, to pay ever higher bond yields financial markets asked for as a risk premium. These three crises were intertwined. If some debt-stressed sovereigns could not pay their debt, the banking system as a whole could collapse because euro-area banks owned a significant amount of sovereign debt. Severe losses in the banks' balance sheets caused by high-risk lending to the private sector risked the solvency of certain sovereigns. To complete the circle, sluggish growth and declining competitiveness threatened the credit worthiness of some highly indebted countries. Restraint lending to the corporate sector stalled an economic rebound and reinforced the vicious downward spiral of higher debt and joblessness in the euro area's periphery.[1] The sovereign debt crisis displayed a close interdependence across national economies and across national governments and national banks.[2]

Greece—a geographically and economically peripheral member of the Eurozone—emerged as epicentre of the euro crisis. Greece's economic boom was propelled by large foreign-funded fiscal deficits which reached 13.6 % at the end of 2009; the stock of debt accounted for 129 % of GDP at the end of 2009. The economic boom was propelled by large foreign-funded fiscal deficits; 75 % of the

[1] Shambaugh (2012), pp. 158–159.

[2] Merler and Pisani-Ferry (2012).

F.-J. Meiers, *Germany's Role in the Euro Crisis*,
DOI 10.1007/978-3-319-20514-4_3

country's debt was held by foreign creditors. The financial upheaval on Wall Street in 2008 caused by the bursting of a debt-fuelled housing bubble at the end of 2006[3] abruptly ended the flow of external private capital on which the Greek growth model so desperately depended. International investors began withdrawing their money from Greece thereby increasing the cost of debt financing and raising troubling questions about the country's solvency and the viability of the monetary union.[4]

3.1 Advice of the Swabian Housewife: Do Your Homework!

The Merkel government concluded that Germany did its homework: the labor market reformed, labor costs cut, the budget on a trajectory towards balance, and the economic outlook improving after the dramatic downturn caused by the upheavals on Wall Street. The crisis confirmed German ordoliberal thinking that all economic policy begins and ends at home. When Merkel learned about the falsification of Greek fiscal accounts she insisted that this was some else's crisis that did not require German involvement. Only Greek discipline could fix the country's misfortune. The survival of a single currency hinged solely on the sinner's readiness to adopt virtuous policies in pursuit of steady growth and sustainable public debt.

From the perspective of a schwäbische Hausfrau—southern Germany's thrifty Swabian housewife—repeatedly invoked by Chancellor Merkel during the peak of the global financial crisis in 2008 to underline the virtues of frugal housekeeping and balanced budgeting[5]—the root cause of the Greek debt malaise was self-evident: by living beyond its means Greece broke the rules of the Stability and Growth Pact and took the country to the edge of default. The "no-bail-out rule" of the Maastricht Treaty of 1993 implied that the problem of soaring spreads of Greek government bonds was for Athens to resolve. By reference to the rules of the Stability and Growth Pact, debt-ridden countries like Greece had to accept their responsibility to take swift and resolute action to cut its debt ratios to meet the agreed fiscal consolidation targets. "The rules must be obeyed", Merkel said.[6]

The message coming from Berlin was that the problem in Greece was for Athens to resolve by adopting the economics of a Swabian housewife by which one can only spend the money one has. The moral hazard fundamentalists within the Merkel government, the coalition parties and the Bundesbank and leading newspapers like the Frankfurter Allgemeine Zeitung kept the upper hand with their argument that

---

[3] Reinhart and Rogoff (2009), pp. 203–239.

[4] International Monetary Fund (2013), pp. 5 and 6.

[5] Christlich Demokratische Union (2008), p. 5; Kollewe (2012).

[6] EU special summit Meeting emphasis shared responsibility, Brussels, February 11, 2010 (http://www.bundeskanzlerin.de/Content/EN/Artikel/2010/02/2010-02-11-eu-sondergipfel_en.html).

the spend-thrift Club Med (Club Méditerranée) tried to avoid paying for their own mistakes by grabbing the German public purse. The expectations that the Greeks themselves could get their house in proper order rested on the firm conviction[7] that the benefits of contractionary economic policies—a return to sustainable public finances and greater competitiveness—would outweigh the negative impact on demand as the positive results of German reform efforts since 2003 had proved.[8] In other words: if Greece wanted to remain a stable and reliable chain-link within the monetary union, it had to take on some heavy lifting and bear the resultant pain.

Consequently, Merkel decided in March 2010 to halt France's early proposal to establish an EU mechanism to aid debt-ridden Greece.[9] Then French President Nicolas Sarkozy in a veiled criticism of Merkel's minimalist approach said, "On the necessity of taking other measures, France is working on it and Germany is thinking about it."[10] As the Greek sinner proved incapable of averting an imminent default Chancellor Merkel began to reverse her non-commitment strategy towards Athens. As expression of "shared responsibility for the stability of the currency area as a whole" she declared that only as an "absolutely last resort" Germany would extend financial assistance if Greece had exhausted all financial alternatives. Assistance would be tied to "rigorous conditions", the full involvement of the IMF,[11] and a unanimous decision of the Eurogroup.[12]

At the same time, the German government began to talk about sanction procedures against delinquent members. "We need to have an agreement under which, as a last resort, it's possible to exclude a country from the euro zone if again and again it doesn't fulfill the requirements," Chancellor Merkel, referring to Eurozone deficit and debt rules, said in a speech to the Bundestag.[13] She also conceded that the sanctions mechanism of the Stability and Growth Pact were "insufficient". She therefore championed more effective and automatic deficit procedures to ensure the compliance of all member countries with the fiscal rules in the future.[14] Finance Minister Wolfgang Schäuble also considered a "Grexit"[15] a plausible—even desirable—strategy. His argument was that with Greece out, would make it easier to build a stronger monetary union with a more credible firewall. If Greece wanted to remain a member, then it "must form a stable government and it must adhere to its

[7] Alesina and Ardagna (2009).

[8] Schäuble (2013c).

[9] Abadi and Germania (2010).

[10] Benhold and Castle (2008), Münchau (2008), and Vinoncur (2009).

[11] The inclusion of the IMF was influenced by the fact that in the past it made its support of financial aid packages conditional on the readiness of lender countries to adjust their macroeconomic and structural policies. IMF Conditionality, March 31, 2014 (https://www.imf.org/external/np/exr/facts/conditio.htm).

[12] Bundesregierung (2010a, b).

[13] Deutscher Bundestag (2010), p. 2719.

[14] Bundesregierung (2010a).

[15] The term "Grexit" has been introduced by Citigroup economist Michael Saunders. Boesler (2012).

obligations as well," he added[16] Countries which seriously infringed the rules of currency union should "in extreme cases" lose EU structural fund payments and "have their voting rights in the Council suspended for at least one year". In a document entitled "Key Proposals to strengthen the Euro Area" he proposed various measures to assure a strict enforcement of fiscal discipline in the future. The proposals included more stringent budgetary surveillance within the EU alongside reinforcement of budgetary discipline. He also called for creating binding national law to respect the European Stability and Growth Pact. He pointed out that his new rules would require changes to EU treaties.[17]

The Merkel government's response to the looming Greek sovereign debt crisis revealed some serious flaws in Germany's legal reference points: the German narrative of the euro crisis and the virtues of the Swabian housewife.

1. Roots of the Crisis. Both the Maastricht Treaty of 1993 and the Stability and Growth Pact (SGP) were directed at constraining fiscal deficits and debts; they were not designed to address persistent structural problems in several Eurozone member countries rooted in private-sector overreach and macroeconomic policies, namely rising account imbalances, trade deficits, housing bubbles, large private debts and high banking leverage. Public debt in the euro area actually declined from 71.7 % in 1999 to 66.2 % in 2007 while private sector debt dramatically increased as a consequence of an unsustainable housing and consumption binge.[18] Policy makers ignored the huge risks of rising private debt to the Eurozone economy. The massive increase of private debt revealed "the obsession of the architects of the Maastricht Treaty with government failures (which) made them blind to market failures."[19] "The insouciance of policy makers about the risk being run" before 2008 ended in "a deep recession and a prolonged post-crisis malaise, as economies not only lost the fuel of extra borrowing but also grappled with the overhang of debt."[20]
2. Lenders' complacency. Adoption of the euro and loose global credit conditions in the 2000s allowed booming economies of the euro periphery like Greece and Spain easy access to foreign borrowing supported by the ECB's decision to keep interest rates at low levels in light of Germany's sweeping labor market reforms. They did not encounter any institutional constraints or market pressure to slow down their precarious expansion of debt-financed private demand with deteriorating competitiveness and labor market rigidities exacerbating these external imbalances. This irresponsible spending binge was made possible by irresponsible cross-border lending especially from German and French banks

[16] Spiegel (2014a, b); and Geithner (2014), p. 483.

[17] Schäuble (2012c) and Thomas and McGroarty (2010).

[18] Lojsch et al. (2011), p. 17; International Monetary Fund (2011), pp. 1–6; Legrain (2014), pp. 46–96; Geithner (2014), p. 447.

[19] Pisani-Ferry (2013), p. 55; Chen et al. (2013), pp. 101–142; Laeven and Tressel (2013), pp. 39–66; Peet and La Guardia (2014), p. 30.

[20] Wolf (2014b).

that helped to inflate the private sector excesses in deficit economies in search for higher yields. “Excess borrowing by fools would have been impossible without excess lending by fools: creditors and debtors are joined at the hip.”[21] This complacency came to an abrupt end in 2009 when the shock waves of the financial earthquake in the United States reached Europe and the falsification of Greek fiscal accounts and the prospect of massive budget deficits became public.

3. Irrational exuberance of the markets. Ordoliberal wisdom states that the market and its participants always act rationally. The exceptional risk taking of financial markets before 2007 generated a housing bubble, soaring housing prices, rising debt and rapidly increasing leverage inside the financial sector itself. The financial markets not only promoted exceptional risk taking but they also ignored the risks that existed long before in the crisis countries. The interest rate differentials between German government bonds to 10-year treasury bonds for Portugal, Italy, Ireland, Greece and Spain were minimal. Interest rates no longer served as signals of macroeconomic pressure points. It was only at the end of 2009, the spread in interest rates abruptly surged when Greece plunged into deep crisis. The negative sentiments within the financial markets spread contagiously to other countries with large external imbalances, notably Italy and Spain, which threatened their creditworthiness and ultimately the survival of the euro area. Thus, financial markets did not “act preventively but simply punitively.”[22]
4. Misreading of the no-bail-out clause. The German failed to see that the no bail-out clause of the Lisbon Treaty (Article 125) is the kind of law “that is irrelevant until needed,” and when needed “it becomes impossible to apply.”[23] Article 125 was designed for good weather. It did not include mechanisms to cope with the gathering storm of the euro crisis, because the German government (wrongly) assumed that the very existence of the macroeconomic convergence criteria would automatically enforce compliance by the member countries. Strict adherence to German constitutional law and a strict application of the convergence criteria within the EU treaties together with deep-held ordoliberal convictions that looked to the past for answers severely circumscribed German policy to take a more accommodative fiscal and monetary policy in support of distressed member states. Furthermore, the no bailout rule was designed as a wall against self-inflicted government defaults. The Maastricht Treaty did not envisage defaults as a result of contagion where financial fundamentals of troubled countries did not point to budgetary excesses.[24]

---

[21] Wolf (2014a), p. 80; Pisani-Ferry (2013), pp. 49–51.

[22] Quitzau (2014), p. 4; Chen et al. (2013); Laeven and Tressel (2013).

[23] Münchau (2010b).

[24] Quitzau (2014), p. 4.

5. Relativization of debt rules. The protective procedures of the Stability and Growth Pact began to unravel on November 25, 2003 when the ECOFIN Council decided not to apply the excessive deficit procedure against France and Germany and to grant both countries an additional year to balance their budgets. Under the pressure of France and Germany, the European Council approved an amended Stability and Growth Pact in March 2005. The ceilings of 3 % for budget deficit and 60 % for public debt were maintained, but the decision to declare a country in excessive deficit could now rely on certain parameters: the behavior of the cyclically adjusted budget, the level of debt, the duration of the slow growth period and the possibility that the deficit is related to productivity-enhancing procedures. The Schröder government relativized the very institution its predecessor so diligently shaped; it thereby set a bad example to peripheral countries that had far more vulnerable economies like Greece.[25]
6. It takes two to tango. The euro crisis unveiled deep macroeconomic imbalances within the euro area. Germany's lending was the other side of the ordoliberal coin in support of an export-led growth strategy. Its success rested on the readiness to provide foreign demand with money to buy German products. The more successful this strategy, the more stock of lending and borrowing was piling up. The German government ignored the two-way street of this structural imbalance between lender and borrower. Instead, Berlin drew the wrong conclusion that piling up of debt in the peripheral countries like Greece or Ireland could be treated by a one-size-fits-all-policy where the discipline rested exclusively on the side of the borrowers while Germany's current account surplus of around 7 % of GDP remained unaffected.
7. Compounding the Greek malaise. Instead of expelling any doubt about Greece's ability to refinance its debt, Merkel's remark to support Greece only once it was denied access to the markets reinforced market doubts in Athens' credibility to manage its outstanding debt and raised anxiety that the monetary union could fall apart in a disorderly heap. The avoidance of the dire consequences of a "Grexit" required exceptional access by Greece to external financial assistance; without which the Greek patient would be unable to get out of his self-made fiscal quagmire and threatened to infect other weak Eurozone economies. In short, Merkel's reassurance made Greece's failure inevitable for which the German purse would pay.[26]
8. Sounding like Herbert Hoover in the 1930s. The Merkel government's iron-clad commitment to a strategy of austerity and its deep scepticism of forceful

---

[25] ECOFIN Council, *Implementation of Stability and Growth Pact*, 2546th Council meeting, 14492/1/03 Rev 1 en) (Presse 320), pp. 15–22 Brussels, November 25, 2003 (http://ec.europa.eu/economy_finance/economic_governance/sgp/pdf/11_council_press_releases/2003-11-25_council_press_release_en.pdf); Council of the European Union (2005), pp. 22–23; European Commission (2006), pp. 36–38; Savage (2007), pp. 165–173; Crawford (2007), pp. 138–140 and 142; Reiermann and Wiegrefe (2012).

[26] Jones (2010), p. 33.

financial rescues made the problem worse. Instead of reacting with "massive preemptive force" to remove the circumstances that made it rational for the markets to panic, the Merkel government adopted the "clear view" of the Swabian housewife: "Greece had binged, so it needed to go on a strict diet. Other nations with unsustainable deficits had to do the same." At the same time, the Merkel government began to slash the German federal budget and introduced a debt brake into the German constitution with the expectation that the euro area partners should emulate the good German example. This "clear view" squandered an opportunity to build credibility with the markets: "Europe continued to burn in the fall" of 2010 and looked "like Herbert Hoover in the 1930s."[27]

9. Sacrificing the strategic to the tactical. Domestic politics, especially the critical state election in North Rhine Westphalia on May 9, 2010, led to a delayed policy response by the Chancellor. The longer Merkel dragged her feet, the more the markets began to doubt her willingness to get ahead of the crisis and spend whatever is necessary to contain the Greek sovereign debt crisis and to prevent it from infecting other parts of the euro area. As the Economist observed, "Thanks to the extraordinary incompetence, Europe's leaders have almost ensured that the Greek rescue failed before it began."[28]
10. Costs of abstention. Doing nothing raised the costs for the German public purse even more. Her initial abstention did not stop but snow-balled the economic and political crisis. It allowed the "fast and furious"[29] Greek contagion to spread into a continent-wide conflagration that threatened the very existence of the euro. A sense of Murphy's Law spread through the markets: everyone was expecting the malaise could get worse—and it got worse. The irony is that Merkel's initial indecisiveness turned Germany from a bystander into a stakeholder who became trapped into providing permanent financial assistance to the ailing economies in the Southern periphery to prevent a default and a subsequent unravelling of the monetary union on which the success of Germany's export-led growth model so critically depends.

3.2 Merkel's Tough Love: Solidity in Return for Solidarity

The escalation of the euro crisis in spring 2010 presented a tricky quandary for the Chancellor. To stand back risked the euro crisis spinning out of control, Dominique Strauß-Kahn, the head of the IMF, warned Chancellor Merkel in late April.[30] Jean Claude Trichet, the head of the ECB, reminded the euro area governments that it

---

[27] Geithner (2014), pp. 447–448 and 475.

[28] The Economist (2010); Schwarzer (2010), pp. 16–17; Roubini (2010a).

[29] Reinhart and Rogoff (2009), pp. 201 and 241.

[30] Bundesregierung (2010c) and Kulish (2010).

was their "primary responsibility to take appropriate measures in order to counter the present severe tensions."[31]

It was the financial markets[32] that forced the German government to give up its initial minimalist approach in the euro crisis management in favour of a committed posture to meet the crisis du jour. As an ominous sign of a Greek contagion Portuguese, Spanish and Italian bond yields began to spike. Financial markets were unconvinced that the efforts of the euro member countries to get the crisis under control were sufficient to remove the threat of a disintegration of the Eurozone. The Royal Bank of Scotland concluded that if Greece, Portugal or Spain were allowed to default, the global financial system would suffer serious damage.[33] A breakup would be a cataclysmic blow and for Germany particularly destabilizing. A Union Banque Suisse (UBS) analysis suggested that Germany might suffer a loss of 20–25 % of GDP in the first year and then roughly half that amount in each subsequent year.[34] Moreover, a disintegration of the euro would threaten the central achievement of the European integration project—the Single European Market (SEM) whose greatest beneficiary was Germany—in 2013, 57 % of German exports went to the wider EU market.[35] Incurring the costs of conditional and temporary financial assistance appeared acceptable compared to the unknown impact of a disorderly default, a subsequent "Grexit" and an unravelling of the monetary union to the German public purse, the economy and the financial institutions which are both intrinsically intertwined with the broader EU market.

Following the logic of the domino theory that the euro would not become stronger if the weakest link, i.e. Greece, were to exit, Chancellor Merkel determined that Germany would be better off with all members remaining in the euro area. Just as the closure of Lehman Brothers in mid-October 2008 had almost brought down the global financial system,[36] a "Grexit" could become the equivalent to a breakdown of the euro area. Merkel drew four conclusions: First, Germany's vital national interests lay with the European Union, the common market and the common currency. Second, swift and targeted measures were essential to keep the damage as limited as possible and to assure the survival of the monetary union as a whole. Third, the shortcomings of EMU's institutional architecture had to be rectified but on German terms to forestall another existential crisis. Fourth, the only solution to the euro crisis was a step-by-step approach. As the debt crisis had been building for years, the solution would also take years. Not allowing Greece to default on its sovereign debt, stabilizing the euro area, and saving the euro in the long-run, have become Merkel's categorical imperatives.

---

[31] Trichet (2010).

[32] Pisani-Ferry (2013), p. 78.

[33] Barber (2010).

[34] Deo et al. (2011), The Economist (2011), Wolf (2011), and Thomas (2012a).

[35] Statistisches Bundesamt (2014), p. 413; Böhmer et al. (2014), pp. 19, 21–22, 26–27, 29.

[36] Pisani-Ferry (2013), p. 81; Geithner (2014), pp. 190 and 198–199.

For Merkel, the stabilization and preservation of the Eurozone is a vital German interest that has to be defended even at the cost of a bail-out of some feckless members. In a speech to the German Bundestag, Merkel summed her changed position to the Greek debt crisis as follows, "To put in a nutshell: the euro which is together with the common market the foundation of growth and prosperity for Germany is in danger. If we do not avert this danger the consequences for Europe will be immense. ...Much more than these numbers are at stake; it is about much more than one currency. Monetary union is a common destiny. It is therefore no more and no less than the preservation and viability of the European idea. This is our historic task, for if the euro fails Europe fails."[37] A year later she told the German public that Germany could not manage the job alone and that "unusual measures" would have to be taken to preserve "the stability of our currency".[38]

By helping Greece "we stabilize the Euro as a whole" declared Merkel and her Foreign Minister Guido Westerwelle in a common statement in early May 2010. Both, however, made plain that Germany was not prepared to issue a blank check to Athens. If Germany had to pay it wanted to ensure that it got its money worth. A shared European approach was contingent upon Greece's readiness to implement deep spending cuts and to adopt an ambitious reform and consolidation package to overcome the lagging competitiveness of the Greek economy. Countries which ignored these rules would face "consequences".[39] In sum, Merkel's answer to the gathering storm of the euro crisis was: "We need to take steps we can control." Foreign Minister Guido Westerwelle put it this way: "Our success could serve as a model to our partners."[40]

After weeks of intensive negotiations, the newly established Troika (IMF, the European Commission and the ECB) reached agreement with the Greek government on May 2, 2010 on a 3-year financial support program for Greece with a total of € 100 billion to which the euro area countries contributed € 80 billion under the Greek Loan Facility and the IMF committed € 30 billion under a Stand-By Arrangement (SBA).[41] The Greece bailout program did not mark the end but only the first step into long and arduous process to keep Greece and the other countries of the arc of crisis afloat. The European leaders met a week later and approved a temporary rescue mechanism. The European Financial Stability Facility (EFSF) had a total volume of € 500 billion in bilateral loan guarantees and balance-of-payment support backed by as much as € 250 billion in IMF loans provided on a country-to-country basis. The emergency fund was scheduled to end in June 2013. Its activation was subject to "strong conditionality" similar to the terms and conditions of the IMF and required unanimous approval by the member states.[42]

---

[37] Deutsche Bundestag (2010), pp. 4125–4126.

[38] Peel (2011).

[39] Bundesregierung (2010d) and Westerwelle (2013).

[40] Westerwelle (2012a, b, 2013).

[41] International Monetary Fund (2010) and European Commission (2010).

[42] Council of the European Union (2010).

In view of the malfunctioning of security markets, the ECB's Governing Council announced its Security Market Program (SMP) that allowed the central bank to buy public and private debt securities in secondary markets. The SMP program was directed to restore "an appropriate monetary transmission mechanism" The liquidity injected through the program into the markets was aimed at stabilizing the bond yields of the crisis-hit countries.[43]

Berlin in recognition of the failure of the original Stability and Growth Pact to prevent the outbreak of the sovereign debt crisis began to call for a "Faustian Pact"[44]: the long-term sustainability of the euro project had to be secured by linking lending facilities to a strengthened set of strict rules for monetary and fiscal stability. Based on a Franco-German initiative[45] the European Council agreed in mid-December 2010 to a revision of Article 136 TFEU. The new permanent European Stability Mechanism (ESM) replaced the European Financial Stability Facility (EFSF) and the European Financial Stabilization Mechanism (EFSM). Its main features are built on the existing EFSF. The authorized capital stock is € 700 billion with a lending capacity of € 500 billion. The ESM offers the same financing instruments as the EFSF including loans, precautionary financial assistance and loans to member states for recapitalizations of financial institutions, as well as primary and secondary bond market purchase. Maturities can extend up to 30 years. When EU member countries approved the revision of Article 136 TFEU, the new mechanism went into force on January 1, 2013 and entered into operation on July 1, 2013—then it became the sole mechanism to new requests for financial assistance by euro area Member States. The new permanent mechanism fulfills Berlin's core demands:

- the moral hazard is restricted by allowing the ESM only to be activated, "if indispensable, to safeguard the stability of the euro area as a whole"
- any requested financial assistance is made subject to "strict conditionality" based "on a stringent program of economic and fiscal adjustment in line with existing arrangements"
- the European Commission has new powers to scrutinize national budgets and impose fines on governments which consistently overshoot deficit guidelines set by the Growth and Stability Pact
- financial assistance required "unanimity of the members participating in the vote", thus giving the German government a veto power over any lending decision
- the total lending capacity is confined to € 500 billion thus limiting Germany's liability to a maximum guarantee commitment of € 190,024,800,000 with a paid

[43] European Central Bank (2010).

[44] Münchau (2011a).

[45] Bundesregierung (2010e, f, g).

in capital contribution of € 21.72 billion to the authorized capital stock of € 80 billion[46]

- the ESM recapitalization fund of € 60 billion can be used to bail out ailing banks in the future and only under specific conditions of the EFSF-ESM facility and contingent upon the establishment of a "single supervisory mechanism".[47]

Lastly, the German government began to push for a legally binding mechanism within an amended EU treaty which would impose sanctions on those member countries which were not in compliance with the stipulations of the Stability and Growth Pact. In a speech to the Bundestag on 7 September 2011, Chancellor Merkel demanded that all members should follow the German example and include a Schuldenbremse (debt brake) into their constitution. She therefore called for changes in the EU Treaty. "In the Lisbon treaty there is no mechanism to force those who can't or don't want to respect the stability pact to do so. Therefore, if we say to ourselves that we need more Europe, a stronger, better Europe in the future, then changes to the treaty should not be taboo to ensure the rules are binding."[48]

Following the German demand of binding reforms to Eurozone governance, all EU member states with the exception of the United Kingdom and the Czech Republic approved an additional, intergovernmental treaty—the Fiscal Compact. Member states adopted a set of country-specific fiscal rules that codify in national law the SGP's limits on government deficits and debt. If a member state is not in compliance with the percent budget deficit ceiling or the 60 % debt-level rules, the Commission initiates an Excessive Deficit Procedure (EDP) and submits a proposal for counter-measures for the member state to correct the situation. If a euro area member country repeatedly breaches its "adjustment path" towards its medium-term-budgetary objectives (MTO) and the SGP fiscal limits, then the Commission may fine the state a percentage of its GDP. In addition, member states are entitled to refer any country that fails to enforce sufficiently robust national fiscal rules to the European Court of Justice (ECJ).[49] For Berlin, the Fiscal Compact provides "real enforcement rights vis-à-vis national budgets" through the introduction of a debt brake and the new control authority of the Commission over national budgets.[50]

---

[46] General Secretary of the Council, *European Council Conclusions, December 16–17, 2010*, Brussels, January 25, 2011 (http://www.consilium.europa.eu/uedocs/cms_data/docs/pressdata/en/ec/118578.pdf); Shareholders. *European Stability Mechanism* (http://www.esm.europa.eu/about/governance/shareholders/index.htm); *Treaty Establishing the ESM* (http://www.european-council.europa.eu/media/582311/05-tesm2.en12.pdf).

[47] European Council (2012).

[48] Deutscher Bundestag (2011), pp. 14471 and 14472.

[49] *Treaty on Stability, Co-ordination and Governance in the EMU*, Title III:- Fiscal Compact; Title IV—Economic Policy Coordination and Convergence (http://european-council.europa.eu/media/639235/st00tscg26_en12.pdf); Hodson (2013), pp. 195 and 198.

[50] See Merkel's speeches to the European Parliament on November 7, 2012 (http://www.bundesregierung.de/ContentArchiv/DE/Archiv17/Reden/2012/11/2012-11-07-merkel-eu.html) and the German parliament on October 18, 2012, *Plenarprotokoll 17/198*, p. 23813 (http://dip21.bundestag.de/dip21/btp/17/17198.pdf) and on December 13, 2012, *Plenarprotokoll 17/214*, pp. 26195–26196 (http://dip21.bundestag.de/dip21/btp/17/17214.pdf).

The Compact also re-assured bailout–weary German voters that the rescue programs were not just the first installment towards a euro transfer union at the expense of German taxpayers but a necessary evil to prevent a disintegration of the currency union and to gain time to rectify the shortcomings of the original institutional architecture of the monetary union. In sum, Berlin succeeded in establishing an "austerity club" whose goal is to "enforce life-long austerity, with balanced budget rules enshrined in national constitutions."[51]

"If the euro fails, Europe fails" became Merkel's mantra. Ever since, she supported stabilizing measures to ensure that such a meltdown never happens again. If Germany could not avoid writing the checks to help struggling countries, it wanted to set the terms. Her preferred sequence of action became clear: fiscal rectitude and improved competitiveness as the prize for German solidarity.[52] The Greek rescue program did prevent an immediate default and allowed Greece to remain in the euro. The Greek bailout, however, left a "toxic legacy"[53] as the IMF conceded in an ex-post evaluation of its 2010 SBA program.[54] The report raised some serious questions about the effectiveness and appropriateness of Berlin's call for "expansionary fiscal contraction" as the only path out of the euro crisis:

1. Constricted German narrative. The Merkel government had spent the first 2 years of the euro crisis telling German voters that the crisis in the peripheral countries was exclusively fiscal in nature and that profligate governments were responsible for the resultant mess. The irresponsible behaviour however, extended far beyond fiscal discipline. Only Greece qualified as a genuine fiscal crisis. Ireland's and Spain's main drag was not fiscal profligacy or excessive current account deficits but a massive expansion of private credit. Italy's and France's problems are not deficit spending, but sluggish economic growth which raised serious questions about the sustainability of the mountain of debt, which in the case of Italy had reached more than 120 % of GDP in 2010 and a gradual erosion of competitiveness paired with the inability of both political systems to address the structural problems of overregulation, job-destroying tax-systems and entrenched interest groups.[55]
2. Myopia of expansionary fiscal contraction. The G-20 summit in Toronto made the case for "synchronized fiscal adjustment" which would "at least halve the deficits by 2013 and stabilize or reduce government debt-to-GDP ratios by 2016."[56] The deleveraging of public and private sectors at the same time however, removed an urgently needed offset for the crisis-hit economies in the southern periphery, especially for the enfeebled Greek patient whose

[51] Münchau (2012b).

[52] Merkel (2013b).

[53] Wolf (2013d).

[54] International Monetary Fund (2013).

[55] Eurostat (2011); Pisani-Ferry (2013), pp. 63–66, 113–114; Peet and La Guardia (2014), pp. 30 and 70–72.

[56] Bundesregierung (2010h), p. 3.

condition worsened. "If we all hit the brakes together, we all get stuck together," former French Finance Minister Pierre Muscovici[57] summed up the paradox of thrift. The central issue was not if public debt at a specific ratio to GDP, presumably above 90 %, were to stunt growth as Rogoff and Reinhard argued.[58] Of more immediate concern was the impact of severe government spending cuts on economic activity as IMF analysts pointed out. A revision of the fiscal multipliers—the effect that adding or subtracting a dollar of government spending would have on the broader economy during a downturn—showed that they were twice as large (1 %) as initially assumed (0.5 %). Instead, rapid fiscal adjustment in the middle of a deep recession turned out to be the best recipe for a toxic mix of economic contraction, staggering unemployment and increasing debt. The standby arrangement assumed that Greece could impose austerity with little effect on growth and employment. The Greek economy encountered a much deeper-recession than expected—the decline in real GDP between 2009 and 2012 was 17 %, the forecast was 5.5 %—with depressingly high unemployment—the jobless rate in 2012 was 25 % to the original projection of 15 %. Debt originally projected to peak at around 155 % of GDP in 2013 increased to 170 % of GDP. The larger than expected downturn in economic activity put pressure on the sustainability of Greece's escalating public debt.[59]

3. Negative effects of post-crisis adjustment. The persistent debt overhang of the private and public sector in the weak peripheral countries and the slow progress that has been made in these countries to bring down the combined debt levels implies that deleveraging will take years, if not decades, to be completed. The corollary of private saving and further fiscal consolidation through a combination of tax increases and spending cuts is lower levels of domestic demand (private consumption, private investment and government spending). The Eurozone's fiscal compact which will kick in 2016 will amplify the negative effects of post-crisis adjustment: national governments can no longer increase their debts to absorb the effects of private-sector deleveraging. Thus, the new fiscal rules will prolong a period of already sluggish growth, a staggering jobless rate, lowflation, a constant threat of insolvency and political upheavals.[60]
4. Fiscal short-sightedness. The Growth and Stability Pact may cause serious policy errors in an environment of prolonged lowflation. Lowflation distorts the fiscal adjustment effectively taken by euro area member countries. Fiscal adjustments implemented by national governments in an environment of persistent lowflation increase the risk of deflationary pressures which will further

[57] Lowry (2013). See also Summers (2012, 2013a, b), Dolan (2012), and Wolf (2013a, c).

[58] Reinhart and Rogoff (2010), pp. 573–578.

[59] International Monetary Fund (2013), pp. 21, 22, 26, 42. See also Legrain (2014), pp. 97–125; Pisani-Ferry (2013), pp. 108–115; Peet and La Guardia (2014), pp. 67, 69, 156; Krugman (2015a, b).

[60] Standard & Poors (2014), pp. 3, 5, 11; Münchau (2014d).

aggravate the debt problems of the weak euro area member countries.[61] The causal relationship between fiscal tightening, sluggish growth, higher debt burden and persistent lowflation raises the cardinal question whether sovereign states still have to implement additional fiscal tightening in order to fulfil the pact's rules that will only exacerbate "the chronic demand deficiency syndrome"?[62]

5. German unilateralism: The introduction of a balanced budget law by the German parliament on May 29, 2009 into the German constitution forbids the federal government from 2016 onwards to run a structural deficit of more than 0.35 % of GDP. From 2020, the states will not be permitted to run any structural deficit at all.[63] A debt brake enshrined in the constitutions of euro area member countries would inspire confidence in the markets that they can adopt exit strategies from excessive fiscal deficits as the "prerequisite for balanced and sustainable growth". The law illustrates German attitude to debt as morally objectionable with zero as the correct level of debt.[64] If the long-term survival of the euro area requires greater fiscal co-ordination, Berlin has tied itself to a standard of the "most dour and simple-minded conservatism" it expects others to follow. And it exemplified Berlin's "policy unilateralism at its most extreme."[65]
6. Beggar-your-neighbour policy. Emulating Germany's neo-mercantilist growth model powered amounts to a "beggar-your-neighbour policy". The snag is that an increase in the exports of one country leads to a decline of other countries "everything else being equal".[66] It is impossible for all Eurozone governments to rebalance their economies all at the same time by exporting and investing more, while their consumers borrow less.[67] The German economy became structurally dependent on foreign demand, particularly from other euro area member countries, to drive economic growth—exports expanded by almost 60 % from 2000 (€ 597.4 billion) to 2010 (€ 951.9 billion); their share to German GDP increased from 28.3 % in 2000 to 37 % ten years later.[68] Germany's trade surpluses steadily increased since 2007 to € 217 billion or 7.4 % of GDP in 2014.[69] German exports were indirectly stimulated and

[61] Smaghi (2014).

[62] Wolf (2015).

[63] Gesetz zur Änderung des Grundgesetzes (Art. 91c, 91d, 104b, 109, 109a, 115, 143d), Bundesgesetzblatt (BGBl.) I 2009, Bonn, July 31, 2009, pp. 2248–2250 (http://npl.ly.gov.tw/pdf/6919.pdf); Deutscher Bundestag (2009).

[64] Schäuble (2010).

[65] Tooze (2010); Tooze (2010), p. 27. See also Münchau (2009a) and Wolf (2010b).

[66] Britain (2013).

[67] Wolf (2013e, f), Ferguson (2013), Krugman (2013a, b), Tilford and Springford (2013), Cohen-Setton (2013), and The Economist (2014a).

[68] Federal Statistical Office (2015b), p. 2; Federal Statistical Office (2015c), p. 3.

[69] Federal Statistical Office (2015a).

subsidized and German imports inhibited by an artificially and systematically undervalued "German euro" that led some observers to brand Germany a "stealth currency manipulator".[70] German obsession with exports not only reinforced downward trends at home—low productivity growth, low public and private investment rate, extremely weak domestic demand and a growing imbalance between corporate profits and worker pay. The imposition of Germany's preferred policy of internal devaluation on the struggling Eurozone economies[71] together with Germany's persistent current account surplus also contributed to "a deflationary bias for the euro area, as well as for the world economy."[72] And Germany as an obedient follower of a rules-based system should know that fiscal rules can work only if applied symmetrically to countries with persistent fiscal deficits and current account surplus. It was Mr. Weidmann who sharply rebutted criticism that Germany must address persistent imbalances of its own economy. Comparing Germany's economy to a top football team, he said it would make no sense to criticize the surplus and handicap Germany by reducing it. "The quality of the Bundesliga doesn't improve by getting the top Bundesliga football teams play all their matches wearing backpacks."[73]

7. The fruits of myopic frugality. Two decades of underinvestment in human and physical capital is a long-standing shortcoming of the Germany economy. The share of investment in GDP has been declining rapidly, from an average of 23 % in the 1990s to 17 % today, well below the 21 % average for industrial countries. The decaying infrastructure—46 % of the bridges, 41 % of its streets and 20 % of its highways need repair—together with low spending on education puts the long-term growth prospect of Europe's largest economy and also of the rest of Europe at risk. The principle constraint on increased public sector investment is the constitutional budget rule that limits the structural deficit to 0.35 % of GDP. Berlin's narrow focus on debt reduction stands in the way to renew the country's aging capital stock and foster growth.[74]
8. "Extend and pretend". Greece's significant debt overhang and a more sustainable debt outlook required debt restructuring from the beginning.[75] Instead, the German government opted for cutting down fiscal deficits and extending the

[70] Prestowitz (2013).

[71] Posen (2013); Dullien (2013); Tilford (2006), pp. 35–40, 51–52, 57–58; Tilford (2010), pp. 1–5; Tooze (2012), p. 23.

[72] U.S. Department of the Treasury. Office of International Affairs (2013), p. 25. See also European Commission (2014d), pp. 8, 9, 13–14; European Commission (2014e), pp. 3, 4, 6; European Commission (2014f), p. 29.

[73] Deutsche Bundesbank (2014a, b).

[74] Tooze (2012), pp. 23, 27; Fratzscher (2013, 2014a); Fratzscher (2014b), pp. 74–95; Baldi et al. (2014), pp. 8–10, 14, 15; European Central Bank (2013b); Dailey and Smale (2013); Storbeck (2014); The Economist (2014b); Wagstyl (2014).

[75] Reinhart and Rogoff (2013), Roubini (2010b), Wolf (2010a, 2013d), Münchau (2010a, 2014c), Buiter (2012), and Taylor (2013b).

payback period of Greece's debt. Berlin's strategy took for granted that an expansionary fiscal contraction would move Greece's debt to a sustainable path that the markets would award. The German-inspired policy prescription assumed that weak countries like Greece could pay back the growing mountain of debt someday. It would require improbable economic growth rates for many years to bring Greece debt down substantially. But without some meaningful debt relief, the mountain of debt will make it extremely difficult for Athens to turn the corner, the IMF concluded. More debt relief is unavoidable—some 7 % of GDP—to meet the debt sustainability target of 124 % in 2020 and of 110 % in 2022.[76] The only question is how far default will occur through inflation, and how much through formal or coercive debt restructuring as Greece's debt problems are becoming more intractable. Berlin's denial of debt restructuring could risk exacerbating the final costs of deleveraging.[77]

9. German banks' fatal Greece exposure. Berlin ignored the warnings from IMF analysts, because it did not want to force German financial institutions to accept huge losses on their Greek bond holdings estimated to be around € 28 billion.[78] These holdings would have dropped in value were the Greek private creditors to be bailed in. Huge Greek write-offs would have exposed the fragility of German lenders. They might have suffered the same fate as the Greek banks: they had to be bailed out, too. Berlin would then be forced to approve huge bank rescue programs to shore up the German banking sector. To avoid crippling losses to German banks, Berlin opted for a transfer of ownership of a large part of the Greek debt from the private to the public sector via two bailout programs. The transfer of ownership of Greek debt provided a window of opportunity for many private lenders to reduce their exposures and to escape unscathed while the German public purse was put on the hook.[79]
10. Targeted Obsessions: The TARGET2 system (Trans-European Automated Real-time Gross Settlement Express Transfer System)—the relationship established between the TARGET2 users and the receptive central bank[80]—generated large claims in the central banks of surplus countries and vice versa large liabilities in the central banks of deficit countries. The Bundesbank's TARGET2 demands rose to € 751 billion in August 2012.[81] The worry that German taxpayers will be trapped by huge TARGET2 liabilities materializes

[76] International Monetary Fund (2013), pp. 26–28.

[77] Plender (2014).

[78] Ewing (2010a, b) and Pisani-Ferry and Sapir (2010).

[79] Frühauf (2012); Fratzscher (2014b), p. 179.

[80] European Central Bank, *TARGET2* (http://www.ecb.europa.eu/paym/t2/html/index.en.html).

[81] Sinn (2012a), pp. 197–206, 271–278; Sinn (2014), pp. 41–42, 45, 50, 94–95, 132, 179; Sinn (2012b, c).

only if the euro area were to collapse and the ECB to be dissolved.[82] Owing to ECB's OMT program the Bundesbank's "targeted" surplus more than halved to € 310 billion a year later.[83] As distressed countries came to depend on their domestic banks which in turn were heavily dependent on national banks, the European System of Central Banks (ECSB) "ended up indirectly funding" them. The ESCB, in effect, allowed these countries to reduce their large current account deficits over several years despite the collapse of private funding, thus providing them "an essential cushion" in rough times.[84]

11. Domino effect of bail-ins. The German government agreed to a restructuring of Greece's debt in March 2012[85] under two conditions: private holders of Greek government bonds (banks, insurers and investment funds) had to defray the costs of a debt restructure agreement while a restructuring of the debt Germany now owns via the EFSF-ESM rescue programs are categorically excluded. Greece's debt swap offer in late February 2012 based on the Private Sector Involvement (PSI) measure planted a "time bomb"[86] that did blow a deep hole into Cyprus' financial system because of their banks' deep exposure to the Greek "haircut". The € 10 billion support package for the ailing Cyprus financial system agreed to by the Troika and the Cyprus government in mid-March 2013, underlined the German determination that a bail in of private creditors had to be part of any rescue program guaranteed by taxpayers.[87] If anything, the Cyprus crisis revealed how far the euro area member countries were from a commonly agreed institutional framework for the resolution of banking sovereign crises.[88]
12. Paradoxes of German assistance. The deeper the German public purse became entangled in Eurozone rescue measures the more insistent Berlin became that shareholders and depositors with bank deposits above € 100,000 had to accept the losses of "haircuts" and bank closures, while troubled states had to repay the public-guaranteed loans in full and in due time. The unequal treatment of public and private creditors helped to prevent a situation emerging that could have triggered the payment of the German guarantees of up to € 190 billion which would be irretrievably lost.[89] But it did not address the further increase of Greece's total debt burden to 175.1 % at the end of 2013; many experts warn

[82] Kaminska (2011); Kaiser (2012a); Hulverscheidt and Roßmann (2012); Jahn and Plickert (2013, 2015); Griechen bringen ich Geld aus dem Land, *Frankfurter Allgemeine Zeitung*, February 7, 2015.

[83] Fratzscher (2014b), p. 178.

[84] Wolf (2014a), pp. 69 and 71.

[85] *Eurogroup Statement on Cyprus*, Brussels, March 25, 2013 (http://eurozone.europa.eu/newsroom/news/2013/03/eg-statement-cyprus-25-03-13/).

[86] Greece launches debt swap offer, *Financial Times*, February 25, 2012; Higgins and Alderman (2013).

[87] Peel (2013a).

[88] Pisani-Ferry (2013), p. 96.

[89] Münchau (2013a), Wolf (2013b), Véron (2013), Barber (2013), and Schäuble (2013b).

that a debt burden above 120 % of GDP is unsustainable for a small economy like Greece. Athens is trapped into a self-reinforcing cycle of greater borrowing and more indebtedness that eventually becomes unsustainable. Because of its staunch refusal to agree to a "haircut" for public holders of Greece's debt Germany is trapped into providing new rescue packages if Athens proves unable to service its maturing debt or to cover its fiscal imbalances—the Commission estimated that Greece would need up to € 14.9 billion in financial help through 2015.[90]

13. Restricted ESM backstops. On German insistence, the power to "directly recapitalize" banks through the ESM, is attached with several strict conditions like "bail-in instruments" which will make it highly unlikely, that the ESM bank recapitalization fund will be used at all. Germany also made clear that the fund could not bail out banks with legacy problems, implying it is of no use for ailing Spanish savings banks (cajas) who could only receive loans via the bank recapitalization fund of the Spanish government.[91] The mutually destructive links between banks and sovereigns, the permanent ESM facility was supposed to severe, may not be broken at all. As Olli Rehn concluded, these conditions would "dilute" the link, but not break it.[92]
14. The doom loop unchecked. The ESM bank recapitalization fund of € 60 billion is insufficient to cover hidden losses by banks of up to € 2.6 trillion. Without a substantial fund of the magnitude of € 2 trillion it barely matters who will become the resolution authority because the fund cannot act timely and effectively to dramatic losses in the banking sector. The restricted access to and the limited volume of the ESM bank recapitalization fund means that the liability of failing banks will remain with domestic institutions and the banks' home states first and foremost and not with the European tax-payers.[93] Debt domestication in the euro area—more sovereign debt has been absorbed by domestic banks since 2011—further tightens the mutually destructive link between sovereigns and banks. The doom loop unchecked could increase the systemic risks for both sovereigns and banks if a fresh crisis erupted in the financial system.[94]
15. German leadership on the cheap. Berlin's measured step-by-step policy to do just enough to prevent the collapse of the euro area has been "a day late and a euro short."[95] Her minimalist approach made the problem more difficult, expensive and protracted. Merkel was not prepared to assume the responsibility Jean-Claude Trichet, the former head of the ECB, had in mind when he announced the Securities Market Program (SMP): that the European partners, in a mutual endeavor, would build an effective firewall to cushion adjustment in embattled Eurozone economies. The Merkel government ruled out the creation

[90] European Commission (2014c), p. 72; Byrne and Hope (2014).

[91] Münchau (2012c, 2013d), Gericano (2013), and Davies (2012).

[92] Spiegel (2013a).

[93] Münchau (2013b, c).

[94] Unmack (2013), Atkins (2012, 2013b, 2013c), and Thompson and Jenkins (2013).

[95] Kleine-Brockhoff (2011), Roubini (2010a), and The Economist (2010).

of a credible firewall of the magnitude of up to € 1–1.5 trillion which would fall disproportionately on the German public purse. The volumes of both the EFSF and the ESM are insufficient to assure the sustainability of Italy's or Spain's mountains of public and private debt—Italy alone has more than € 2 trillion of public debt outstanding.[96] Successful German resistance to the establishment of a reliable firewall may again raise doubts in the markets about the sustainability of sovereign debt and the viability of the monetary union.[97]

In sum, the Merkel government's attitude toward the Greek sovereign debt crisis began to change in spring 2010. The Chancellor recognized that, given the reality of extensive trade and financial interconnectedness, a disorderly euro area hurts not just the periphery, but the core. German officials began to support extensive bailout packages to ensure that the threat of a disintegration of the euro area would gradually recede. It was in the overriding German interest to keep the euro area intact. The financial markets rightly concluded that Berlin was prepared to bailout the indebted Eurozone member countries. Merkel's change was more revealing about underlying German attitudes toward the crisis than about practical solutions to address the root causes of the problem. The message from Berlin to Eurozone member countries remained the same: no gain without pain! Merkel's austerity-driven approach protected her domestic flanks but exacerbated the economic and fiscal woes of the misery belt: it tried to remove a cancer while the patient's heart was on the brink of failure.[98] Lastly, Berlin's measured step-by-step policy to do just enough to prevent the collapse of the euro area has been a day late and a euro short. The logic of Merkel's minimalist policy made the German public purse an ever bigger stakeholder in the euro crisis while never willing "to devote enough resources to ensure they were effective."[99]

3.3 Merkel's Acquiescence to Draghi's Bazooka

When the markets conceived the ESM rescue fund as insufficient and Spanish and Portuguese bond yields subsequently shot up to dangerous levels in summer 2012, the ECB stepped in to prevent a further escalation of the crisis.[100] Mario Draghi declared that the ECB would do "whatever it takes" to protect the Eurozone from collapse. "And belief me, it will be enough."[101] In early September he announced the bold but controversial decision that the ECB would, if necessary, buy the sovereign debt of distressed countries in unlimited quantities in secondary markets.

[96] Eurostat (2014).

[97] Geithner (2014), pp. 473–474; Gurria (2012); Münchau (2012a, 2013b, d).

[98] Privitera (2012), p. 4.

[99] Wren-Lewis (2013). See also Roubini (2012, 2013a, b).

[100] Carrel et al. (2012), Irwin (2013), and Spiegel (2014c).

[101] European Central Bank (2012c).

Draghi explained the rationale of the OMT program as follows, "We aim to preserve the singleness of our monetary policy and to ensure the proper transmission of our policy stance to the real economy throughout the area. OMT will enable us to address severe distortions in government bond markets which originate from, in particular unfounded fears on the part of investors of the reversibility of the euro. ...You have in large parts of the euro area what we call a 'bad equilibrium' ... so, there is the case for intervening ... to break these expectations, which ... do not concern only the specific countries, but the euro area as a whole." The ECB will buy only short-term bonds with maturities up to 3 years on the secondary market. Money pumped into the financial markets will later be removed through the sales of securities or through regular lending to banks The ECB's intervention is contingent upon the country's willingness to submit to a structural adjustment program administered by the ESM.[102] The Markets believed Draghi. The OMT has not yet been applied, although the very existence of the facility has been credited for having restored confidence in the markets about the longevity of the euro. Subsequently, Italian and Spanish government bond yields fell to more tolerable levels. The OMT program has thus removed "dangerous tail risks related to a euro breakup."[103]

Draghi's unlimited, but ultimately untested pledge calmed markets because the German Chancellor acquiesced despite public objections by the Bundesbank.[104] The ECB bond buying revealed a split between the stand of principle taken by the Bundesbank and the more pragmatic attitude of the Chancellor. In an interview with Der Spiegel, Weidmann reiterated his visceral opposition to possible ECB bond purchases. "We should not underestimate the risk that central bank financing can become addictive like a drug." It would be a mistake for the ECB "to guarantee that every member remains in the euro zone no matter what the price." The decision to take on government debt should be made "by parliaments and not central banks", he added.[105]

Draghi's "bazooka" won the tacit backing of the Chancellor. She recognized that the bond buying program was helpful to back her step-by-step strategy to prevent an unravelling of the monetary union with unknown risks for Germany's export-dependent economy and its financial institutions. A Grexit would confront Berlin with the unenviable choice between the devil and the deep blue sea: a transfer union or the collapse of the euro.[106] From the G-8 summit meeting in Camp David, the OECD and the IMF to national capitals across Europe the message to Berlin was unanimous: the misery belt countries could not cut their way to fiscal health; some might be even tempted to take the risk of default. Germany the island of bliss could

---

[102] European Central Bank (2012a, b).

[103] IMF Report (2013), p. 5; de Grauwe and Ji (2012), pp. 34, 35, 37, 40; Wolf (2012b).

[104] Spiegel (2014c); Geithner (2014), p. 484.

[105] Weidmann (2012a), Deutsche Bundesbank (2012a, b, 2013), Jones and Peel (2012), and Ewing and Thomas (2014).

[106] Faiola (2012), Peel (2012b), von Hammerstein et al. (2012), and Spiegel (2014c).

not detach itself from the crisis that according to Berlin's narrative belonged to the others, namely the PIIGS. The front cover of the Economist featured the sinking of a ship symbolizing the world economy with the title: "Please can we start the engines now, Mrs. Merkel?"[107] In response to growing disenchantment with her insistence on lock-step austerity that others must suffer to preserve the system Merkel conceded the euro crisis demonstrated that "national answers are not sufficient to secure stability of the euro area."[108]

In-mid-August, she backed the ECB chief unequivocally for the first time, stating that the central bank "is following fully the same line" of the European heads of governments "to do everything possible to preserve the common currency." She concluded "that monetary stability issues justify the ECB's latest decisions", but she insisted that the development of the euro could be moved into a "positive" direction only if "conditions" were fulfilled. She defended Weidmann's right to openly criticize the OMT, but reminded him and other critics "to weigh their words very carefully" in a "very decisive phase".[109] Finance Minister Schäuble, who originally was a strong advocate of a "Grexit", began to criticize speculation among German politicians and economists about a possible Greek exit. "That achieves nothing. It simply stirs up insecurity and provokes a corresponding market reaction." He affirmed that "we will do whatever it takes to defend the euro."[110] As in spring 2010, Merkel concluded that the gathering storm of the euro crisis could undermine "European unity" and seriously threaten the competitiveness of the "export nation Germany" in the era of globalization. "We are all in the same boat. No European country can be strong in the long-run if others are not doing well."[111]

Weidmann's vociferous opposition served Merkel's purposes well, ensuring that any rescue program for Greece would come with many strings attached. As she said after a meeting with Greek Prime Minister Antonis Samaras, "I made clear in the talks that we of course expect from Greece that the commitments that were made be implemented, that deeds follow words."[112] With her renewed call of solidity in return for solidarity she remained in control of the delicate balancing act she had performed for 2 years: to assist struggling countries only if they accepted "irreversible steps towards a lasting stability union" while reassuring the German public that she was staunchly defending the German public purse. "Common liability can only take place, if sufficient control is assured," she told the Bundestag. However, she categorically excluded any form of debt mutualisation "as long as I live".[113]

[107] Birnbaum (2012); Jolly (2012); Castle (2012); Spiegel and Barker (2012); Junker (2012); de Vigo (2012); Schröder (2012); Kaiser (2012b); The Economist (2012a, pp. 11–12), The Economist (2012b); Wolf (2012a); Thomas (2012b); Altman (2012); Thomas (2012c); Ferguson and Roubini (2012).

[108] Deutscher Bundestag (2012c), p. 22223. See also Schäuble's speech to the Bundestag on July 19, 2012, Deutscher Bundestag.

[109] Bundesregierung (2012), Ewing (2012), and Bryant (2012).

[110] Peel (2012a) and Birnbaum and Schaeuble (2012).

[111] Merkel (2013a, b).

[112] Eddy (2012) and Ewing and Eddy (2012).

[113] Deutscher Bundestag (2012b), p. 22700; Deutscher Bundestag (2012c), p. 22224; Merkel (2012); Bannas (2012); Kundnani (2012).

The German public and the legislature proved to be a force manageable for Merkel. Her diligence in demanding strict standards of fiscal spending and structural reforms as the prize for German limited financial assistance to preserve the euro played well among German voters who were deeply opposed to more financial bailouts to profligate southern partners or to rushed steps towards more integration.[114] She effectively turned the euro crisis into a political opportunity to bolster her public standing and that of the CDU/CSU. Her cautious pragmatism in the euro crisis that had protected her countrymen from the mess elsewhere together with Germany's resilient economy won her a resounding endorsement from German voters in the federal elections in September 2013.[115] The Bundestag supported Merkel's linkage policy of solidity in return for solidarity as well. All bailouts for Greece,[116] Spain,[117] Cyprus,[118] Ireland[119] and

---

[114] Kulish (2012a, b), Atkins (2013a), and Peel (2013b).

[115] Kirkegaard (2013), Stephens (2013), and Davies (2013a, b).

[116] Deutscher Bundestag, *Gesetzentwurf der Fraktionen der CDU/CSU und FDP über den Entwurf eines Gesetzes zur Übernahme von Gewährleistungen zum Erhalt der für die Finanzstabilität in der Währungsunion erforderliche n Zahlungsfähigkeit der Hellenischen Republik (Währungsunion-Finanzstabilitätsgesetz-WFStG)*, Drucksachen 17/1544, 17/1561 and 17/1562 (**Greece I**); ibid., *Antrag des Bundesministeriums der Finanzen Finanzhilfen zugunsten der Hellenischen Republik; Einholung eines zustimmenden Beschlusses des Deutschen Bundestages nach § 3 Absatz 1 des Stabilisierungsmechanismusgesetzes (StabMechG) für Notmaßnahmen der Europäischen Finanzstabilisierungsfazilität zugunsten der Hellenischen Republik*, Drucksachen 17/8730, 17/8731 and 17/8735 (**Greece II**).

[117] Deutscher Bundestag, *Antrag des Bundesministeriums der Finanzen Finanzhilfe zugunsten Spaniens; Einholung eines zustimmenden Beschlusses des Deutschen Bundestages nach § 3 Absatz 1 in Verbindung mit § 3 Absatz 2 Nummer 1 und 4 des Stabilisierungsmechanismusgesetzes (StabMechG) für Notmaßnahmen der Europäischen Finanzstabilisierungsfazilität zugunsten Spaniens*, Drucksachen 17/10320 und 17/10321 (**Spain**).

[118] Deutscher Bundestag, *Antrag des Bundesministeriums der Finanzen Einholung eines zustimmenden Beschlusses des Deutschen Bundestages nach § 4 Absatz 1 Nummer 1 und 2 des ESM-Finanzierungsgesetzes, nach § 3 Absatz 1 des Stabilisierungsmechanismusgesetzes im Rahmen der Haftungsanpassungen nach Artikel 8 Absatz 2 des EFSF-Rahmenvertrages sowie nach § 3 Absatz 1 i.V.m. Absatz 2 Nummer 2 des Stabilisierungsmechanismusgesetzes hier: betreffend die Gewährung einer Stabilitätshilfe an die Republik Zypern in Form einer Finanzhilfefazilität des ESM gemäß Paragraf 4 Absatz 1 Nummer 1 des ESM-Finanzierungsgesetzes*, Drucksache 17/13060 (**Cyprus I**); ibid.; *Antrag des Bundesministeriums der Finanzen Einholung eines zustimmenden Beschlusses des Deutschen Bundestages nach § 4 Absatz 1 Nummer 1 und 2 des ESM-Finanzierungsgesetzes, nach § 3 Absatz 1 des Stabilisierungsmechanismusgesetzes im Rahmen der Haftungsanpassungen nach Artikel 8 Absatz 2 des EFSF-Rahmenvertrages sowie nach § 3 Absatz 1 i.V.m. Absatz 2 Nummer 2 des Stabilisierungsmechanismusgesetzes hier: betreffend die Annahme einer Vereinbarung über eine Finanzhilfefazilität zwischen der Republik Zypern und dem ESM und der Zustimmung zu einem Memorandum of Understanding gemäß Paragraf 4 Absatz 1 Nummer 2 des ESM-Finanzierungsgesetzes*, Drucksache 17/13060 (**Cyprus II**).

[119] Deutscher Bundestag, *Antrag des Bundesministeriums der Finanzen Einholung eines zustimmenden Beschlusses des Deutschen Bundestages nach § 4 Absatz 1 Nummer 1 und 2 des ESM-Finanzierungsgesetzes, nach § 3 Absatz 1 des Stabilisierungsmechanismusgesetzes im Rahmen der Haftungsanpassungen nach Artikel 8 Absatz 2 des EFSF-Rahmenvertrages sowie nach § 3 Absatz 1 i.V.m. Absatz 2 Nummer 2 des Stabilisierungsmechanismusgesetzes hier:*

Portugal[120] as well as the temporary and permanent rescue programs EFSF[121] and ESM[122] easily passed the Bundestag with large bipartisan majorities. The broad legislative approval of all measures related to the euro crisis had two minor flaws: the two coalition parties denied Chancellor Merkel the "chancellor's majority" of 312 votes in half of the twelve votes—Greece II, Spain, Cyprus I and II, Ireland and Portugal.[123]

---

betreffend die Verlängerung der maximalen durchschnittlichen Laufzeit des EFSF-Darlehens an Irland um sieben Jahre, Drucksache 17/13060 (**Ireland**).

[120] Deutscher Bundestag, *Antrag des Bundesministeriums der Finanzen Einholung eines zustimmenden Beschlusses des Deutschen Bundestages nach § 4 Absatz 1 Nummer 1 und 2 des ESM-Finanzierungsgesetzes, nach § 3 Absatz 1 des Stabilisierungsmechanismusgesetzes im Rahmen der Haftungsanpassungen nach Artikel 8 Absatz 2 des EFSF-Rahmenvertrages sowie nach § 3 Absatz 1 i.V.m. Absatz 2 Nummer 2 des Stabilisierungsmechanismusgesetzes hier: betreffend die Verlängerung der maximalen durchschnittlichen Laufzeit des EFSF-Darlehens an Portugal um sieben Jahre*, Drucksache 17/13060 (**Portugal**).

[121] Deutscher Bundestag, *Gesetzentwurf der Fraktionen der CDU/CSU und FDP über den Entwurf eines Gesetzes zur Änderung des Gesetzes zur Übernahme von Gewährleistungen im Rahmen eines europäischen Stabilisierungsmechanismus*, Drucksachen 17/6916, 17/7067 and 17/7130 (**EFSF**).

[122] Deutscher Bundestag, *Gesetzentwurf der Fraktionen der CDU/CSU und FDP Entwurf eines Gesetzes zu dem Vertrag vom 2. März 2012 über Stabilität, Koordinierung und Steuerung in der Wirtschafts- und Währungsunion*, Drucksachen 17/9046, 17/10125 and 17/10171 (**ESM I**), ibid., *Gesetzentwurf der Fraktionen der CDU/CSU und FDP über den Entwurf eines Gesetzes zu dem Vertrag vom 2. Februar 2012 zur Einrichtung des Europäischen Stabilitätsmechanismus*, Drucksachen 17/9045, 17/10126 and 17/10172 (**ESM II**); ibid., *Gesetzentwurf der Fraktionen der CDU/CSU und FDP Entwurf eines Gesetzes zur finanziellen Beteiligung am Europäischen Stabilitätsmechanismus (ESM-Finanzierungsgesetz – ESMFinG)*, Drucksachen 17/9048, 17/10126 and 17/10172 (**ESM III**); ibid., *Gesetzentwurf der Fraktionen der CDU/CSU und FDP Entwurf eines Gesetzes zu dem Beschluss des Europäischen Rates vom 25. März 2011 zur Änderung des Artikels 136 des Vertrags über die Arbeitsweise der Europäischen Union hinsichtlich eines Stabilitätsmechanismus für die Mitgliedstaaten, deren Währung der Euro ist*, Drucksachen 17/9047 and 17/10159 (**ESM IV**).

[123] Deutscher Bundestag, *Endgültiges Ergebnis der Namentlichen Abstimmung Nr. 1* (**Greece I**), Berlin, May 7, 2010 (http://www.bundestag.de/blob/191296/08bc1702033a6f7d957b652575a473b8/20100507_1-data.pdf); ibid., *Endgültiges Ergebnis der Namentlichen Abstimmung Nr. 1* (**Greece II**), February 27, 2012 (https://www.bundestag.de/blob/192300/0bf0d28ba709cc4f70b6f67673aab975/20120227_griechenland-data.pdf); ibid., *Endgültiges Ergebnis der Namentlichen Abstimmung Nr. 1* (**Spain**), July 19, 2012 (http://www.bundestag.de/blob/192516/30dc80a20d8daf827769e868aea2e360/20120719-data.pdf); ibid., *Endgültiges Ergebnis der Namentlichen Abstimmung Nr. 1* (**Cyprus I**), April 18, 2013 (http://www.bundestag.de/blob/194292/9f3595783042385616ad696e57effb86/20130418_zypern1-data.pdf); ibid., *Endgültiges Ergebnis der Namentlichen Abstimmung Nr. 2* (**Cyprus II**), April 18, 2013 (http://www.bundestag.de/blob/194288/ed1614aca818d0fb7f723fc664b60e82/20130418_zypern2-data.pdf); ibid., *Endgültiges Ergebnis der Namentlichen Abstimmung Nr. 3* (**Ireland**), April 18, 2013 (http://www.bundestag.de/blob/194298/eaa4df6081ccfc37c9728824080c40ea/20130418_irland3-data.pdf); ibid., *Endgültiges Ergebnis der Namentlichen Abstimmung Nr. 4*, April 18, 2013 (**Portugal**) (http://www.bundestag.de/blob/194294/ae275e49b7924f7d151d9da2b2750540/20130418_portugal4-data.pdf); ibid., *Endgültiges Ergebnis der Namentlichen Abstimmung Nr. 1* (**EFSF**), September 29, 2011 (http://www.bundestag.de/blob/192038/eb43e22bdfd4a1aeff0f0135a04c51cf/20110929_euro-data.pdf); ibid., *Endgültiges Ergebnis der Namentlichen Abstimmung Nr. 2* (**ESM I**), June 29, 2012 (http://www.bundestag.de/blob/192486/5deeda3e97f6b068f67dcfc0a170e3d5/20120629_17_9046-data.pdf); ibid., *Endgültiges*

Chancellor Schröder's risky decision in early November 2001 to tie the critical vote on Germany's participation in Operation Enduring Freedom in Afghanistan has taught Chancellor Merkel to avoid unneeded political controversy in the legislative chamber. Secondly, The Bundesbank and the Bundesverfassungsgericht emerged as Merkel's most formidable veto players at the domestic bargaining table.

Voting Record of the Merkel Government (CDU/CSU and FDP) on Euro Area Assistance Programs (2010–2013)

	Greece I	Greece II	Spain	Cyprus I	Cyprus II	Ireland
Yes	391	496	473	487	486	500
CDU/CSU	234	219	221	220	221	223
FDP	92	85	80	83	84	83
No	72	90	97	101	103	90
CDU/CSU	04	13	13	10	08	07
FDP	01	04	09	08	08	06
Abstention	30	05	13	103	11	13
CDU/CSU	0	02	0	08	01	01
FDP	0	01	01	08	0	0
Absent	30	29	37	19	20	26
CDU/CSU	01	03	03	06	07	06
FDP	0	03	03	01	01	04

	Portugal	EFSF	ESM I	ESM II	ESM III	ESM IV
Yes	494	523	488	493	495	504
CDU/CSU	220	226	231	218	218	218
FDP	84	89	87	82	83	83
No	92	85	110	106	101	97
CDU/CSU	07	10	03	16	16	16
FDP	07	03	04	10	08	08
Abstention	05	03	06	05	05	01
CDU/CSU	01	01	01	01	01	01
FDP	0	01	01	0	0	0
Absent	29	09	16	16	19	18
CDU/CSU	09	0	02	02	02	02
FDP	02	0	01	01	02	02

It was the Bundesbank, which began to raise its principled concern about the wisdom of collective actions to assist the Greek patient to prevent a meltdown of the monetary union. The ECB's active monetary policy since May 2010 turned out

Ergebnis der Namentlichen Abstimmung Nr. 3 (**ESM II**), June 29, 2012 (http://www.bundestag.de/blob/192484/bcbd6a39bdd611136188d1857950ec1d/20120629_17_9045-data.pdf); ibid., *Endgültiges Ergebnis der Namentlichen Abstimmung Nr. 4* (**ESM III**), June 29, 2012 (http://www.bundestag.de/blob/192490/859d2eb66c57c3739bf153360cc43d88/20120629_17_9048-data.pdf); ibid., *Endgültiges Ergebnis der Namentlichen Abstimmung Nr. 5* (**ESM IV**), June 29, 2012 (http://www.bundestag.de/blob/192488/a4d5085aac601e5f83c75d031bfc7b1d/20120629_17_9047-data.pdf).

to be the red flag to the its orthodox monetary policy. The SMP program enjoyed an overwhelming majority of the ECB's Governing Council members. Subsequent press accounts indicated that only Axel Weber, the head of the Bundesbank, and Jürgen Stark, a member of the ECB Governing Board and former member of the Bundesbank's Executive Board, strongly argued against the ECB role in a bond buying program of debt-ridden European countries in the markets. Both feared that the ECB's unconventional action would raise doubts about its prized independence from political influence, blur the responsibilities between monetary and fiscal policies and kindle inflation. "Buying government bonds entail considerable stability policy risks and thus I regard this program of the ECB's Council decision critically even in this exceptional situation", Weber said. By lending tens of billions of euros against bonds classed as "junk", the ECB would reward institutions that bought shaky sovereign debt and countries that issue it.[124] He, therefore, called for the SMP program to be phased out without delay.[125] Strains over the SMP came to a head in early 2011, when Weber, Berlin's favored candidate to succeed Jean-Claude Trichet as head of the ECB, announced his resignation as Bundesbank president in February 2011. With his misgivings over the ECB's decision to reactivate its SMP program in August, Stark resigned from the ECB Executive Board a month later.

Jens Weidmann, like his predecessor, turned out to be the defender of the Maginot Line of German orthodox monetary policy.[126] The insistence that the currency area could not become a community of shared liability became his recurrent refrain. Weidmann resisted the ECB's decision in August 2011 to buy Italian and Spanish sovereign bonds at a brisk pace.[127] He was the only member within the Governing Council who opposed the ECB's OMT program and turned into its constant critique. "Herr Nein" used the same arguments[128] against the ECB's OMT program he had directed against the SMP program.

- The decision goes beyond its monetary policy responsibilities. It "blurred the boundaries between monetary policy and fiscal policy". Instead of leaving the repair of the transmission mechanism to national fiscal authorities, the ECB compromised its independence.
- The open-ended purchase of national assets via the money press is effectively financing sovereign debt which the ECB is expressly prohibited from doing by Article 123 TFEU.
- The move towards a debt union amounted to "an extensive surrender of national fiscal sovereignty" The control over national budgetary policies was in danger to slip from "democratically elected parliaments" to a "central entity" currently not envisaged in European treaties.

[124] Taylor (2013a).

[125] Münchau (2010c) and Weber (2010).

[126] Fichtner (2014) and Schelkle (2012).

[127] Atkins (2011) and Evans-Pritchard (2011).

[128] Deutsche Bundesbank (2011b), pp. 66–69; Deutsche Bundesbank (2011c); Atkins and Sandbu (2011).

- The purchase of a large amount of assets from a specific country takes on the ECB's balancing sheet financial risks that could have budgetary consequences outside the control of national parliaments.
- The monetary financing of sovereign debt removed an incentive for highly indebted countries to adopt strict fiscal and structural adjustment programs; instead, it increased "the euro-area countries' propensity to incur debt even further".
- By shifting extensive additional risks to the countries providing assistance and to their taxpayers, "the euro area has taken a major step towards communitising risks arising from unsound public finances and misdirected macroeconomic policies."

In short, the ECB's assumed role as lender of last resort weakened "the underlying principle of national fiscal responsibility on which the European monetary union is founded." The emergence of a "reversibility risk in bond yields does not justify unlimited purchases. Instead of relying on ECB's extra liquidity measures it was "imperative that the bail-out rule . . . and the associated disciplining function of the capital markets be strengthened, and not fatally weakened."[129] He concluded that the ECB's mandate should be changed to limit its scope of action in policy areas such as OMT: In this regard, the German Constitutional Court could issue a decision demanding the German government to seek changes to the ECB's mandate to force the ECB's Governing Council to a narrow definition of its mandate that would ensure a clear dividing line between fiscal and monetary policy.[130]

Weidmann's concern is seconded by the German Constitutional Court. Since the Maastricht Case in 1993, the court never impeded steps towards deeper integration. It made such moves contingent upon a meaningful participation of the Bundestag in all matters related to its constitutional responsibilities for European affairs (Article 23) and budgetary spending.[131] In its ruling of 30 June 2009, the court did not find constitutional objections against the Lisbon Treaty. At the same time, the court reasserted the power of the German parliament over EU legislation on the grounds that democratic control in an association of sovereign nation states can only be exercised at national level. A decision by a German government to abolish the sovereign German state in favour of a newly created European entity would require approval not only of the Bundestag and Bundesrat but also of the German public via a referendum.[132]

---

[129] Deutsche Bundesbank (2011a).

[130] Bundesbank chief backs further curbs on ECB, *Financial Times*, June 13, 2013; Weidmann (2013a).

[131] Bundesverfassungsgericht *89, 155 vom 12.10.1993, Az: 2 BvR 2134, 2159/92* (http://dejure.org/dienste/vernetzung/rechtsprechung?Gericht=BVerfG&Datum=12.10.1993&Aktenzeichen=2%20BvR%202134/92).

[132] Bundesverfassungsgericht, *2 BvE 2/08 vom 30.6.2009*, Absatz-Nr. (1–421) (http://www.bverfg.de/entscheidungen/es20090630_2bve000208.html).

With its two rulings in 2011 and 2014 the Court began to seriously challenge the wisdom of the German government to agree to various euro rescue measures with significant German financial guarantees. On 7 September 2011 it rejected three complaints about German involvement in the first Greek bailout and the establishment of the EFSF as "unfounded". Both measures did not infringe the budgetary authority of the Bundestag. Andreas Vosskuhle, president of the court's Second Senate, said that the "very close decision"—only one of the eight judges actually dissented—should not be "mistakenly interpreted as a constitutional blank check authorizing further rescue measures." The court declared that any euro rescue package remained compatible with the Basic Law (Grundgesetz) only if the stability-oriented character of the monetary union was preserved. The ESM cannot "become a vehicle of unconstitutional state financing by the ECB." In this regard, the judges reiterated the complaints the Bundesbank had made against the Greece bailout measure, "... such a course [i.e. a long-term support facility] would additionally weaken the personal responsibility of the national financial policies, and it would be a further step in the direction of a liability and transfer community...thus the incentive for a cautious budgetary policy would be weakened."[133] The decision endorsed the Bundesbank's principal argument that the responsibility for fiscal policy rested exclusively at the national level. The court's criticism of a long-term rescue facility was an open invitation to the plaintiffs to submit a new complaint, this time against the ESM measure.[134]

In second ground-breaking ruling, six of the eight judges followed the basic argument of Mr. Weidmann against the ECB's unlimited emergency government bond buying facility in his oral presentation to the Court's hearings on the ESM Treaty.[135] The Second Senate ruled that the OMT program is "incompatible with primary law" because it "exceeds the European Central Bank´s monetary policy mandate and thus infringes the jurisdiction of member countries as well as violates the prohibition of monetary fiscal funding."[136] The German Constitutional Court agreed to three interrelated objections the German Central Bank made against the ECB's OMT program: it might breach the principle that budget deficits must not be monetized; it might imply a mutualization of government debt, which is considered an "economic" policy, beyond the ECB's strictly defined monetary policy mandate; it might breach the principle of "no bail out" of governments by European institutions. As the German court has no judicial authority over the ECB to repeal its controversial OMT program, it handed the case to the European Court of Justice, but expressed strong disapproval about its legality. In a preliminary ruling, Pedro Cruz Villalón, an ECJ Advocate-General, declared the OMT-program "compatible with Article 123(1) TFEU". He considered the program "suitable for bringing about

[133] Bundesverfassungsgericht, *2 BvR 987/10 vom 7.9.2011*, Absatz-Nr. (1–142) (http://www.bverfg.de/entscheidungen/rs20110907_2bvr098710.html).

[134] Münchau (2009b, 2011b).

[135] Weidmann (2012b), pp. 9–17, 29; Weidmann (2013b).

[136] Bundesverfassungsgericht (2014a, b).

a reduction in interest rates on government bonds of the States concerned." He also considered the program "necessary" as well as "proportionate in the strict sense" since the central bank was not about "to assume a risk that will necessarily make it vulnerable to insolvency."[137] The final decision, expected in 4–6 months, is likely to follow the advocate-general's opinion. If the ECJ then sides with the ECB, the currency union will find itself in the invidious situation of where EU law contradicts the constitutional law of its most important member—Germany.[138]

Germany's reluctant acceptance that its institutions have no formal jurisdiction over the management of the euro comes at a heavy political price. Two of the country's most respected institutions—the Bundesbank and the Bundesverfassungsgericht—have declared that the ECB cannot legally buy unlimited quantities of sovereign bonds of selected Eurozone governments. Their legal objections could further undermine the support and political legitimacy of the euro project in Germany and strengthen the political position of eurosceptic groups like the Alternative für Deutschland (AfD), the only avowedly anti-euro party in Germany which rose sharply in the election to the European Parliament and three recent state elections.[139] With the thick fog of uncertainty hanging over the ECB's remit, policymakers in Berlin may feel more comfortable to do "too little, not too much".[140] Or, as a weapon of last resort, the Merkel government might be tempted to render the controversial OMT program ineffective by blocking potential beneficiaries' access to the conditional credit line of the ESM program which does require Berlin's approval.[141]

3.4 The Banking Union: Merkel's "New Union Method"

The euro crisis exposed the serious flaws in the design of the monetary union by creating a common currency without a political union, a centralizing bank supervision and mutual economic and fiscal decision making convergence. At the height of the panic over Spain's ailing cajas the Eurozone countries agreed on the initial step toward the banking union. The banking union's central goals have been to better administer insolvent banks, avoid contagion to other financial institutions, and break the lethal embrace between banks and sovereigns as happened in Ireland and Spain when the cost of bank rescues undermined public finances. The proposed bank-failure program, known as Single Resolution Mechanism (SRM), is conceived as part of a broader European banking union whose other provisions include a Single Supervisory Mechanism (SSM) who writes common rules and enforces

[137] Court of Justice of the European Union (2015a, b).

[138] Barber (2014) and Münchau (2014a).

[139] Münchau (2014e), Rachman (2014), and Wolf (2013g).

[140] The Economist (2013).

[141] Münchau (2014a) and Jones and Wagstyl (2014).

them uniformly, a Resolution Mechanism (SRM) to "resolve" failed banks, and a harmonized system of deposit guarantee schemes (DGS), a euro-wide guarantee of deposits to reassure savers. The movement towards breaking the mutually destructive links between banks and sovereigns confronted Berlin with two fundamental problems: who has the ultimate decision-making power for setting up the rules for imposing losses on bank creditors and implementing them? Under what conditions can member states draw on a shared bailout fund to inject money directly into troubled banks? In short: who decides and who pays?

From the beginning, the German government supported the creation of a Europe-wide supervisory system for banks. Following the same script as in the bailout cases, Berlin insisted on various conditions which strongly rejected a centralized authority exercised by the ECB and the Commission and instead called for a vibrant political control exercised by national governments and national parliaments amid fears of establishing a transfer union through the back door. The "socialisation" of all bank debts in the Eurosystem would render German taxpayers liable for bank debts elsewhere. The ESM funds would not only cover the public debt of crisis countries, but also the debts of their banks thereby protecting bank creditors "from any losses". Economically sound countries would be "exposed to constant pressure to widen the limits of this liability or to soften the requirements for its provision", criticised 172 German-speaking economic professors in an open letter.[142] Chancellor Merkel dismissed the signers' central critique that a joint liability for banking debt had been approved at the Brussels summit in late June 2012.[143] "Assuming any liability for banks remains as prohibited ('verboten') as assuming liability for states. In this respect, the Brussels decisions have not changed the present situation."[144] But Berlin's conceptual ideas about an integrated financial framework, called a "banking union", mirrored the major concern of the more than 200 German-speaking economics professors. The German position[145] can be summarized as follows:

- the daily supervision responsibilities of the ECB should be limited to around 130 banks that pose a systemic risk at the European level
- the presence of a "Chinese wall" should ensure that ECB decision-making in supervisory and monetary policy matters are "strictly separated"
- strong bail-in rules should protect European taxpayers adequately against bank failures. The liability for cleaning up banks must be borne by senior creditors and shareholders that finance banks, followed by national resolution funds' contributions, before European rescue funds step in as a last resort
- the € 500 billion ESM rescue fund should not be readily accessible as a backstop for ailing banks

[142] Sinn and Krämer (2012a, b). See also Sinn (2014), pp. 96–98, 101.

[143] Council of the European Union (2012); Deutscher Bundestag, Drucksache 17/10320, Anlage 3: European Commission (2012), pp. 15–34.

[144] Die Bundeskanzlerin (2012). See also Die Bundesregierung (2012).

[145] Schäuble (2012a, b, d, 2013a); Schäuble (2012a), p. 22987; Schäuble (2012b), p. 26195.

- the ECB's supervisory role should be held "accountable to the European Parliament and the European Council"
- to strengthen "democratic legitimation", the power of a single authority to take a bank into resolution should remain in the hands of national authorities and be coordinated at the European level but not centralized within the Commission
- the European resolution fund should be based on an intergovernmental agreement outside EU treaties.

In early July 2013, the European Commission put itself on a collision course with Germany when it proposed the creation of a single EU authority that "would decide whether and when to place a bank into resolution and would set out a framework for the use of resolution tools and the fund." Michel Barnier, the EU Commissioner for Internal Market and Services, summarized the central goal of his proposal as follows: "We need a system which can deliver decisions quickly and efficiently, avoiding doubts on the impact on public finances, and with rules that create certainty in the market."[146] The ECB also declared that a new bank bailout authority should be "strong and independent" with "efficient and timely decision-making" powers to force failing banks to either recapitalize or shut down. "A single mechanism is better placed to guarantee optimal resolution action than a network of national resolution authorities. Co-ordination between national resolutions systems has not proved sufficient to achieve the most timely and cost-effective resolution decisions, particularly in cross-border context." Both the Commission and the ECB argued that provisions in current EU treaties (Article 114) were adequate to create a strong centralized authority.[147]

In a swift and negative response, Berlin warned that the EU Commission overstepped its legal powers with its proposal to make itself the single authority for winding down ailing banks in the Eurozone. "In our view, the commission proposal oversteps [its] authorities," Steffen Seibert, Germany's government spokesman, declared.[148] Finance Minister Schäuble argued that a single authority was out of step with existing European treaty law which limits the power of the EU institutions over national finances. Instead he proposed a "two-step approach". The first phase should build on national resolution authorities taking coordinated decision with a board at the central level, "to ensure quick effective and coherent decision-making. The second phase would require a treaty revision that would make a long-term centralized resolution authority legally unchallengeable. "Much stronger budget protection must be given to participating member states in order to ensure legitimacy and compliance with constitutional requirements," he wrote in a letter to Michel Barnier. "The proposal regrettably envisages too high a degree of centralisation with regard to the boundaries of the existing (EU) law."""[149]

---

[146] EU Commission (2013).

[147] European Central Bank (2013a), pp. 2, 3, 4–5.

[148] Fairless (2013).

[149] Bundesministerium der Finanzen (2013).

The German government concluded that EU treaties "do not suffice to anchor beyond doubt a new and strong central resolution authority." They have to be changed to provide firm legal underpinning of a new banking union, particularly a new bank bailout system. A new treaty should be examined outside the Lisbon requirements to avoid a time-consuming and free-wheeling process. Treaty changes takes as a model two recently adopted treaties on the creation of the ESM permanent rescue fund and the Fiscal Compact, both written and ratified within months.[150]

A French-German paper called for a resolution board effectively controlled by the Eurozone members than the Commission. Bank bailout would be handled by "a single resolution board involving national authorities." The ECB would have the authority to declare Eurozone banks insolvent, but the power to do anything about it still rests with national governments. The Franco-German plan envisages a less ambitious "specific fund" that could only be tapped under the condition of implementing tough economic reform measures. With representatives of national authorities, the ECB and the Commission, a board would undertake preparatory work before the Commission would decide whether and when to place a bank in resolution.[151]

The details of how this hybrid scheme—essentially a network of national funds under a single European authority—will operate had been hammered out by European finance ministers and members of the European Parliament in mid-December 2013 and mid-March 2014. Under the deal, the ECB assumed responsibility for supervision of banks[152] on November 4, 2014. The new single supervisory mechanism consists of both the ECB and the national financial supervision authorities under the overall oversight of the ECB. The ECB directly supervises "120 significant banking groups" which represents 82 % (by assets) of the euro area banking sector while about 3500 banks, including German Landesbanken as well as local and regional German saving banks (Sparkassen and Raiffeisenbanken), will be left for the "national competent authorities" who will "work closely" with the ECB.[153]

A common rule book on bank resolution will apply across the EU from 2015. A central bank resolution authority is directly responsible for proposing decisions to recapitalize or wind up all crossborder Eurozone banks, should they face severe difficulties. The SRM relies on the ECB to signal when a financial institution in the

[150] Schäuble (2013a) and Spiegel and Peel (2013).

[151] Presse- und Informationsamt der Bundesregierung (2013), pp. 4–5.

[152] The new task "concerning policies relating to the prudential supervision of credit institutions and other financial institutions" is enshrined in Article 126(7) of the *Treaty on the Functioning of the European Union*, Official Journal of the European Union, 2012/C 326/103, Vol. 55, October 26, 2012 (https://www.ecb.europa.eu/ecb/legal/pdf/c_32620121026en.pdf).

[153] European Central Bank (2014d). The task is enshrined in Article 126(7) of the *Treaty on the Functioning of the European Union*, Official Journal of the European Union, C 326/49, October 26, 2012 (http://eur-lex.europa.eu/legal-content/EN/TXT/PDF/?uri=CELEX:12012E/TXT&from=EN).

euro area was facing severe difficulties reinforcing its role as supervisor. The Commission is given a formal role to approve resolution decisions to shut down or shrink a bank. An independent resolution board supported by a staff of around 300 and made up of representatives from the central bank, the European Commission, and member states will be able to recommend a lender to be closed or restructured. Its recommendations would need the approval of the European Commission or—in the event of Brussels rejecting a board proposal—a majority vote of banking union member states.

The so-called bail-in rules for senior shareholders, bondholders and depositors with deposits above € 100,000 are brought forward from 2018 to 2016, with an intergovernmental treaty defining how the costs can be gradually shared. The minimum bail-in amounts to 8 % of total liabilities and the intervention is capped at 5 % of the bank's total liabilities and contingent on Brussels' approval. National resolution funds should be established and fully available by 2023 (originally 2025), with money coming from levies on banks equivalent to 1 % of covered deposits which amounts up to € 55 billion across the EU. The common fund will be allowed to borrow in the markets against its future cash flows. Big countries are given greater voting power to block the release of common resolution funds. The requirement for a two-thirds majority, based on the ECB capital key, would give Germany, the Netherlands and Finland a blocking majority. A decision of the resolution board would require the bank's home state to agree to the measures.[154]

The German Finance Minister Wolfgang Schäuble praised the compromise. "Our goal was a sensible decision-making mechanism with effective control of the resources deployed and minimal risk for the taxpayer." The deal ensures that "the mutualized liability . . . remained ruled". The agreement does not put Germany in a position of "taking on any irresponsible risks." Lastly, the principle purpose of the rescue fund is "to have it in order not to use it."[155] The agreement on the banking union largely bears the characteristic trademark of Merkel's cautious step-by-step policy approach:

- No common backstop. The German government fears that the risk-sharing element of deeper integration (the ESM's recapitalization of banks, a common resolution fund for insolvent banks and greater EU fiscal authority) result in a politically unacceptable transfer union whereby Germany permanently pays for the periphery. Consequently, Berlin successfully torpedoed anything that could be conceived as an assurance of joint-liability, the core principle on which an effective banking union rests. Thanks to unyielding German resistance to tap the ESM rescue fund as a credit line, the principle of national responsibility has been firmly established during the transition, according to which each national government will be responsible for dealing with its own troubled banks. "The priority will be to make creditors and owners responsible, and we get away

[154] European Commission (2014a, b), Council of the European Union (2013), and Spiegel (2013b).
[155] Kanter and Ewing (2014a, b); Higgins and Eddy (2013); Deutscher Bundestag (2014), p. 4886.

from taxpayers always putting up for the banks," Chancellor Merkel summed up the German understanding of sharing bank losses.[156]

- Drowning of the remit of a Eurozone bank supervisor. Germany's concern over the Commission's banking union proposal reflects deeper unease over ceding national supervision power, especially over the network of saving banks. National bank authorities will play a prominent role in the repair and recapitalization of Eurozone banks: controversies should be resolved through greater co-ordination between them. Schäuble's proposal of a network of national resolution authorities together with the decision-role given to the European Council ensures that all vital decisions on the bailed out or winding down of failing European banks require the consent of national governments involved.
- Merkel's preference to a "new union method". Berlin's vision of the Eurozone bank rescue plan would give more control to Brussels on fiscal matters but more leeway for national authorities on banks. The Commission's role is strictly limited to verify the process towards fiscal probity with more intrusive budget surveillance and statistical auditing of states with high debts and deficits. But the German government is highly hesitant to cede any new executive powers to a central body ultimately overseen by the Commission which would loosen Germany's control over decisions with a direct impact on the German public purse. The member states still are "the masters of the treaties."[157] The German preference for intergovernmental cooperation gives the individual member states the discretion if and how the bank rescue fund is used.
- Byzantine decision-making setup. The agreement did not establish a single resolution authority to deal with failed banks. Berlin's unwillingness to cede national control to the commission led to a hybrid system of three separate agencies—a new resolution board, the European Commission and the EU council of national ministers—which hampers the ability of a central authority to function quickly if a defunct bank needs to be rescued or wound down over a weekend. "And it is certain that it does not work when hundreds of people across Europe have to discuss what needs to be done," declared Mario Draghi.[158]
- Lack of sufficient joint funds. The € 55 billion bank resolution fund to be set up over 8 years lacks the financial firepower for tackling even a modest crisis. The bailout fund covers only 0.2 % or € 30.749 trillion of the aggregate balance sheet of the Eurozone financial sector in February 2014. Most of the banks concerned have assets of more than € 30 billion. The Irish government was forced to pump € 30 billion into just one financial institution, Anglo Irish Bank, during the financial crisis in 2010.[159]
- Hierarchy of losses. During the 8-year transition, each national government, not Europe as a whole, will have to take care of its troubled national banks. From the

[156] Deutscher Bundestag (2013), pp. 31887–31888; Deutscher Bundestag (2014), pp. 4885–4886.
[157] Bundeskanzlerin (2011); Deutscher Bundestag (2012a), p. 23815.
[158] European Central Bank (2013c, 2014c).
[159] European Central Bank (2014b) and Münchau (2013g).

bail in of bank creditors, the use of national deposit insurance funds to the limit of a maximum of 5 % of the bank's balance sheet, there are several hurdles before bank-financed resolution funds can be used to inject new capital into other countries' failing banks or to share the costs of defunct banks in the future.
- Delay. Germany insists that decisions on closure of ailing banks involving billions of euros must be based on a water-tight legal framework. The treaty change is the only way to achieve this legal clarity. The legal reservation will delay the banking union. Such treaty changes take years. It is an intricate, time–consuming process requiring unanimous consents among all EU member countries. Time is not a luxury at the euro's disposal.
- No third pillar of a Federal Deposit Insurance Corporation (FDIC). As Germany rejected the idea of common deposit insurance which would put German taxpayers on the hook for bailing out other countries' banks, only "two pillars of the banking union are now in place", Mario Draghi concluded.[160]

Many of the main elements of a banking union have been watered down, delayed, or not implemented.[161] The agreement falls short of what is needed to stabilize the euro area's banking system without reinforcing the pernicious link between weak banks and fragile sovereigns ("doom loop"). Instead, it will "produce the financial sector equivalent of austerity – a secular credit crunch."[162] The compromise raises doubts if and when the euro area will have an effective banking union. Should the crisis flare up again, decision makers may find themselves again being trapped over arguments on reforms that could take some years when markets require action in days or hours.

Time and again, Merkel proved unwilling to agree to a joint liability program or to sacrifice national sovereignty to a common European resolution authority. What matters for Germany foremost are the hierarchy of losses and the legal foundations of the banking union. The Chancellor put again into her pocket on what the bailout programs have already been premised: "more Eurozone fiscal discipline, at no cost for Germany."[163] The agreement on the banking union underlines Merkel's clear preference for domestic needs which validates Schröder's dictum that "all existential questions of the German nation will be decided in Berlin and nowhere else"[164]

---

[160] European Central Bank (2014a).

[161] Münchau (2013d, g, 2014b), Smaghi (2013), and Kapoor (2013a, b).

[162] Münchau (2013e, h) and Frieda (2013).

[163] Münchau (2013f, h).

[164] Deutscher Bundestag (2002), p. 25583.

References

Abadi, C., & Germania, F. (2010, May 24). *Foreign Policy*. http://www.foreignpolicy.com/articles/2010/05/24/frau_germania

Alesina, A., & Ardagna, S. (2009, October). *Large changes in fiscal policy* (NBER Working Paper No. 15438). National Bureau of Economic Research, Boston. http://www.nber.org/papers/w15438

Altman, R. C. (2012, June 4). Euro zone on the brink. *Washington Post*.

Atkins, R. (2011, August 23). Bundesbank opposes ECB bond buying. *Financial Times*.

Atkins, R. (2012, September 3). Eurozone. Convergence in reverse. *Financial Times*.

Atkins, R. (2013a, March 21). Athens crisis highlights pressure on Merkel. *Financial Times*.

Atkins, R. (2013b, June 11). Eurozone banks retreat behind borders. *Financial Times*.

Atkins, R. (2013c, October 28). Debt: A deceptive calm. *Financial Times*.

Atkins, R., & Sandbu, M. (2011, November 14). FT interview transcript: Jens Weidmann. *Financial Times*.

Baldi, G., Fichtner, F., Michelsen, C., & Richter, M. (2014). Weak investment dampens Europe's growth. *DIW Economic Bulletin, 4*(7). http://www.diw.de/documents/publikationen/73/diw_01.c.469261.de/diw_econ_bull_2014-07-3.pdf

Bannas, G. (2012, June 28). Merkel gegen Eurobonds. *Frankfurter AllgemeineZeitung*.

Barber, T. (2010, May 25). World is dangerously exposed to European default. *Financial Times*.

Barber, T. (2013, July 22). Schäuble keeps quiet on mounting cost to Germany on Europe's woes. *Financial Times*.

Barber, T. (2014, February 8). Courts and contradictions. *Financial Times*.

Benhold, K., & Castle, S. (2008, November 25). Germany and France out of sync. *International Herald Tribune*.

Birnbaum, M. (2012, May 22). Merkel's isolation among G-8 on economic policy reflects sentiment in Germany. *Washington Post*.

Birnbaum, M., & Schaeuble, W. (2012, June 16). Germany 'will do whatever it takes to defend the euro'. *Washington Post*.

Boesler, M. (2012, May 23). Citi: 'Greece will Leave euro on 1 January 2013'. *Business Insider*. http://www.businessinsider.com/buiter-greece-will-leave-emu-on-1-january-2013-2012-5?IR=T

Böhmer, M., Weisser, J., & Drechsler, K. (2014, July 28). *20 Jahre Binnenmarkt. Wachstumseffekte der zunehmenden europäischen Integration*. Gütersloh, Germany: Bertelsmann Stiftung. http://www.bertelsmann-stiftung.de/cps/rde/xbcr/SID-25A7AD77-878BD41F/bst/xcms_bst_dms_40166_40167_2.pdf

Britain, S. (2013, January 1). The folly of beggar-your-neighbour policies. *Financial Times*.

Bryant, C. (2012, August 26). Merkel supports Bundesbank chief. *Financial Times*.

Buiter, W. (2012, October 16). Only widespread debt restructuring can save the euro. *Financial Times*.

Bundeskanzlerin. (2011, November 2). Rede von Bundeskanzlerin Merkel anläßlich der Eröffnung des 61. Akademischen Jahres des Europakollegs Brügge, Bruges. http://m.bundeskanzlerin.de/ContentArchiv/DE/Archiv17/Reden/2010/11/2010-11-02-merkel-bruegge.html?nn=819844

Bundesministerium der Finanzen. (2013, July 13). *DOK 2013/0674605*. Berlin. http://www.banking-union-watch.eu/wp-content/uploads/2013/08/Brief-Sch%C3%A4uble-Barnier.pdf

Bundesregierung. (2010a, March 26). *An important day for the euro*. Brussels. http://www.bundeskanzlerin.de/Content/EN/Artikel/2010/03/2010-03-26-eu-rat-hilfen-griechenland_en.html

Bundesregierung. (2010b, April 23). *Pressestatement von Bundeskanzlerin Merkel zum Antrag Griechenlands auf Finanzhilfe*. Berlin. http://www.bundesregierung.de/Content/DE/Mitschrift/Pressekonferenzen/2010/04/2010-04-23-statement-griechenland.html

Bundesregierung. (2010c, April 28). *Pressestatements von Bundeskanzlerin Merkel und dem geschäftsführenden Direktor des IMF, Dominique Strauß-Kahn*, Berlin. http://www.bundeskanzlerin.de/ContentArchiv/DE/Archiv17/Mitschrift/Pressekonferenzen/2010/04/2010-04-

Bundesregierung. (2010d, May 3). *Pressestatements von Bundeskanzlerin Merkel und Bundesaußenminister Westerwelle*. Berlin. http://www.bundesregierung.de/Content/DE/Mitschrift/Pressekonferenzen/2010/05/2010-05-03-statement-griechenland.html;

Bundesregierung. (2010e, October 19). *Pressekonferenz Merkel, Sarkozy und Medwedew in Deauville*. http://www.bundeskanzlerin.de/ContentArchiv/DE/Archiv17/Mitschrift/Pressekonferenzen/2010/10/2010-10-19-pk-deauville.html

Bundesregierung. (2010f, October 27). *Regierungserklärung von Bundeskanzlerin Merkel zum EU-Gipfel in Brüssel und zum Gipfel der G-20 in Seoul*. Berlin. http://www.bundeskanzlerin.de/ContentArchiv/DE/Archiv17/Regierungserklaerung/2010/2010-10-27-merkel-regerklaerung-eu-g20.html

Bundesregierung. (2010g, December 10). *Pressestatements von Bundeskanzler Merkel und Staatspräsident Sarkozy in Freiburg im Breisgau*. http://www.bundeskanzlerin.de/ContentArchiv/DE/Archiv17/Mitschrift/Pressekonferenzen/2010/12/2010-12-10-pressestatement-merkel-sarkozy.html

Bundesregierung. (2010h). *The G-20 Toronto Summit Declaration, June 26–27, 2010*. http://www.bundesregierung.de/Content/DE/StatischeSeiten/Breg/G8G20/Anlagen/G20-erklaerung-toronto-en.pdf?__blob=publicationFile

Bundesregierung. (2012, August 17). *Pressekonferenz von Bundeskanzlerin Angela Merkel und dem kanadischen Premierminister Stephen Harper, Ottawa*. http://www.bundesregierung.de/ContentArchiv/DE/Archiv17/Mitschrift/Pressekonferenzen/2012/08/2012-08-16-merkel-kanada.html

Bundesverfassungsgericht. (2014a, February 7). *BVerfG, 2 BvR 2728/13 vom 14.01.2014, Absatz-Nr. (1–105)*. Karlsruhe. http://www.bverfg.de/entscheidungen/rs20140114_2bvr272813.html

Bundesverfassungsgericht. (2014b, February 7). *BVerfG, 2 BvR 1390/12 vom 17.12.2013*. Karlsruhe. http://www.bverfg.de/entscheidungen/rs20131217_2bvr139012.html

Byrne, A., & Hope, K. (2014, April 26/27). Greece warned of € 14.9 bn financing gap. *Financial Times*.

Carrel, P., Barkin, N., & Breithardt, A. (2012, September 25). Special Report: Inside Mario Draghi's euro Rescue plan. *Reuters*. http://www.reuters.com/article/2012/09/25/us-ecb-draghi-plan-idUSBRE88O09A20120925

Castle, S. (2012, June 23). Pressure mounts on Merkel as I.M.F. urges action on crisis. *New York Times*.

Chen, R., Milesi-Ferreti, G. M., & Tressel, T. (2013). External imbalances in the Euro area. *Economic Policy, 28*(73), 101–142.

Christlich Demokratische Union. (2008, December 1). *Rede der Vorsitzenden der CDU Deutschlands, Frau Bundeskanzlerin Dr. Angela Merkel, auf dem Bundesparteitag 2008 der CDU Deutschlands in Stuttgart*. http://www.stuttgart08.cdu.de/wp-content/uploads/2008/12/081201-rede-merkel-pressefassung.pdf

Cohen-Setton, J. (2013, November 11). The deflationary bias of Germany's current account. *Bruegel*. http://www.bruegel.org/nc/blog/detail/article/1186-blogs-review-the-deflationary-bias-of-germanys-current-account/

Council of the European Union. (2005, March 23). *Presidency conclusions, Annex II: Improving the implementation of the stability and growth pact*. Brussels. http://www.consilium.europa.eu/uedocs/cms_data/docs/pressdata/en/ec/84335.pdf

Council of the European Union. (2010, May 9/10). *Extraordinary Council meeting Economic and Financial Affairs, Press Release 9596/10* (Presse 108), Brussels. http://europa.eu/rapid/press-release_PRES-10-108_en.htm?locale=en

Council of the European Union. (2012, June 29). *Euro Area Summit Statement*, SN 2999/12, Brussels. https://www.consilium.europa.eu/uedocs/cms_data/docs/pressdata/en/ec/131359.pdf

Council of the European Union. (2013, December 18). *Council agrees general approach on SRM*. Brussels. http://www.consilium.europa.eu/uedocs/cms_data/docs/pressdata/en/ecofin/140190.pdf

Court of Justice of the European Union. (2015a, January 14). *Opinion of Advocate General Cruz Villalòn delivered on January 14, 2015 Case C-62/14 Peter Gauweiler and Others v Deutscher Bundestag*. Luxembourg. http://curia.europa.eu/juris/document/document.jsf?text=&docid=161370&pageIndex=0&doclang=EN&mode=req&dir=&occ=first&part=1&cid=205492

Court of Justice of the European Union. (2015b, January 14). *Press Release No 2/15*. Luxembourg. http://curia.europa.eu/jcms/upload/docs/application/pdf/2015-01/cp150002en.pdf

Crawford, B. (2007). *Power and German Foreign Policy*. Basingstoke, UK: Palgrave Macmillan.

Dailey, S., & Smale, A. (2013, November 21). Germany is burdened as physical state buckles. *International New York Times*.

Davies, G. (2012, June 10). The consequences of Spain rescue. *Financial Times*.

Davies, G. (2013a, September 16). Angela Merkel – Lame duck or savior of the euro? *Financial Times*.

Davies, G. (2013b, September 14). One woman to rule them all. *The Economist*. http://www.economist.com/news/leaders/21586343-german-voters-should-re-elect-angela-merkel-their-chancellorand-europes-leader-one-woman

de Grauwe, P., & Ji, Y. (2012). From panic-driven austerity to symmetric macroeconomic policies in the Eurozone. *Journal of Common Market Studies, 51*(51), 866–880.

de Vigo, M. (Spanish Europe Minister). (2012, July 29). Wenn Deutschland weiter so diskutiert, zerbricht die Eurozone. *Frankfurter AllgemeineZeitung*.

Deo, S., Donovan, P., & Hathaway, L. (2011, September 6). *Euro break-up. The consequences*. London: UBS Investment Research, Global Economic Perspectives. http://bruxelles.blogs.liberation.fr/UBS%20fin%20de%20l%27euro.pdf

Deutsche Bundestag. (2010, May 19). *Plenarprotokoll17/42*. Berlin, 2010. http://dipbt.bundestag.de/dip21/btp/17/17042.pdf

Deutsche Bundesbank. (2011a, July 22). *Statement by Bundesbank President Dr. Jens Weidmann on the outcome of the European Council meeting*. Frankfurt am Main. http://www.bundesbank.de/Redaktion/EN/Pressemitteilungen/BBK/2011/2011_07_22_statement_by_bundesbank_president_dr_jens_weidmann_on_the_outcome_of_the_european_council_meeting.html

Deutsche Bundesbank. (2011b, August). *Zu den Beschlüssen der Staats- und Regierungschefs des Euro-Währungsgebiets und der EU-Organe vom 21. Juli 2011, Monatsbericht*. Frankfurt am Main 2011. http://www.bundesbank.de/Redaktion/DE/Downloads/Veroeffentlichungen/Monatsberichte/2011/2011_08_monatsbericht.pdf?__blob=publicationFile

Deutsche Bundesbank. (2011c, September 19). *Stellungnahme von Dr. Jens Weidmann*. Berlin. http://www.bundesbank.de/Redaktion/DE/Kurzmeldungen/Stellungnahmen/2011_09_19_%C3%BCbernahme_von_gew%C3%A4hrleistungen.html

Deutsche Bundesbank. (2012a, March 28). *Rebalancing Europe*, Speech by Dr. Jens Weidmann at Chatham House, London. http://www.bundesbank.de/Redaktion/EN/Reden/2012/2012_03_28_weidmann_rebalancing_europe.html

Deutsche Bundesbank. (2012b, May 8). Monetary policy is no panacea for Europe. *Financial Times*.

Deutsche Bundesbank. (2013, April 23). Global economic outlook – What is the best policy mix? Speech at the Economic Club of New York. http://www.bis.org/review/r120425a.pdf

Deutsche Bundesbank. (2014a, March 14). Bundesbank posts €4.6 billion profit in 2013. Frankfurt am Main. http://www.bundesbank.de/Redaktion/EN/Topics/2014/2014_03_13_annual_report.html

Deutsche Bundesbank. (2014b, March 17). *External imbalances in the euro area*, Speech by Dr. Jens Weidmann at the International Business Cycle Conference Kiel Institute for the World Economy. Kiel. http://www.bundesbank.de/Redaktion/EN/Reden/2014/2014_03_17_weidmann.html

Deutscher Bundestag. (2002, September 13). *Plenarprotokoll 14/253*. Berlin. http://dip21.bundestag.de/dip21/btp/14/14253.pdf
Deutscher Bundestag. (2009, March 24). *Bundestagsdrucksache 16/12410*. Berlin. http://dip21.bundestag.de/dip21/btd/16/124/1612410.pdf
Deutscher Bundestag. (2010, March 17). *Plenarprotokoll 17/30*. Berlin. http://dipbt.bundestag.de/dip21/btp/17/17030.pdf
Deutscher Bundestag. (2011, September 7). *Plenarprotokoll 17/123*. Berlin. http://dipbt.bundestag.de/dip21/btp/17/17123.pdf
Deutscher Bundestag. (2012a, October 18). *Plenarprotokoll 17/198*. Berlin. http://dip21.bundestag.de/dip21/btp/17/17198.pdf
Deutscher Bundestag. (2012b, June 29). *Plenarprotokoll, 17/188*. Berlin. http://dip21.bundestag.de/dip21/btp/17/17188.pdf
Deutscher Bundestag. (2012c, June 27) *Plenarprotokoll, 17/186*. Berlin. http://dipbt.bundestag.de/dip21/btp/17/17186.pdf
Deutscher Bundestag. (2013, June 27). *Plenarprotokoll 17/250*. Berlin. http://dip21.bundestag.de/dip21/btp/17/17250.pdf
Deutscher Bundestag. (2014, September 25). *Plenarprotokoll 18/54*. Berlin. http://dipbt.bundestag.de/doc/btp/18/18054.pdf
Deutscher Bundestag. *Plenarprotokoll, 17/189*. Berlin. http://dip21.bundestag.de/dip21/btp/17/17189.pdf
Die Bundeskanzlerin. (2012, July 5). *Pressestatements von Bundeskanzlerin Angela Merkel und dem Präsidenten des Ministerrates der Republik Libanon, Najib Mikati*. Berlin. http://www.bundeskanzlerin.de/ContentArchiv/DE/Archiv17/Mitschrift/Pressekonferenzen/2012/07/2012-07-05-merkel-mitaki.html
Die Bundesregierung. (2012, June 29). *Pressestatements von Bundeskanzlerin Angela Merkel zum Europäischen Rat*. Brussels. http://www.bundesregierung.de/ContentArchiv/DE/Archiv17/Mitschrift/Pressekonferenzen/2012/06/2012-06-29-merkel-eu-rat.html
Dolan, M. (2012, May 3). Austerity can't be the only answer. *International Herald Tribune*.
Dullien, S. (2013). *A German model for Europe?* London: European Council on Foreign Relations.
Eddy, M. (2012, August 25). Merkel vows to help Greeks stay in Euro Zone. *New York Times*.
European Central Bank. (2010, May 10). *Press release – ECB decides on measures to address severe tensions in financial markets*. Frankfurt am Main. http://www.ecb.europa.eu/press/pr/date/2010/html/pr100510.en.html
European Central Bank. (2012a, September 6). *Introductory statement to the press conference (with Q&A) by Mario Draghi, President of the ECB, and VítorConstâncio, Vice-President of the ECB*, Frankfurt am Main. http://www.ecb.europa.eu/press/pressconf/2012/html/is120906.en.html
European Central Bank. (2012b, October 22). *Interview of Mario Dragh, President of the ECB, with Der Spiegel*, Frankfurt am Main. http://www.ecb.europa.eu/press/inter/date/2012/html/sp121029.en.html
European Central Bank. (2012c). *Speech by Mario Draghi, President of the ECB, at the Global Investment Conference in London, July, 26, 2012*. https://www.ecb.europa.eu/press/key/date/2012/html/sp120726.en.html
European Central Bank. (2013a, November 6). *Opinion of the European Central Bank on a proposal by the European Parliament (No 1093/2010) and the Council (Con/2013/76)*. Frankfurt am Main. https://www.ecb.europa.eu/ecb/legal/pdf/en_con_2013_76_f_sign.pdf
European Central Bank. (2013b, November 21). Speech by Mario Draghi, President of the ECB, at Führungstreffen Wirtschaft "Strategies for more growth" organised by Süddeutsche Zeitung, Berlin. http://www.ecb.europa.eu/press/key/date/2013/html/sp131121.en.html
European Central Bank. (2013c, December 30). *Interview of Mario Draghi with Der Spiegel*. https://www.ecb.europa.eu/press/inter/date/2013/html/sp131230.de.html
European Central Bank. (2014a, March 20). *Statement of the ECB on SRM Agreement*. Frankfurt am Main. https://www.ecb.europa.eu/press/pr/date/2014/html/pr140320.en.html

European Central Bank. (2014b, April 10). *Money, banking and other financial corporations.* Frankfurt am Main. http://sdw.ecb.europa.eu/reports.do?node=100000137

European Central Bank. (2014c, March 18). Introductory statement of Danièle Nouy, Chair of the Supervisory Board, Single Supervisory Mechanism, ECB, at the hearing of the Committee on Economic and Monetary Affairs of the European Parliament, Brussels. http://www.ecb.europa.eu/press/key/date/2014/html/sp140318.en.html

European Central Bank. (2014d, November 4). *ECB assumes responsibility for euro area banking supervision.* Press Release, Frankfurt am Main. http://www.ecb.europa.eu/press/pr/date/2014/html/pr141104.en.html

European Commission. (2006). Directorate-General for Economic and Financial Affairs. *European Economy No. 3/2005 – Public Finances in EMU 2005.* Brussels. http://ec.europa.eu/economy_finance/publications/publication421_en.pdf

European Commission. (2010, May 3). *Euro area and IMF agreement on financial support programme for Greece.* Brussels. http:/ec.europa.eu/economy_finance/articles/eu_economic_situation/2010-05-03-statement-commissioner-rehn-imf-on-greece_en.htm

European Commission. (2012, July 9). *Spain. Memorandum of Understanding on Financial-Sector Policy Conditionality.* Brussels. http://dip21.bundestag.de/dip21/btd/17/103/1710320.pdf

EU Commission. (2013, July 10). Commission proposes single resolution mechanism for the banking union. *Press Release IP/13/674*, Brussels. http://europa.eu/rapid/press-release_IP-13-674_en.htm

European Commission. (2014a, March 20). *Statement 14/77.* Brussels. http://europa.eu/rapid/press-release_STATEMENT-14-77_en.htm?locale=en

European Commission. (2014b, April 19). *A single resolution mechanism for the banking union.* Brussels. http://ec.europa.eu/internal_market/finances/banking-union/index_en.htm

European Commission. (2014c, April). *The second adjustment programme for Greece fourth review.* Brussels. http://ec.europa.eu/economy_finance/publications/occasional_paper/2014/pdf/ocp192_en.pdf

European Commission. (2014d, March 5). *Results of in-depth reviews under Regulation (EU) No. 1176/2011.* Brussels. http://ec.europa.eu/economy_finance/economic_governance/documents/2014-03-05_in-depth_reviews_communication_en.pdf

European Commission. (2014e, June 2). *Council Recommendation on Germany's 2014 national reform programme and delivering a Council opinion on Germany's 2014 stability programme.* Brussels. http://ec.europa.eu/europe20120/pdf/csr2014_Germany_en.pdf

European Commission. (2014f, November 4). *European Economic Forecast Autumn 2014.* Brussels. http://ec.europa.eu/economy_finance/publications/european_economy/2014/pdf/ee7_en.pdf

European Council. (2012, June 29). *Euro area statement.* Brussels. http://www.consilium.europa.eu/uedocs/cms_data/docs/pressdata/en/ec/131359.pdf

Eurostat. (2011, December). *Structure of Government debt in Europe in 2010.* Statistics in focus 68/2011, Luxembourg. http://epp.eurostat.ec.europa.eu/cache/ITY_OFFPUB/KS-SF-11-068/EN/KS-SF-11-068-EN.PDF

Eurostat. (2014, April 23). *Euro area and EU28 government deficit at 3.0% and 3.3% of GDP respectively*, News Release 64/2014. Luxembourg. http://epp.eurostat.ec.europa.eu/cache/ITY_PUBLIC/2-23042014-AP/EN/2-23042014-AP-EN.PDF

Evans-Pritchard, A. (2011, September 2). EU law "gutted" by bail outs, growls Bundesbank. *The Telegraph.* http://www.telegraph.co.uk/finance/financialcrisis/8736194/EU-law-gutted-by-bail-outs-growls-Bundesbank.html

Ewing, J. (2010a, April 29). Already holding junk, Germany hesitates. *New York Times.*

Ewing, J. (2010b, June 5). European banks murky books make exposure anyone's guess. *International Herald Tribune.*

Ewing, J. (2012, August 26). German official opposes European debt purchases. *New York Times.*

Ewing, J., & Eddy, M. (2012, August 28). German E.C.B. officials split over plan for saving euro zone. *International Herald Tribune.*
Ewing, J., & Thomas, L. (2014, October 17). Regulators are Gauging Health of Europe's Banks, and the Remedy May Sting a Little. *New York Times.*
Faiola, A. (2012, September 14). As Germany rises, Frau Nein say 'Yes'. *Washington Post.*
Fairless, T. (2013, July 10). Germany objects to EU proposal for restructuring banks. *Wall Street Journal Online.* http://online.wsj.com/news/articles/SB10001424127887324425204578597213438213952
Federal Statistical Office. (2015a, February 9). *German exports in 2014: +3.7% compared with 2013*, Press Release 038/2015-02-09, Wiesbaden. https://www.destatis.de/EN/PressServices/Press/pr/2015/02/PE15_038_51.html
Federal Statistical Office. (2015b, February 20). *Foreign Trade. Overall development in foreign trade since 1950.* Wiesbaden. https://www.destatis.de/EN/FactsFigures/NationalEconomyEnvironment/ForeignTrade/OverallDevelopment/Tables/OverallDevelopmentForeignTrade.pdf?__blob=publicationFile
Federal Statistical Office. (2015c, February 24). *Volkswirtschaftliche Gesamtrechnungen.* Wiesbaden. https://www.destatis.de/DE/ZahlenFakten/GesamtwirtschaftUmwelt/VGR/Inlandsprodukt/Tabellen/Volkseinkommen1925_pdf.pdf?__blob=publicationFile
Ferguson, N. (2013, July 11). Merkel's 'deutscher Michel' ploy is bad economics. *Financial Times.*
Ferguson, N., & Roubini, N. (2012, June 9). Germany is failing to learn the lessons of the 1930s. *Financial Times.*
Fichtner, U. (2014, January 24). Herr Nein: The Bull in the Euro Zone's China Shop. *Spiegel Online.* http://www.spiegel.de/international/europe/bundesbank-president-weidmann-stands-opposed-to-euro-rescue-measures-a-945348.html
Fratzscher, M. (2013, November 19). Investment, not the surplus, is Germany's big problem. *Financial Times.*
Fratzscher, M. (2014a, August 28). The German locomotive has become Europe's liability. *Financial Times.*
Fratzscher, M. (2014b). *Die Deutschland-Illusion: Warum wir unsere Wirtschaft überschätzen und Europe brauchen.* München: Carl Hanser Verlag.
Frieda, G. (2013, December 10). A weak banking union risks deflation. *Financial Times.*
Frühauf, M. (2012, August 31). Banken reduzieren ihre Risiken. *Frankfurter Allgemeine Zeitung*
Geithner, T. (2014). *Stress test reflections on financial crises.* London: Random House.
Gericano, L. (2013, May 16). Banking union on the cheap will fail. *The Economist.* http://www.economist.com/blogs/freeexchange/2013/05/european-central-bank-2
Gurria, A. (2012, March 27). The unfinished business of making Europe work. Brussels. http://www.oecd.org/about/secretary-general/theunfinishedbusinessofmakingeuropework.htm
Higgins, A., & Alderman, L. (2013, March 27). Europeans planted seeds of crisis in Cyprus. *International Herald Tribune.*
Higgins, A., & Eddy, M. (2013, December 12). E.U. Ministers stagger toward banking deal. *New York Times.*
Hodson, D. (2013). The Eurozone in 2012, whatever it takes to preserve the Euro? *Journal of Common Market Studies, 51.*
Hulverscheidt, C., & Roßmann, R. (2012, August 2). Ein Risiko von 730 Milliarden Euro. *Süddeutsche Zeitung.*
International Monetary Fund. (2010, May 2). *IMF reaches staff level agreement with Greece on € 30 Billion stand-by arrangement.* Press Release No. 10/176. http://www.imf.org/external/np/sec/pr/2010/pr10176.htm
International Monetary Fund. (2011, May). World economic and financial surveys. Regional economic outlook Europe: Strengthening the recovery. Washington, DC. http://www.imf.org/external/pubs/ft/reo/2011/eur/eng/ereo0511.pdf

International Monetary Fund. (2013, May 20). *Ex post evaluation of exceptional access under the 2010 stand-by-arrangement*. Washington, DC. https://www.imf.org/external/pubs/ft/scr/2013/cr13156.pdf

Irwin, N. (2013, March 29). Three days that saved the world financial system. *Washington Post.*

Jahn, J., & Plickert, P. (2013, August 17). Schäuble: Gesamtrisiko beträgt 310 Milliarden Euro. *Frankfurter Allgemeine Zeitung*

Jahn, J., & Plickert, P. (2015, February 7). Griechen bringen ich Geld aus dem Land. *Frankfurter Allgemeine Zeitung.*

Jolly, D. (2012, May 23). O.E.C.D. sees Euro-Zone crisis hurting world economy. *New York Times.*

Jones, E. (2010). Merkel's Folly. *Survival, 52*(3), 21–38.

Jones, C., & Peel, Q. (2012, August 2). Bundesbank urges ECB to keep within remit. *Financial Times.*

Jones, C., & Wagstyl, S. (2014, February 8/9). Q&A: Germany's constitutional court and the bond-buying plan. *Financial Times.*

Junker, J-.C. (2012, July 30). Esgeht um das Überleben des Euro. *Süddeutsche Zeitung.*

Kaiser, S. (2012a, March 6). The Hundred-Billion-Euro-Bomb: Euro-Zone Central Bank System Massively Imbalanced. *Spiegel Online.* http://www.spiegel.de/international/europe/the-hundred-billion-euro-bomb-euro-zone-central-bank-system-massively-imbalanced-a-818966.html

Kaiser, S. (2012b, May 6). The end of Germany's illusions. *Spiegel Online.* http://www.spiegel.de/international/europe/why-germany-must-give-up-power-to-save-the-euro-a-837063.html

Kaminska, I. (2011, December 6). How Germany is paying for the Eurozone crisis anyway. *Financial Times.* http://ftalphaville.ft.com/2011/12/06/782821/how-germany-is-paying-for-the-eurozone-crisis-anyway/.

Kanter, J., & Ewing, J. (2014a, March 20). Europe strikes a deal to compete banking union. *Reuters.* http://www.reuters.com/article/2014/03/20/us-eu-bankingunion-idUSBREA2J0ZJ20140320

Kanter, J., & Ewing, J. (2014b, March 21). European officials reach deal on failed-bank system. *New York Times.*

Kapoor, S. (2013a, December 20). European banking union is a sham that solves nothing. *Financial Times.*

Kapoor, S. (2013b, December 22). Europe's Flawed Banking Deal. *New York Times.*

Kirkegaard, J. F. (2013, September 13). *Germany's sleepy but significant elections*. Washington, DC: Peterson Institute for International Economics. http://blogs.piie.com/realtime/?p=3996

Kleine-Brockhoff, T. (2011, December 2). Why isn't Germany stepping up to save the euro zone? *Washington Post.*

Kollewe, J. (2012, September 19). Angela Merkel's austerity postergirl: The thrifty Swabian housewife. *The Guardian.* http://www.theguardian.com/world/2012/sep/17/angela-merkel-austerity-swabian-housewives

Krugman, P. (2013a, November 3). The depressing Germans. *New York Times*

Krugman, P. (2013b, November 16). Brussels v Berlin. The fuss over Germany's surplus misses the point. *The Economist.* http://www.economist.com/news/europe/21589892-fuss-over-germanys-surplus-misses-point-brussels-v-berlin

Krugman, P. (2015a, January 25). The Greek Stand-By Arrangement. *New York Times.* http://krugman.blogs.nytimes.com/2015/01/25/the-greek-stand-by-arrangement/

Krugman, P. (2015b, April 19). Crowding In and the Paradox of Thrift. *New York Times.* http://krugman.blogs.nytimes.com/2015/04/19/crowding-in-and-the-paradox-of-thrift/?_r=0

Kulish, N. (2010, April 29). Merkel tested as escalating Greek crisis hurts euro. *New York Times.*

Kulish, N. (2012a, February 28). Germany Backs Greece aid, but at a cost to Merkel. *New York Times*

Kulish, N. (2012b, August 9). German voters face real choice on euro. *Financial Times.*

Kundnani, H. (2012, August 26). The German people will decide Europe's fate. *The Guardian.* http://www.theguardian.com/commentisfree/2012/aug/26/merkel-push-treaty-may-tear-eu-apart

Laeven, L., & Tressel, T. (2013). European financial integration before the crisis. In C. Enoch, et al. (Eds.), *From fragmentation to financial integration in Europe*. Washington, DC: International Monetary Fund.
Legrain, P. (2014). *European spring: Why our economies and politics are in a mess and how to put them right*. London: CB Books.
Lojsch, D. H., Rodriguez-Vives, M., & Slavik, M. (2011, October 2011). *The size and composition of government debt in the Euro Area* (European Central Bank Occasional Paper Series No. 132). Frankfurt am Main. https://www.ecb.europa.eu/pub/pdf/scpops/ecbocp132.pdf
Lowry, A. (2013, April 10). Europe brushes off American advice. *International Herald Tribune*.
Merkel, A. (2012, June 27). No Euro bonds as long as I live. *Spiegel Online*. http://www.spiegel.de/international/europe/chancellor-merkel-vows-no-euro-bonds-as-long-as-she-lives-a-841163.html
Merkel, A. (2013a, June 3). Weare all in the same boat. *Spiegel Online*. http://www.spiegel.de/international/europe/spiegel-interview-with-angela-merkel-on-euro-crisis-and-arms-exports-a-903401.html
Merkel, A. (2013b, August 18). Es wird sehr, sehr knapp. *Frankfurter Allgemeine Zeitung*.
Merler, S., & Pisani-Ferry, J. (2012, March 29). *Sudden stops in the Euro Area*. Brussels, Belgium: Bruegel. http://www.bruegel.org/publications/publication-detail/publication/718-sudden-stops-in-the-euro-area/
Münchau, W. (2008, November 30). German complacency poses a real threat. *Financial Times*.
Münchau, W. (2009a, June 22). Berlin weaves a deficit hair-shirt for us all. *Financial Times*.
Münchau, W. (2009b, July 13). A damning verdict. *Financial Times*.
Münchau, W. (2010a, April 18). Greece's bailout only delays the inevitable. *Financial Times*.
Münchau, W. (2010b, May 10). Germany pays for Merkel's miscalculation. *Financial Times*.
Münchau, W. (2010c, June 6). Frankfurt's Shroud of Secrecy should be Shed. *Financial Times*.
Münchau, W. (2011a, February 21). A misguided German narrative. *Financial Times*.
Münchau, W. (2011b, September 13). Stop rejoicing. This is no victory for the Eurozone. *Financial Times*.
Münchau, W. (2012a, May 28). How to build a fiscal union to save the Eurozone. *Financial Times*.
Münchau, W. (2012b, December 4). France and Germany look set to fudge it yet again. *Financial Times*.
Münchau, W. (2012c, December 16). Politics undermine hope of banking union. *Financial Times*.
Münchau, W. (2013a, March 24). Eurozone break-up edges even closer. *Financial Times*.
Münchau, W. (2013b, June 16). Bond markets nerves threaten to end Europe's calm. *Financial Times*.
Münchau, W. (2013c, June 23). Europe is ignoring the scale of bank losses. *Financial Times*.
Münchau, W. (2013d, June 30). The EU will regret terminating a banking union. *Financial Times*.
Münchau, W. (2013e, November 4). Worry about the euro, not the European Union. *Financial Times*.
Münchau, W. (2013f, December 11). Der fatale Triumph der Deutschen. *Spiegel Online*. http://www.spiegel.de/wirtschaft/bankenunion-wolfgang-muenchau-ueber-die-fatalen-folgen-a-938464.html
Münchau, W. (2013g, December 16). This is not the banking union Europe is looking for. *Financial Times*.
Münchau, W. (2013h, December 23). An exercise in prolonging a banking credit crunch. *Financial Times*.
Münchau, W. (2014a, February 10). Germany's constitutional court has strengthened the eurosceptics. *Financial Times*
Münchau, W. (2014b, March 16). Europe should say no to a flawed banking union. *Financial Times*.
Münchau, W. (2014c, April 13). This could be the moment of Greece to default. *Financial Times*.
Münchau, W. (2014d, June 16). Europe faces the horrors of its own house of debt. *Financial Times*.
Münchau, W. (2014e, September 29). Germany's eurosceptics plant turmoil. *Financial Times*.

Peel, Q. (2011, September 27). Germany and the Eurozone: Besieged in Berlin. *Financial Times.*

Peel, Q. (2012a, July 30). Schäuble view at odds with US. *Financial Times.*

Peel, Q. (2012b, September 17). Merkel reaffirms backing of Draghi Plan. *Financial Times.*

Peel, Q. (2013a, March 19). Cyprus shows German line is hardening. *Financial Times.*

Peel, Q. (2013b, September 3). Germans hostile to further transfer of funds to eurozone. *Financial Times.*

Peet, J., & La Guardia, L. (2014). *Unhappy union: How the Euro crisis – And Europe – Can be fixed.* London: Profile Books Ltd.

Pisani-Ferry, J. (2013). *The Euro crisis and its aftermath.* Oxford, UK: Oxford University Press.

Pisani-Ferry, J., & Sapir, A. (2010, April 22). Germany should share the blame for the Greek crisis. *Bruegel.* http://www.bruegel.org/nc/blog/detail/article/264-germany-should-share-the-blame-for-the-greek-crisis

Plender, J. (2014, December 30). Forgive the debt or earn the wrath of its victims. *Financial Times.*

Posen, A. S. (2013, June 14). Getting Germany past internal devaluation. *Die Welt.* http://www.iie.com/publications/opeds/oped.cfm?ResearchID=2424

Presse- und Informationsamt der Bundesregierung. (2013, May 30). *France and Germany – Together for a stronger Europe of stability and growth.* Press Release 187/13, Berlin. http://www.bundesregierung.de/ContentArchiv/DE/Archiv17/_Anlagen/2013/05/2013-05-30-dt-frz-erklaerung-englisch.pdf;jsessionid=679D5BA027312BCF0F47926DAAD2BE53.s1t2?__blob=publicationFile&v=5

Prestowitz, C. (2013, July 18). Stealth Currency Manipulation. *Foreign Policy.* http://foreignpolicy.com/2013/07/18/stealth-currency-manipulation/

Privitera, A. (2012). *The need to think bigger.* Washington, DC: American Institute for Contemporary German Studies. http://www.aicgs.org/issue/the-need-to-think-bigger/

Quitzau, J. (2014, June 20). *The European Monetary Union: More stable than ever.* Washington, DC: American Institute for Contemporary German Studies. http://www.aicgs.org/publication/the-european-monetary-union-more-stable-than-ever/

Rachman, G. (2014, February 11). Courts, voters and the threat of another euro crisis. *Financial Times.*

Reiermann, C., & Wiegrefe, K. (2012, July 16). Germany's leading role in weakening the Euro. *Spiegel Online.* http://www.spiegel.de/international/germany/chancellor-gerhard-schroeder-key-in-weakening-the-euro-stability-pact-a-844458-druck.html

Reinhart, C., & Rogoff, K. S. (2010). Growth in a time of debt. *American Economic Review, 100* (2).

Reinhart, C. M., & Rogoff, K. S. (2009). *This time is different: Eight centuries of financial folly.* Princeton, NJ/Oxford, MS: Princeton University Press.

Reinhart, C. M., & Rogoff, K. S. (2013, December). *Financial and sovereign debt crisis: Some lessons learned and those forgotten* (IMF Working Paper 13/266). Washington, DC. http://www.imf.org/external/pubs/wp/2013/wp13266.pdf

Roubini, R. (2010a, May 10). We will have even more crisis in the future. *Spiegel Online.* http://www.spiegel.de/international/business/spiegel-interview-with-economist-nouriel-roubini-we-will-have-even-more-crises-in-the-future-a-693991.html

Roubini, N. (2010b, June 28). Greece best option is an orderly default. *Financial Times.*

Roubini, N. (2012, December 17). The Eurozone's delayed reckoning. *Project Syndicate.* http://www.project-syndicate.org/commentary/the-inevitable-return-of-europe-s-crisis-by-nouriel-roubini

Roubini, N. (2013a, August 10). What Angela isn't saying, *The Economist.* http://www.economist.com/news/finance-and-economics/21583257-euro-zone-rescues-have-left-sovereign-debt-too-high-be-sustainable-what-angela

Roubini, N. (2013b, August 22). Berlin's consistency on Greece rescue. *Financial Times.*

Savage, J. D. (2007). *Making the EMU. The politics of budgetary surveillance and the enforcement of Maastricht.* Oxford, UK: Oxford University Press

Schäuble, W. (2010, June 24). Maligned Germany is right to cut spending. *Financial Times.*

Schäuble, W. (2012a). Merkel's speeches to the German parliament on September 12, 2012. *Plenarprotokoll, 17/191*. http://dipbt.bundestag.de/dip21/btp/17/17191.pdf
Schäuble, W. (2012b). Merkel's speeches to the German parliament on December 13, 2012. *Plenarprotokoll 17/214*. http://dip21.bundestag.de/dip21/btp/17/17214.pdf
Schäuble, W. (2012c, May 10). Grexit would be regrettable, but not fatal. *Spiegel Online*. http://www.spiegel.de/international/europe/european-leaders-warn-greece-may-have-to-leave-euro-zone-a-832464.html
Schäuble, W. (2012d, August 31). How to protect EU taxpayers against bank failures. *Financial Times*.
Schäuble, W. (2013a, May 12). Banking union must be built on firm foundations. *Financial Times*.
Schäuble, W. (Finance Minister). (2013b, August 23). Ich kann keine Zahlennennen. *Handelsblatt*.
Schäuble, W. (2013c, September 17). Ignore the doom-mongers: Europe is being fixed. *Financial Times*.
Schelkle, W. (2012, February 23). Der Fanatismus der Zentralbank. *Frankfurter Allgemeine Zeitung*.
Schröder, G. (2012, May 4). Austerity is strangling Europe. *New York Times*.
Schwarzer, D. (2010). German cooperative capitalism and EU economic policy: The sources of the tension. In R. Dehousse & E. Fabry (Eds.), *Where's Germany heading?* Paris: Notre Europe. http://www.swp-berlin.org/fileadmin/contents/products/fachpublikationen/1007_where_is_germany_heading_ swd_ks.pdf
Shambaugh, J. C. (2012, Spring). *The Euro's three crises* (Brooking's Papers on Economic Activity).
Sinn, H.-W. (2012a). *Die Target Falle: Gefahren für unser Geld und unsere Kinder*. München: Carl HanserVerlag.
Sinn, H.-W. (2012b, April 12). A crisis in full flight. *Project Syndicate*. http://www.project-syndicate.org/commentary/a-crisis-in-full-flight
Sinn, H.-W. (2012c, June 13). Why Berlin is balking on a bailout. *New York Times*.
Sinn, H.-W. (2014). *Gefangen im Euro*. München: Redline Verlag.
Sinn, H.-W., & Krämer, W. (2012a, July 5). *Aufruf von 283 deutschspachigen Wirtschaftsprofessoren*. Universität Dortmund. http://www.statistik.tu-dortmund.de/kraemer.html
Sinn, H.-W., & Krämer, W. (2012b, July 10). Eine Antwort auf die Kritiker. *Frankfurter Allgemeine Zeitung*.
Smaghi, L. B. (2013, December 19). The European banking union is a disappointment. *Financial Times*.
Smaghi, L. B. (2014, October 11/12). The eurozone's low inflation problem, *Financial Times*.
Spiegel, P. (2013a, June 19). EU struggles to unlink banks from states as summit looms. *Financial Times*.
Spiegel, P. (2013b, December 10). Q&A: EU banking union. *Financial Times*.
Spiegel, P. (2014a, May 12). It was the point where the Eurozone could have exploded. *Financial Times*.
Spiegel, P. (2014b, May 15). Inside Europe's Plan Z. *Financial Times*.
Spiegel, P. (2014c, May 16). If the euro falls, Europe falls. *Financial Times*.
Spiegel, P., & Barker, A. (2012, June 22). IMF challenges Berlin's crisis response. *Financial Times*.
Spiegel, P., & Peel, Q. (2013, May 20). Berlin plans to streamline EWU but avoid wholesale treaty. *Financial Times*.
Standard & Poors. (2014, June 10). *The long haul: Eurozone deleveraging could stunt growth for years*. Frankfurt am Main. http://twitdoc.com/upload/lisa_nugent/the-long-haul-eurozone-deleveraging-could-stunt-growth-for-years-10-jun-14-.pdf
Statistisches Bundesamt. (2014). *Statistisches Jahrbuch 2014*, Chapter 16: Foreign Trade. https://www.destatis.de/DE/Publikationen/StatistischesJahrbuch/Aussenhandel.pdf?__blob=publicationFile
Stephens, P. (2013, September 12). The audacity of stealth – Merkel's plan for the euro. *Financial Times*.

Storbeck, Q. (2014, January 20). Germany needs more infrastructure spending. *International New York Times.*

Summers, L. (2012, October 10). The world is stuck in a vicious circle. *Financial Times*

Summers, L. (2013a, January 22). End the damaging obsession with deficits. *Financial Times.*

Summers, L. (2013b, February 10). The growth agenda we need. *Washington Post.*

Taylor, P. (2013a, May 13). The disunity at Europe's central bank. *International Herald Tribune.*

Taylor, P. (2013b, June 11). Moments muffed by the troika. *International Herald Tribune.*

The Economist. (2010, April 29). Acropolis now. *The Economist.* http://www.economist.com/node/16009099

The Economist. (2011, September 17). After the fall. *The Economist.* http://www.economist.com/node/21529046

The Economist. (2012a, May 26). Europe's choice. *The Economist.*

The Economist. (2012b, June 9). Start the engines, Angela. *The Economist.* http://www.economist.com/node/21556577

The Economist. (2013, November 9). The perils of falling inflation. *The Economist.* http://www.economist.com/node/21589424

The Economist (2014a, February 1). http://www.economist.com/news/europe/21595503-views-economics-euro-and-much-else-draw-cultural-archetype-hail-swabian/comments?page=2

The Economist. (2014b, June 7). Clouds ahead. *The Economist.* http://www.economist.com/node/21603439

Thomas, L. (2012a, May 21). Big worry for Europe: A double meltdown. *International Herald Tribune.*

Thomas, L. (2012b, June 4). Eurozone approaching its moment of truth. *International Herald Tribune.*

Thomas, L. (2012c, June 4). Euro zone approaching its moment of truth. *International Herald Tribune.*

Thomas, A., & McGroarty, P. (2010, May 20). Germany wants more political Euro Zone. *Wall Street Journal.* http://online.wsj.com/news/articles/SB10001424052748703559004575256281619635818

Thompson, C., & Jenkins, P. (2013, October 13). Bank exposure to EU states' bonds on. *Financial Times.*

Tilford, S. (2006, September). Will the eurozone crack, London: Centre for European Reform, September 2006. http://cer-staging.thomas-paterson.co.uk/sites/default/files/publications/attachments/pdf/2011/p_688_eurozone_crack_42-892.pdf

Tilford, S. (2010, September). *How to safe the euro.* London: Centre for European Reform, September 2010. http://www.cer.org.uk/sites/default/files/publications/attachments/pdf/2011/essay_euro_tilford_14sept10-196.pdf

Tilford, S., & Springford, J. (2013, December 3). Deflating German excuses. *International New York Times.*

Tooze, A. (2010, May 5). The message from Berlin that Europe failed to grasp. *Financial Times.*

Tooze, A. (2012). Germany's Unsustainable Growth. *Foreign Affairs, 91*(5), 23–30.

Trichet, J.-C. (2010, May 15). A 'Quantum Leap' in governance of the euro zone is needed. *Spiegel Online.* http://www.spiegel.de/international/europe/european-central-bank-president-jean-claude-trichet-a-quantum-leap-in-governance-of-the-euro-zone-is-needed-a-694960.html

U.S. Department of the Treasury. Office of International Affairs. (2013, October 30). *Report to Congress on International Economic and Exchange Rate Policies.* Washington, DC. http://www.treasury.gov/resource-center/international/exchange-rate-policies/Documents/2013-10-30_FULL%20FX%20REPORT_FINAL.pdf

Unmack, N. (2013, July 19). 'Home bias' for bonds puts euro at risk. *International Herald Tribune.*

Véron, N. (2013, March 29). With Cyprus, Europe risks being too tough on banking moral hazard. *Financial Times.*

Vinoncur, J. (2009, January 6). German comfort zone: Oblivious and proud. *International Herald Tribune.*
von Hammerstein, K., Reiermann, C., & Schult, C. (2012, October 9). Why Merkel wants to keep Greece in the Euro Zone. *Spiegel Online.* http://www.spiegel.de/international/europe/merkel-wants-to-keep-greece-in-the-euro-zone-a-854879.html
Wagstyl, S. (2014, September 1). Germany: In a spin. *Financial Times.*
Weber, A. (2010, October 12). *Monetary policy after the crisis: A European perspective.* New York City. http://www.bis.org/review/r101018a.pdf
Weidmann. J. (2012a, August 29). Too close and to state financing via the money press. *Spiegel Online.* http://www.spiegel.de/international/europe/spiegel-interview-with-bundesbank-presi dent-jens-weidmann-a-852285.html
Weidmann, J. (2012b, December 21). *Stellungnahme gegenüber dem Bundesverfassungsgericht zu den Verfahren mit den Az 2BvR 1390/2, 2 BvR 1421/12, 2 BvR 6/12.* Frankfurt am Main. http://www.handelsblatt.com/downloads/8124832/1/stellungnahme-bundesbank_handelsblatt-online.pdf
Weidmann, J. (2013a, June 24). Nichtallesisterlaubt. *Süddeutsche Zeitung.*
Weidmann, J. (2013b, September 30). Stop encouraging banks to buy government debt. *Financial Times.*
Westerwelle, G. (2012a, May 23). A growth pact for Europe. *Washington Post*
Westerwelle, G. (2012b, May 11). Europas Weg aus der Krise: Wachstum durch Wettbewerbsfähigkeit – Regierungserklärung Außenminister Westerwelles vor dem Deutschen Bundestag. Berlin. http://www.auswaertiges-amt.de/DE/Infoservice/Presse/Reden/2012/120511-BM_Reg_Erkl_Europa.html
Westerwelle, G. (2013, March 14). EU needs austerity and reform, not spending. *Financial Times.*
Wolf, M. (2010a, May 4). A bail-out for Greece is just the beginning. *Financial Times.*
Wolf, M. (2010b, May 20). The eurozone stumbles into a beggar-my-neighbour policy. *Financial Times.*
Wolf, M. (2011, September 20). Why breaking up is so hard to do. *Financial Times.*
Wolf, M. (2012a, May 30). Fate of euro zone lies with Germany. *Financial Times.*
Wolf, M. (2012b, September 12). Draghi alone cannot save the euro. *Financial Times.*
Wolf, M. (2013a, February 26). The sad record of fiscal austerity. *Financial Times.*
Wolf, M. (2013b, March 27). Cyprus adds to Europe's confusion. *Financial Times.*
Wolf, M. (2013c, April 14). Europe: bitter medicine, *New York Times.*
Wolf, M. (2013d, June 18). The toxic legacy of the Greek crisis. *Financial Times.*
Wolf, M. (2013e, September 24). Germany's strange parallel universe. *Financial Times.*
Wolf, M. (2013f, November 5). Germany is a weight on the world. *Financial Times.*
Wolf, M. (2013g, November 12). Why Draghi was right to cut rates. *Financial Times.*
Wolf, M. (2014a). *The shifts and the shocks. What have we Learned – And have still to Learn – From the financial crisis.* London: Allen Lane.
Wolf, M. (2014b, September 4). Financial reform: Call to arms. *Financial Times.*
Wolf, M. (2015, January 21). Bolder steps from Europe's central bankers. *Financial Times.*
Wren-Lewis, S. (2013, June 13). *How a Greek drama became a global tragedy.* Oxford University. http://mainlymacro.blogspot.de/2013/06/how-greek-drama-became-global-tragedy.html

Chapter 4
Germany's Ordoliberal Lodestar and the Shifting Euro Crisis, 2014 –

Fears of a breakup the monetary union have subsided since 2014. Dogged by meagre feeble and uneven growth, towering unemployment and lowflation becoming a chronic condition, the euro crisis has shifted from the acute to the chronic, from the periphery to the centre. The current economic problems of the euro area economy result from a "negative aggregate demand shock". This is different from the situation in 2011 and 2012, when the euro area suffered from a financial shock. "The default risk is now the result of the risk of a prolonged depression", concluded ECB Vice-President Vitor Constâncio.[1] Of central concern is the persistent stagnation of the euro area economy, particularly in France and Italy, the rising deflationary pressure as a result of prolonged weakness of aggregate demand within the currency zone together with the inability of the ECB to meet its inflation target of below, but close to 2 % in 2 years, and the snap election in Greece on January 25, 2015 which brought back the spectre of the country's default.

4.1 Nein, Nein, Nein to Fiscal Leniency

The recovery that started in late 2013 is mired in a slow-growth track. The weak performance of the second and third largest economies of the currency area endangers the ability of France and Italy to comply with Eurozone budget and debt rules within the next 3 years (Wolf 2014). In its annual report, the Cour des Comptes, reminded French policymakers that France was still in a "danger zone". "The current situation of public finances remains worrying. Deficits remain large

[1] In his speech, he attacked what he called a "misguided view" that the euro area economic problems were "solely the result of supply side problems." European Central Bank, *Monetary policy challenges in the euro area*, Speech by ECB Vice-President Vitor Constâncio at the Annual Conference of the Marshall Society, Cambridge, January 31, 2015 (https://www.ecb.europa.eu/press/key/date/2015/html/sp150131_1.en.html).

F.-J. Meiers, *Germany's Role in the Euro Crisis*,
DOI 10.1007/978-3-319-20514-4_4

and debt continues to rise. We can't close our eyes in the face of such a serious situation," said Didier Migaud, head of the Cour des Comptes. Missing the deficit target of 3 % in 2015 "would be a serious blow to the financial credibility of France," he warned. "We will respect our European commitments to reduce the deficit. This is an unmovable point," pledged Finance Minister Michel Sapin (Roger 2014; Horobin 2014; Carnegy 2014a; Thomson 2014a, b).

As a direct consequence of sluggish growth, French Finance Minister Michel Sapin acknowledged that the country "will not meet its public deficit target [of 3.8 of GDP] this year", a level he had set necessary only 4 months earlier to meet the EU's ceiling of 3 % next year. Given the bleaker economic outlook, France could only reduce its deficit "at an appropriate pace." Europe should take "firm, clear action by deeply adapting its decisions to the particular and exceptional situation of our continent." Prime Minister Manuel Valls admitted in a letter to the President of the European Commission that "the economic situation weighs more heavily than we anticipated in the spring and prevents us from achieving a reduction in our deficit as rapidly as planned". France would aim to reach the required level of 3 % of GDP only in 2017, concluded Mr. Sapin (Sapin 2014; Thomson 2014c; Schaeffer 2014).[2] French President Hollande acknowledged that the austerity measures France had been compelled to follow made it impossible to produce a recovery. "The diagnosis is clear: due to the austerity policies of the last several years, there is a problem of demand throughout Europe, and a growth rate that is not reducing unemployment." He called on the EU leaders to make growth their highest priority.[3] Instead of focusing on each individual case, the European Commission needed to look at the fiscal position of the euro area as a whole before continuing to impose cuts on individual countries. Surplus countries needed "to pose the question" of what more they ought to do to recover growth", Mr. Sapin observed. "...if we want a global fiscal policy which is more growth friendly, maybe some other countries could compensate a little bit," he added (Roger 2015; Carnegy 2014b; Spiegel 2014b).[4] He and Emmanuel Macron, the French Economics Minister, called upon Germany to fully assume its responsibilities by accepting a grand bargain: raise investment by € 50 billion by 2017 to match the planned € 50 billion the French government is proposing in budget cuts in the same period to meet Berlin's

---

[2] Ministère de l'économie et des finances, *Projet de Loi des Finance 2015. Intervention de Michel Sapin, Ministre des Finances et des Comptes publics*, Bercy, September 10, 2014 (http://proxy-pubminefi.diffusion.finances.gouv.fr/pub/document/18/17929.pdf). Le gouvernement confronté à un grave dérapage du déficit public, *Le Monde*, September 10, 2014 (http://www.lemonde.fr/economie/article/2014/09/10/le-gouvernement-confronte-a-un-grave-derapage-du-deficit-public_4484822_3234.html).

[3] Interview de François Hollande accordée au Monde, *op. cit.*; François Hollande, Discours d'ouverture de la Conférence des Ambassadeurs, Paris, August 28, 2014 (http://www.elysee.fr/chronologie/#e7213,2014-08-28,conference-des-ambassadeurs-4).

[4] Projet de Loi des Finance 2015, Intervention de Michel Sapin, Ministre des Finances et des Comptes publics. Bercy, October 1, 2014 (http://www.economie.gouv.fr/files/files/PDF/2014101_Discours_Michel_Sapin__PLF_2015.pdf)

demands for deficit reductions (Spiegel 2014c; Carnegy and Chassany 2014).[5] The message from the Elysée to the German chancellery, the European Commission and the ECB is clear: France won't take measures that would exacerbate the slowdown in growth. The country will not reach its deficit targets more quickly merely by making deeper budget cuts at a time of absent growth and inflation. "Mais reformer oui, regresser non," summed up Mr. Valls the French position. It is now the turn of the European partners to approve a faster growth policy, and to give France a "feu vert" to slow down the deficit reduction pace without imposing sanction procedures in 2015. The French government will reduce the budget deficit "at our speed" and "our priorities" while "not tumbling into austerity." Mr. Valls concluded (Alderman 2014; Smale and Alderman 2014).[6]

Prime Minister Matteo Renzi said that Italy would use the rotating 6-month EU presidency starting on July 1, 2014 to push for an adjustment of the fiscal rule book to spur growth and to provide countries implementing reforms extra time to meet debt targets. The rules should promote "a more investment-friendly implementation of fiscal discipline at the national level"; i.e., productive investment spending in national budgets should be excluded from public deficit calculations. Pier Carlo Padoan, Italy's Economic Minister, denounced the EU's measure of output gaps as outdated. If the OECD's measure of the Italian output gap of 5.1 % of GDP in 2014 were taken instead of the lower EU figure of 3.5 %, the country "would be in structural surplus now and…for a long time."[7] Rome, like Paris, is asking the European partners to adjust the fiscal rule book to foster a growth-friendly fiscal policy in return for his commitment to resolve the country's long-standing structural problems, to remain within the fiscal rule of 3 % of the "out-dated Maastricht world" and to bring down the excessively high debt ratio of close to 135 % of GDP. Renzi's ambitious reform program fuels worries whether he can fulfill his declared aim of raising growth and reducing the ratio of public debt to GDP at the same time without falling back into "excessive deficit procedure" (Dinmore 2014; Dinmore and Segreti 2014; Kanter 2014a; Hadas 2014; Politi 2014).[8]

---

[5] Paris: Berlin soll 50 Milliarden investieren, *Frankfurter Allgemeine Zeitung*, October 20, 2014.

[6] Dépenses publiques: Sapin ferait machine arrière, *Le Monde*, September 10, 2014 (http://www.lemonde.fr/economie/article/2014/09/10/depenses-publiques-sapin-ferait-machine-arriere_4484756_3234.html); 16 septembre 2014: la déclaration de politique générale de Manuel Valls, *Le Figaro*, September 18, 2014 (http://www.lefigaro.fr/politique/le-scan/2014/09/18/25001-20140918ARTFIG00208-16-septembre-2014-la-declaration-de-politique-generale-de-manuel-valls.php); Gouvernment Française, *Discours de Manuel Valls à Londres*, London, October 6, 2014 (http://www.gouvernement.fr/partage/2086-discours-de-manuel-valls-a-londres).

[7] Peter Spiegel, Stefan Wagstyl and Hugh Carnegy, Renzi leads centre-left drive to loosen Eurozone fiscal rules, *Financial Times*, June 20, 2014; Mario Monti, Europe's leaders need to back shift on rules on public investment, *Financial Times*, October 9, 2014; James Politi, Italy accuses Brussels of 'shaky' accounting, *Financial Times*, November 21, 2014.

[8] Transcript: interview with Italy's prime minister, *Financial Times,* October 3, 2014 (http://www.ft.com/intl/cms/s/0/f26a9cea-4b26-11e4-8a0e-00144feab7de.html). Gambler in a rush, *The Economist*, March 22, 2014. (http://www.economist.com/news/europe/21599391-italian-prime-minister-hopes-be-let-some-europes-fiscal-austerity-gambler-rush).

The ECB noted that France, even with an extra 2 years, may miss the Commission's 2015 deadline for correcting the excessive deficit situation; Italy has made "no tangible progress" in implementing the Commission's recommendations. Without direct reference to both France and Italy it added: "...underlying measures to achieve these targets are often either missing or not sufficiently well specified." (European Central 2014) Mr. Draghi urged both governments to revive economic growth through fundamental and far-reaching reforms rather than to ask the ECB for more assistance. "It's pretty clear that the countries that have undertaken a convincing program of structural reforms are performing better—much better—than the countries that have not done so, or have done so to a limited extent." Progress on structural reforms—more flexible labor markets, less bureaucracy, lower taxes—"is clearly too slow", he bemoaned (European Central 2014; European Central Bank 2014e).[9] The EU authorities advised the French and Italian government to continue with their structural adjustment programs over an extended period of time to ensure that the correction of their excessive public debts and deficits and weak external competitiveness remain on track.[10]

In a first step, the outgoing European Commission cleared the French and Italian governments of "serious non-compliance" with EU budget rules, after they agreed to additional fiscal tightening measures that bring them closer to meeting EU targets. France agreed to adjust its budget by an additional € 3.6 billion though lower interest payments, lower than expected contributions to the EU budget and additional revenue of € 900 million from crackdown on tax evasion. The measures would cut France's structural deficit by 0.5 %—an improvement over the 0.2 % submitted, but short of the 0.8 % the European Commission had sought. Italy decided to move cash from a € 3.3 billion fund originally set aside for tax cuts and allocate it to deficit reduction instead. Italy's structural deficit will be reduced by 0.3 %, better than the 0.1 % in the original draft, but still short of the 0.7 % the Commission had sought.[11] "I think that France has presented the details and

---

[9] ibid., European Central Bank, *Introductory statement by Mario Draghi to the press conference (with Q&A)*, Frankfurt am Main, September 4, 2014 (https://www.ecb.europa.eu/press/pressconf/2014/html/is140904.en.html). ibid., *Interview by Mario Draghi with Handelsblatt*, Frankfurt am Main, January 2, 2015 (http://www.ecb.europa.eu/press/key/date/2015/html/sp150102_1.en.html).

[10] European Commission, *Results of in-depth reviews under Regulation (EU) No1176/2011 on the prevention and correction of macroeconomic imbalances*, Brussels, March 5, 2014, pp. 10, 15, 16–17 (http://ec.europa.eu/economy_finance/economic_governance/documents/2014-03-05_in-depth_reviews_communication_en.pdf); ibid; *Council Recommendation on France's 2014 national reform programme and delivering a Council opinion on France's 2014 stability programme*, Brussels, June 2, 2014, pp. 3, 4, 8 (http://ec.europa.eu/europe2010/pdf/csr2014_France_en.pdf); ibid., *Council Recommendation on Italy's 2014 national reform programme and delivering a Council opinion on Italy's 2014 stability programme*, Brussels, June 2, 2014, pp. 2, 3, 5 (http://ec.europa.eu/europe2010/pdf/csr2014_Italy_en.pdf).

[11] Le Ministre des Finances et des Comptes Publics, *Lettre au Vice-Président Jyrki Katainen*, Paris, October 27, 2014 (http://www.economie.gouv.fr/files/files/PDF/Courrier_de_Michel_Sapin_Jyrki_Katainen_27_octobre_2014.pdf); Il Ministro dell Economica e delle Finanze, *Letter*

elements that will allow it to remain within bounds," Mr. Sapin argued. "The Italian economy is going through one of the most severe and lengthy recessions in its history," Mr. Padoan wrote in his letter to the commission, noting that the country's GDP had declined by 9 % since 2008. "A fourth year of recession is to be avoided by all means as it would be extremely problematic to pull the country out of such an economic environment." In order to deal with such "exceptional circumstances" in 2014 and 2015, the Italian government had decided "to postpone the achievement of the MTO [Medium-Term Budgetary Objective] to 2017".[12] The decision did not mean that the Commission found the draft budgetary plans in full compliance with the Stability and Growth Pact. "We are not prejudging the outcome," declared Jyrki Katainen, the outgoing Commissioner for Economic and Monetary Affairs (European Commission 2014a; Kanter 2014b).[13]

The new European Commission postponed a decision whether to initiate sanction procedures under the Stability and Growth Pact against Paris and Rome until early March 2015. "By then, we will have a clearer picture of whether governments are delivering on their reform commitments", said Pierre Moscovici, the Commissioner for Economic Affairs. France and Italy were asked to provide a "clear calendar, with clear indication" when they will undertake "supplementary efforts", emphasized the new European Commission President Jean-Claude Junker. Günter Öttinger, EU Commissioner for the Digital Economy and Society, wrote that "any extension of the deadline" should be linked "to concrete, measurable policy steps", in particular the implementation of "deep structural reforms" to solve the "economic and fiscal problems in the long term." As Paris has not taken "effective action" to meet deficit targets, the Commission was keeping "all options" open for dealing with rule breakers, added Valdis Dombrovskis, the Commission's Vice-President for the Euro and Social Dialogue (European Commission 2011; Spiegel 2014a; Öttinger, G 2014).[14]

In response to Italy's amended 2014 Economic and Financial Document (DEF), the Commission concluded that "the effective implementation of policy measures adopted recently and in previous years remains the country's Achilles' heel." "The beneficial effects of structural reforms will be delayed and reduced if the many

to the Vice-President Jyrki Katainen, Rome, October 27, 2014 (http://www.mef.gov.it/primo-piano/documenti/2014/Lettera_Padoan.pdf); Peter Spiegel, Brussels clears France and Italy's budgets, *Financial Times*, October 29, 2014.

[12] EurAct.fr, *La France et l'Italie modifient leur budget 2015 pour amadouer Bruxelles*, October 27, 2014 (http://www.euractiv.fr/sections/euro-finances/la-france-et-litalie-modifient-leur-budget-2015-pour-amadouer-bruxelles); Il Ministro dell Economica e delle Finanze, *Letter to the Vice-President Jyrki Katainen*, op. cit.; David Jolly, E.U. Blinks in Budget Fight With Italy and France, *New York Times*, October 29, 2014.

[13] ibid., *Statement by Vice-President Katainen on the Draft Budgetary Plans*, Strasbourg, October 29, 2014 (http://europa.eu/rapid/press-release_STATEMENT-14-344_en.htm?locale=en)

[14] ibid., *Introductory Remarks by Commissioner Pierre Moscovici*, Brussels, November 28, 2014 (http://europa.eu/rapid/press-release_SPEECH-14-2241_en.htm). ibid., *Introductory Remarks by Vice-President Valdis Dombrovskis*, Brussels, November 28, 2014 (http://europa.eu/rapid/press-release_SPEECH-14-2240_en.htm)

institutional bottlenecks, implementation barriers and the weak enforcement capacity are not tackled as a matter of priority." With regard to France's Draft Programming Law for Public Finances for 2014–2017, the European Commission reiterated its criticism that "there is limited progress on public finances and taxation reform. The correction of the excessive deficit and the achievement of the MTO have been postponed. Progress on improving the long-term sustainability of public finances has been limited." Only reforms "ambitious in content, properly designed and promptly implemented", can provide "a stimulus to economic activity" (European Commission 2014b).[15]

The new guidance on the Stability and Growth Pact gives the European Commission greater flexibility when judging whether member countries have violated the EU budget rules. Under the new guidelines, a country facing economic hardship would only have to cut its deficit by 0.25 % instead of 0.5 % before. They could provide a waiver of EU deficit rules if countries like France or Italy just propose a significant economic plan." (European Commission 2015a)[16] Benoît Coeuré, the ECB Executive Board member responsible for handling relations with Brussels, said the ECB was "frustrated" that the debt rules were "already being sidelined". "Not taking any further measures" against France and Italy "increases uncertainty because nobody knows whether the rules are currently being applied in full or not." Any unravelling of the strict deficit rules would only create more instability. "If member states stop here, they will leave the eurozone in a state of permanent fragility," he said, Mr. Draghi in a veiled criticism of the Commission's decision warned that the rules needed "full and consistent" implementation (Spiegel 2015f).[17] The ECB's views are widely shared in Berlin. The more lenient application of the rules of the Stability and Growth Pact would encourage recalcitrant governments in Paris and Rome "to get out from under the chancellor's whip" of fiscal discipline and "allocate their money to lavish deficit spending." (Joffe 2015) A senior German official put it this way, "There will be joyful celebrations in the Elysée and probably in Rome, too, if we go down this path" (Wagstyl 2015c).

The lobbying efforts of the French and Italian governments to persuade the Commission to reward its belated reform efforts finally paid off. The Commission granted a reprieve to France and Italy both found in need of an in-depth analysis

[15] ibid., *France – Monitoring of Policy Progress under the Macroeconomic Imbalances Procedere*, Brussels, December 2014, pp. 2, 3, 24 (http://ec.europa.eu/economy_finance/economic_governance/documents/20141224_fr_imbalances_epc_report_en.pdf).

[16] ibid., *Making the Best Use of the Flexibility within the Existing Rules of the Stability and Growth Pact*, Strasbourg, January 13, 2015 (http://ec.europa.eu/economy_finance/economic_governance/sgp/pdf/2015-01-13_communication_sgp_flexibility_guidelines_en.pdf). ibid., *Presentation of a communication providing new guidance on the Stability and Growth Pact*, Strasbourg, January 13, 2015 (http://europa.eu/rapid/press-release_SPEECH-15-3242_en.htm).

[17] European Central Bank, *Interview with Benoît Cœuré, Member of the Executive Board of the ECB, with Die Welt*, Published on 13 January 2015. https://www.ecb.europa.eu/press/inter/date/2015/html/sp150113.en.html. ibid., *Introductory statement to the press conference (with Q&A) by Mario Draghi*, Nicosia, March 5, 2015 (https://www.ecb.europa.eu/press/pressconf/2015/html/is150305.en.html).

under the Macroeconomic Imbalances Procedure in November 2014. In Italy's case the Commission concluded that given the "weak growth and implementation of structural reforms" the opening of Excessive Deficit Procedures at this stage was "not warranted." For France it decided to set a new deadline to correct its excessive deficit situation "by 2017". The extension should "give France sufficient time to implement ambitious structural reforms." In a clear signal that France still needed to take remedial measures to put its public finances in proper order and to boost the competitiveness of its sluggish economy, the Commission added that "France needs to step up its efforts both on fiscal and structural reforms side." The French government was asked "to deliver an additional 0.2 % of GDP in structural effort" this year. On the basis of France's National Reform Programs and other commitments to structural reforms, Paris would be re-evaluated in "three months." (European Commission 2015b)[18] Finance Minister Sapin declared that the deficit would fall to 3.8 % of GDP this year, 3.3 % next year and 2.7 % in 2017. Prime Minister Valls added that the reduction of the budget deficit below the critical threshold of 3 % in 2017 would be achieved "at our pace and by always promoting our priorities."[19] The Commission's decision to apply the EU budget rules more flexible to France and Italy reflects the major concern that the second and third-largest Eurozone economies are not moving fast enough to overhaul their economies and to create sufficient growth to reduce their debts and budget deficits. Both countries represent the euro area's central problem: economic stagnation despite a long history of deficit spending—both have not registered a budget surplus since the 1970s.

Berlin has remained unmoved by the calls from Paris and Rome. Chancellor Merkel still insists that following the fiscal rule book is essential to financial stability and sustainable growth. "...one really must question whether we can continue to have lesser revenues than expenditures, so that our debts keep on growing. Indeed, a whole crisis of confidence has grown out of that." The European partners should follow the German example of strict budget discipline and structural reforms. "What holds for Germany, applies unchanged to Europe, too." A softening of reform efforts would be "the greatest risk to the continuing recovery." She therefore asked "all—I emphasize here again—all member states [to] accept in full the strengthened rules." Only when the Eurozone's rules were seen as trustworthy could they fulfil their role as "central anchor for stability and

[18] ibid., *Statement by Vice-President Dombrovskis at European Semester 2015 press conference* Brussels, February 25, 2015 (http://ec.europa.eu/commission/content/statement-vice-president-dombrovskis-european-semester-2015-press-conference_en). ibid., *Commissioner Moscovici's remarks at the Press Conference on college decisions on 2015 European Semester*, Brussels, February 25, 2015 (http://europa.eu/rapid/press-release_SPEECH-15-4510_en.htm).

[19] *Valls et Sapin réaffirment l'objectif d'un déficit au-dessous de 3 % du PIB en 2017*, AFP, February 25, 2015 (https://fr.news.yahoo.com/valls-sapin-r%C3%A9affirment-lobjectif-dun-d%C3%A9ficit-au-dessous-185056081.html); Michel Sapin: 'Nous serons sous les 3 % de deficit en 2017', *Le Monde*, December 3, 2014 (http://www.lemonde.fr/politique/article/2014/12/03/Michel-sapin-nous-serons-sous-les-3-de-deficit-en-2017_4533219_823448.html).

above all, trust in the Eurozone." That means that "we stick to what we have agreed upon—that is the Stability and Growth Pact." She called on France to make additional reforms before the European Commission passes a verdict on French fiscal policy in March 2015. "What is now on the table is not yet enough."[20] Mr. Schäuble warned that countries with high debt could not backslide on their fiscal commitment to meet the euro area's fiscal deficit target. "The only problem that some countries have is that they have to stick to the rules." More debt would only lead to a "deepening of the problems instead of solving them." In a speech to the Bundestag he summed up Berlin's understanding of budgetary discipline. "The use of more and more public money and the acceptance of higher deficits and debts are leading us astray." Expansionary fiscal and monetary policies would "cause significant costs and risks with regard to sustainability of public debt, financial stability, and reform effort". Only "innovation, structural reforms, investment and reliable conditions and above all, trust in the sustainability [of public finances]" can deliver growth and employment. At a G20 meeting of finance ministers and central bankers he warned against debt-financed growth. "There's not much leeway from the demand side and from monetary policy to support sustainable growth."[21] Mr. Weidmann objected that the "not…particularly tough" budget rules needed to be strengthened rather than weakened to secure the progress that has been made during the crisis. France should "restore competitiveness and reduce the very high level of public spending." Like Finance Minister Schäuble, he concluded that expansionary fiscal and monetary policies would "risk a further deterioration with regard to the sustainability of public debt, financial stability and reform effort."

[20] Die Bundeskanzlerin, *Merkel empfängt Valls in Berlin. Herausforderungen gemeinsam bewältigen*, Berlin, September 22, 2014 (http://www.bundeskanzlerin.de/Content/DE/Artikel/2014/09/2014-09-22-besuch-mp-valls.html;jsessionid=369FC207AEF75668F5C3BF27E78E0BF6.s2t2); Die Bundesregierung, *21. Cicero Foyergespräch: BK'in Merkel im Gespräch mit Christoph Schwennike und Frank A. Meyer*, Berlin, August 27, 2014 (http://www.bundesregierung.de/Content/DE/Mitschrift/Pressekonferenzen/2014/08/2014-08-28-merkel-cicero.html); Deutscher Bundestag, *Plenarprotokoll 18/50*, Berlin, September 10, 2014, p. 4554 (http://dipbt.bundestag.de/doc/btp/18/18050.pdf); ibid, *Plenarprotokoll 18/60*, Berlin, October 16, 2014, p. 5485 (http://dip21.bundestag.de/dip21/btp/18/18060.pdf); ‚Verlässlichkeit ist ein hohes Gut', Interview mit Bundeskanzlerin Angela Merkel, *Welt am Sonntag*, December 7, 2014 (http://www.bundeskanzlerin.de/Content/DE/Interview/2014/12/2014-12-07-merkel-wams.html).

[21] Peter Spiegel, Stefan Wagstyl and Hugh Carnegy, Renzi heads centre-left drive to loosen eurozone fiscal rules, *Financial Times*, June 20, 2014; 'Die Fehler von vor zehn Jahren nicht wiederholen', Interview of Finance Minister Wolfgang Schäuble with *ARD-Tagesthemen*, June 24, 2014 (http://www.bundesfinanzministerium.de/Content/DE/Interviews/2014/2014-06-24-tagesthemen-textfassung.html?view=renderPrint); Deutscher Bundestag, *Plenarprotokoll 18/49*, Berlin, September 9, 2014, pp. 4460, 4464 (http://dipbt.bundestag.de/doc/btp/18/18049.pdf); International Monetary Fund, Statement by Mr. Wolfgang Schäuble to the International Monetary and Financial Committee, Washington, D.C., October 11, 2014, pp. 1–2 (https://www.imf.org/External/AM/2014/imfc/statement/eng/deu.pdf); Bundesfinanzministerium, *Aktuelle Lage im Euroraum (1): Zum Stand des Reformprozesses im Euroraum insgesamt*, Berlin, September 22, 2014 (http://www.bundesfinanzministerium.de/Content/DE/Monatsberichte/2014/09/Inhalte/Kapitel-3-Analysen/3-1-euroraum-reformprozess-europa-startseite.html).

What are needed are "structural reforms...to overcome the weak pace of growth", and no attempts "to fight debt with more debt."[22] The message from Berlin and Frankfurt to the Eurozone partners is unequivocal: a steadfast commitment to price stability, sound public finances and structural reforms is crucial for confidence, demand, investment and growth as well as a stable currency union.[23] There was one exception to the rule: France. German Finance Minister Schäuble supported a 2-year waiver for France, adopted by EU finance ministers in early March 2015. Even though he approved the decision rather reluctantly—he warned that if the European Commission applied the Stability and Growth Pact too flexible, she would risk losing "trust" and "credibility"—he was anxious to avoid any further political damage to the jaded relationship with France.[24]

The capacity for an expansionary fiscal policy that could help to offset the depressing impact of fiscal consolidation lies "almost uniquely in Germany" where the federal government with a balanced budget has "fiscal space to do so" without violating fiscal rules.[25] Leading international organizations—the IMF and OECD—European authorities—the ECB and the European Commission -, and governments in the United States, France and Italy are urging Germany to loosen

[22] 'Ist er zu stark, bist du zu schwach', Interview mit Bundesbankpräsident Jens Weidmann, *Süddeutsche Zeitung*, May 22, 2014 (http://www.bundesbank.de/Redaktion/DE/Interviews/2014_05_22_weidmann_sz.html); Interview avec le Dr. Jens Weidmann, président de la Deutsche Bundesbank, dans Le Monde du 13/08/2014 (http://www.bundesbank.de/Redaktion/DE/Interviews/2014_08_13_weidmann_le_monde_frz.html); 'The Euro Crisis Is Not Yet Behind Us', Interview with Jens Weidmann, *Spiegel Online*, September 24, 2014 (http://www.spiegel.de/international/business/interview-with-bundesbank-head-jens-weidmann-on-euro-crisis-and-ecb-a-993409.html); Q&A With German Bundesbank President Jens Weidmann, *Wall Street Journal*, October 7, 2014 (http://blogs.wsj.com/economics/2014/10/07/qa-with-german-bundesbank-president-jens-weidmann/); International Monetary Fund, *Statement by the Hon. Jens Weidmann*, Governor's Statement No. 22, Washington, D.C., October 10, 2014, pp. 1–2 (https://www.imf.org/external/am/2014/speeches/pr22e.pdf); Deutsche Bundesbank, ‚*Special Responsibility*', Joint interview with Jens Weidmann published in El Pais, Le Figaro and La Republicca, Frankfurt am Main, December 12, 2014 (http://www.bundesbank.de/Redaktion/EN/Interviews/2014_12_12_weidmann_le_figaro_el_pais_la_repubblica.html).

[23] Germany's ordiliberal principles are well summarized by Jürgen Stark, German prudence is not to blame for the eurozone ills, *Financial Times*, February 12, 2015.

[24] European Council, *National briefing by Wolfgang Schäuble, Federal Minister for Finance of Germany following the ECOFIN Council*, Brussels, March 10, 2015 (http://tvnewsroom.consilium.europa.eu/video/national-briefing-germany-part-11608371); Werner Mussler, Schäuble scheinheilig, *Frankfurter Allgemeine Zeitung*, March, 11, 2015.

[25] European Central Bank, *Speech by Mario Draghi at the Smposium in Jackson Hole*, op. cit.; ibid., *Keynote speech by Mario Draghi, President of the ECB, Eurofi Financial Forum*, Milan, September 11, 2014 (https://www.ecb.europa.eu/press/key/date/2014/html/sp140911_1.en.html); ibid., *Recovery and Reform in the euro area*, Opening remarks by Mario Draghi, President of the ECB, Brookings Institution, Washington D.C., October 9, 2014 (https://www.ecb.europa.eu/press/key/date/2014/html/sp141009.en.html); ibid., *A three-pillar-strategy for the Euro*, Opinion piece by Benoît Cœuré, Member of the Executive Board of the ECB, and by Jörg Asmussen for Berliner Zeitung and Les Echos, Frankfurt am Main, September 19, 2014 (https://www.ecb.europa.eu/press/inter/date/2014/html/sp140919.en.html).

the purse strings and to invest more in infrastructure in order to boost aggregate demand.[26] German policy makers, however, still fail to comprehend the urgency of addressing today's demand shortfall and Germany's "pivotal role" to do more for a flexible, growth-promoting fiscal policy (Greetham 2014; Portes and Weil 2014; Fratzscher 2014; Smaghi 2014).[27] Sigmar Gabriel, deputy Chancellor and leader of the Social Democratic Party (SPD), declared there were "no economic policy grounds" for the government to either abandon or change its fiscal policy. Increasing Germany's national debt for the German infrastructure was no answer to the economic problems of countries like Italy and France which could only be resolved by "structural reforms, growth through investments and higher competiveness."[28]

In a symbolic shift, Wolfgang Schäuble announced on November 6, 2014 an additional € 10 billion in public spending.[29] The infrastructure spending will start only in 2016 and run to 2018, amounting to 0.1 % of annual GDP; the extra spending can be accommodated without breaking the government's two overriding goals of a balanced budget in 2015 ("black zero") and a reduction of the overall national debt from presently 75 % of GDP to 60 % in the 2020s.[30] The extra funding

---

[26] International Monetary Fund, *Euro Area Policies*, op. cit., pp. 8–12; ibid., *Germany*, IMF Country Report No 14/216, Washington, D.C., June 26, 2014 (http://www.imf.org/external/pubs/ft/scr/2014/cr14216.pdf); ibid., Group of Twenty, *Global Prospects and Policy Challenges*, op. cit., p. 9; ibid., *World Economic Outlook*, October 2014, op. cit., pp. 75–89; ibid., *Transcript of a Press Briefing on the World Economic Outlook* (WEO), Washington, D.C., October 7, 2014 (http://www.imf.org/external/np/tr/2014/tr100714.htm); Organization for Economic Cooperation and Development, *Interim Economic Assessment*, op. cit., p. 7; ibid., Shifting into higher gear and rebuilding the engines of growth, Editorial by Catherine Mann, OECD Chief Economist, Paris, November 6, 2014 (http://www.oecd.org/eco/outlook/shifting-into-higher-gear-and-rebuilding-the-engines-of-growth-by-catherine-mann.htm); ibid., *Economic Outlook, Volume 2014/2*, Paris, November 2014 (Preliminary Version), pp. 41, 42–44, 48 (http://www.oecd-ilibrary.org/economics/oecd-economic-outlook-volume-2014-issue-2_eco_outlook-v2014-2-en); European Central Bank, *Speech by Mario Draghi, at Symposium in Jackson Hole*, op. cit.; European Commission, *European Economic Forecast Autumn 2014*, op. cit., pp. IX, 66–67; U.S. Department of the Treasury, Remarks of Secretary Jacob J. Lew at the World Affairs Council of Seattle on *Building a Stronger Global Economy*, Seattle, November 12, 2014 (http://www.treasury.gov/press-center/press-releases/Pages/jl2696.aspx); Hugh Carnegy and Anne-Sylvaine Chassany, France warns EU investment fund will flop without 'real money'. *Financial Times*, November 19, 2014.

[27] ibid., *Die Deutschland-Illussion*, op. cit., pp. 74–95; Lawrence Summers, Why public investment really is a free lunch, *Financial Times*, October 7, 2014.

[28] Bundesministerium für Wirtschaft und Energie, *Herbstprojektion 2014 der Bundesregierung*, Berlin, October 14, 2014 (http://www.bmwi.de/DE/Presse/reden,did=662996.html); Deutsche Bundesbank, *Reforms for Recovery and Resilience*, op. cit.

[29] The Finance Ministry announced in early March 2015 that the federal government would commit an additional € 5 billion to helping struggling municipalities. Of the new money, €1.5 billion will be made available through a supplementary budget this year, and the remaining €3.5 billion from a special fund that can be used through 2018. Bundesministerium der Finanzen, *Bund bringt zusätzliche Investitionen auf den Weg und unterstützt finanzschwache Kommunen*, Berlin, March 3, 2015 (http://www.bundesfinanzministerium.de/Content/DE/Pressemitteilungen/Finanzpolitik/2015/03/2015-03-03-PM09.html).

[30] Bundesministerium der Finanzen, *Pressekonferenz zu den Ergebnissen der 145. Sitzung des Arbeitskreises Steuerschätzungen*, Berlin, November 6, 2014 (http://www.bundesfinanzministerium.de/Content/DE/Video/2014/2014-11-06-steuerschaetzung/2014-11-06-

is in "the very small ballpark what is needed", Ms Lagarde said in a veiled critique (Jones and Wagstyl 2014). The new plan is inadequate to address the huge investment gap in public services. Plugging the investment gap would require 3 % of GDP, or € 80 billion annually (Fratzscher 2013; Smaghi 2014; Harris 2014).[31] As investors are prepared to pay for the privilege of holding Germany's debt—the yields of German 2-year and 5-year bonds are negative (−0.27 % and −0.10 %), those of 10- and 30-year bonds near zero percent (0.15 % and 0.61 %)[32]—and as all government levels—central government, state government, local government and social security funds—achieved a surplus of € 18 billion or +0.6 % of the Maastricht ratio in 2014 for the first time since German reunification and is expected to rise to € 20,7 billion or 0.7 % of GDP this year and € 25,6 billion or 0.8 % in 2016,[33] the federal government sticks to the deep anti-debt consensus—growth can come only as a result of thriftiness—and the constraints of the balanced budget amendment. It deliberately denies itself the unprecedented opportunity presented by the historically low interest rates to address the significant investment gap in public services. Maintaining a budget balanced made "perfect sense" for a country with debts of more than € 2 trillion set to face the "huge" burden from its aging society in the coming decades, argued Mr. Weidmann. "The demographic outlook in particular should deter us from saddling the younger generations with more and more debt," he added.[34] The reflexive opposition of German policy makers to fiscal deficits as inherently hazardous, regardless of their actual costs and benefits, is "pathological". The monetary union "may fail, not because of irresponsible profligacy but rather because of pathological frugality" (Wolf 2015a; Storbeck 2015)[35].

steuerschaetzung.html); Deutscher Bundestag, *Plenarprotokoll 18/68*, Berlin, November 25, 2014, p. 6420 (http://dip21.bundestag.de/dip21/btp/18/18068.pdf) (ibid., Plenarprotokoll, 18/69, Berlin, November 26 2014);, p. 6502 (http://dip21.bundestag.de/dip21/btp/18/18069.pdf); Michael Klein, Ausgaben sollen bis 2018 wieder steigen, *Das Parlament*, December 1, 2014, p. 1.

[31] ibid., The German locomotive has become Europe's liability, *Financial Times*, August 28, 2014. ibid., *Die Deutschland-Illusion*, op. cit., pp. 74–95.

[32] Bloomberg, *German Government Bunds*, April 24, 2015 (http://www.bloomberg.com/markets/rates-bonds/government-bonds/germany/).

[33] Federal Statistical Office, *General government recorded surplus of 18 billion euros in 2014*, Press Release 062/2015-02-24, Wiesbaden, February 24, 2015 (https://www.destatis.de/EN/PressServices/Press/pr/2015/02/PE15_062_813.html); Gemeinschaftsdiagnose, *Eckdaten Prognose für Deutschland Frühjahr 2015*, Munich April 14, 2015, p. 67 (https://www.cesifo-group.de/de/ifoHome/facts/Forecasts/Gemeinschaftsdiagnose/Archiv/GD-20150416.html).

[34] Deutsche Bundesbank, *Die demographischen Herausforderungen Deutschlands*, Rede von Bundesbankpräsident Jens Weidmann im Rahmen der "Wirtschaftsgespräche am Main", Frankfurt am Main, November 27, 2014 (http://www.bundesbank.de/Redaktion/DE/Reden/2014/2014_11_27_weidmann.html); ibid., *Wachstumkräfte stärken – Reformen für mehr Wohlstand*, Rede von Bundesbankpräsident Jens Weidmann beim Wirtschaftsgipfel der Süddeutschen Zeitung, Berlin, November 28, 2014 (http://www.bundesbank.de/Redaktion/DE/Reden/2014/2014_11_28_weidmann.html); ibid., *‚Special Responsibility‘*, op. cit. See also Otmar Issing, Blame Germany for bad policies, not its reluctance to spend more, *Financial Times*, October 24, 2014.

[35] Adam Tooze, Germany's Unsustainable Growth, op. cit., p. 30

4.2 In Defense of the Maginot Line of Monetary Stability

Despite interest rates cut to a record low level and extra liquidity pumped into the banking system, bank lending to the real economy remains weak and has so far not reached all corners of the euro zone evenly. Particularly small and medium-sized enterprises (SME) in stressed southern economies are severely affected by the credit crunch. They face "very pressing problems" in gaining access to bank credit at affordable rates.[36] Even a stabilizing banking sector—the ECB's bank stress tests found only 13 of the 130 largest euro area banks under review wanting[37]—cannot be counted for a more meaningful recovery in demand growth. The ECB's third quarterly bank lending survey points to growing concerns among banks about firms' business outlook and macroeconomic uncertainty, particularly the prolonged weakness of aggregate demand.[38] The inability of the euro area member countries to agree on a credible strategy for boosting growth and the sober outlook of the euro area economy with no obvious sources of new demand act as a further drag on banks' lending readiness.[39]

The loss of economic momentum in the second quarter of 2014 increased the pressure on the ECB to embark on large-scale asset purchases to spur faster growth. The ECB emphasized that its mandate "includes the possibility of buying, under the

---

[36] European Central Bank, *Survey on the Access to Finance of Small and Medium-Sized Enterprises in the Euro Area*, Frankfurt am Main, April 2014, p. 5 (http://www.ecb.europa.eu/pub/pdf/other/accesstofinancesmallmediumsizedenterprises201404en.pdf); Speech by Mario Draghi, at the ECB Forum on Central Banking in Sintra on May 26, 2014, op. cit.; Liz Alderman, Little Guys still face a euro credit crunch, *International New York Times*, May 13, 2014; Sarah Gordon, Give them some credit, *Financial Times*, February 19, 2014; Gert Wehringer, SMEs and the Credit Crunch: Current financing difficulties, policy measures and a review of literature, *OECD Journal: Financial Market Trends*, Vol. 2013/2, Paris, March 20, 2014, pp. 2–4 (http://www.oecd.org/finance/financial-markets/SMEs-Credit-Crunch-Financing-Difficulties.pdf); Marco Giuli, What Does the Banking Union Mean for the Real Economy? in: *Banking Union and Beyond. Discussion papers for Brussels Think Tank Dialogue*, Bruegel, January 28, 2014, pp. 8–9 (http://www.bruegel.org/publications/publication-detail/publication/808-banking-union-and-beyond-discussion-papers-for-brussels-think-tank-dialogue/).

[37] European Central Bank, *Aggregate Report on Comprehensive Assessment*, Frankfurt am Main, October 26, 2014 (https://www.ecb.europa.eu/pub/pdf/other/aggregatereportonthecomprehensiveassessment201410.en.pdf).

[38] European Central Bank, *The Euro Area Bank Lending Survey 3rd Quarter of 2014*, Frankfurt am Main, October 29, 2014, pp. 5, 7, 8, 11 (http://www.ecb.europa.eu/stats/pdf/blssurvey_201410.pdf?2c94dc05dc5cd40aadb6f077dc320999).

[39] Ian Fleming and Patrick Jenkins, Unanswered questions hang over the eurozone bank tests, *Financial, Times*, October 24, 2013; Lorenzo Bini Smaghi, What to do with the eurozone banking system, *Financial Times*, November 7, 2013; Ralph Atkins, Eurozone crisis fears re-emerge, *Financial Times*, October 24, 2014; Gavyn Davies, Stress test alone will not bring the eurozone back to health, *Financial Times*, October 27, 2014 (http://www.ft.com/intl/cms/s/0/63f168e2-5dee-11e4-b7a2-00144feabdc0.html#axzz3HRnfvszQ); Bank stress tests fail to tackle deflation spectre, *Financial Times*, October 28, 2014; Martin Wolf, Europe's banks are too feeble to spur growth, *Financial Times*, October 29, 2014; Erik Nielsen, Hopes for a Eurozone bank lending appear to be misguided, *Financial Times*, November 14, 2014.

appropriate conditions, government bonds on the secondary market should this be necessary from a monetary policy perspective."[40] The scale of the ECB's actions in early June 2014 to avert the alarming threat of persistent lowflation illustrated the central bank's preference for complete unity. The 23-members of the Governing Council did approve only those measures unanimously—a € 400 billion long-term funding for lending operation, a negative deposit rate of −0.1 % on banks' holdings at the ECB and a further cut of the main lending rate to 0.15 %—which do not address the problem of lowflation directly.[41] The IMF called for more forceful and immediate action by the ECB to invigorate the euro area meagre growth in economic activity and address "stubbornly low" levels of inflation by buying "a large scale asset purchase program, primarily of sovereign assets." (International Monetary Fund 2014a)[42] "We are not done here", Mr. Draghi admitted (European Central Bank 2014a).[43] In early September, the ECB's Governing Council agreed to another incremental step. The Council decided to lower the interest rate on the main refinancing operations of the eurosystem by 10 basis points to 0.05 % while charging banks on deposits they leave with it, through a negative rate 0.20 %. "Should it become necessary to further address risks of too prolonged a period of low inflation, the Governing Council is unanimous in its commitment to using additional unconventional instruments within its mandate", he emphasized (European Central Bank 2014b).

In view of the euro area's inability to achieve any sustainable growth at all and the growing risk of lowflation tipping into outright deflation, Mr. Draghi declared that the ECB will meet its responsibility—"we will do what we must" to reverse the "challenging inflation situation" and "raise inflation expectations as fast as possible", because "the firm anchoring of inflation expectations is critical under any circumstances." The bank's Governing Council had agreed to prepare "for further

[40] European Central Bank, Keynote Speech of Yves Mersch: Member of the Executive Board of the ECB, at the 'Welt' Währungskonferenz, Berlin, May 14, 2014 (http://www.ecb.europa.eu/press/key/date/2014/html/sp140514.en.html); ibid., *Introductory statement to the press conference (with Q&A) by Mario Draghi*, Frankfurt am Main, April 3, 2014 (http://www.ecb.europa.eu/press/pressconf/2014/html/is140403.en.html); ibid., *Monetary policy communication in turbulent times*, Speech by Mario Draghi at the Conference De Nederlandsche Bank 200 years, Amsterdam, April 24, 2014 (http://www.ecb.europa.eu/press/key/date/2014/html/sp140424.en.html).

[41] European Central Bank, *Introductory statement by Mario Draghi to the press conference (with Q&A)*, Frankfurt am Main, June 5, 2014 (http://www.ecb.europa.eu/press/pressconf/2014/html/is140605.en.html); ibid., *Recent challenges to monetary policy in the euro area*, speech by Vitor Constâncio, Vice-President of the ECB, at the Athens symposium on Banking Union, Monetary Policy, and Economic Growth, Athens, June 19, 2014 (http://www.ecb.europa.eu/press/key/date/2014/html/sp140619.en.html); ibid., *Introductory statement by Mario Draghi to the press conference (with Q&A)* on September 4, 2014, op. cit.

[42] ibid, *Euro Area Policies*, op. cit., pp. 8–12.

[43] ibid., *Recent challenges to monetary policy in the euro area*, speech by Vitor Constâncio, Vice-President of the ECB, at the Athens symposium on Banking Union, Monetary Policy, and Economic Growth, Athens, June 19, 2014 (http://www.ecb.europa.eu/press/key/date/2014/html/sp140619.en.html).

measures, which could if needed, be implemented in a timely manner." During the first quarter of 2015 the ECB "intends" to expand the size of its balance sheet by € 1 trillion to around € 3 trillion that it had reached in early 2012. Should it become necessary, the ECB will "broaden even more the channels through which we intervene, by altering accordingly the size, pace and composition of our purchases". Like the Federal Reserve, the Bank of Japan and the Bank of England, the ECB is determined to provide further monetary policy accommodation, even without the support from all its Governing Council members, if the economic outlook worsened or the existing measures—the purchase of asset-backed securities (ABS) and covered bonds coupled with liquidity injections through its targeted longer-term refinancing operations (TLTRO)—fell short to stave off economic stagnation and to boost inflation to a level below, but close to 2 %. The ECB would buy sovereign bonds of euro area members in the secondary market in proportion to the percentage of each country's shareholding in the Central Bank. As the "risks of not fulfilling our mandate of price stability are. . .higher than they were six months ago," Mr. Draghi is determined to do what it takes to achieve the central bank's price stability target (European Central Bank 2014c; Praet 2014).[44] Without QE the intended target cannot be reached because the existing programs are not big enough to elevate the size of its balance sheet to the high of € 3 trillion—as of January 2, 2015 the ECB had bought € 29,632 billion of covered bonds and € 1.744 billion of asset-backed securities as part of a program of asset purchases that began in September 2014—and the ECB cannot rely upon banks to expand its balance sheet—banks are continuing to pay off longer-term refinancing loans (LTROs), while the take up of TLTROs has been disappointing: banks borrowed only € 212 billion of the € 400 billion tenders in September and December (European Central Bank 2015a; Jones 2014b; Münchau 2014; Ewing 2014; Mackintosh 2014). In fact, the ECB's balance sheet has shrunk from 32 % to about 21 % of the Eurozone economy since 2012, in effect withdrawing monetary stimulus as credits contracted while the U.S. and Japanese central banks expanded rapidly. "The ECB has taken away the punch bowl and the party hasn't even started yet," Catherine Mann, the OECD Chief Economist, noted.[45] In view of the peripheral risk and potential volatility on the horizon financial institutions did not put their money into the real economy as the ECB expected when it imposed a penalty on bank deposits in June 2014. Private investment activities, especially along Europe's southern rim,

---

[44] ibid., *The role of the banking union in achieving financial stability*, speech by Vítor Constâncio, Vice-President of the ECB, at the FT Banking Summit "Ensuring Future Growth", London, November 26, 2014 (https://www.ecb.europa.eu/press/key/date/2014/html/sp141126.en.html). ibid., *Introductory statement of Mario Draghi to the press conference (with Q&A)*, Frankfurt am Main, December 4, 2014 (https://ecb.europa.eu/press/pressconf/2014/html/is141204.en.html). ibid., *Monthly Bulletin*, Frankfurt am Main, December 2014, p. 5 (https://www.ecb.europa.eu/pub/pdf/mobu/mb201412en.pdf). ibid., *Interview by Mario Draghi with Handelsblatt*, op.cit.

[45] Organization for Economic Cooperation and Development, *Putting the euro area on a road to recovery*, Presentation of the OECD Economic Outlook by Catherine L. Mann, OECD Chief Economist, Paris, November 25, 2014 (http://www.oecd.org/eco/outlook/economicoutlook.html).

remain "persistently weak", with few signs of a significant recovery. Overall lending to non-financial companies fell 1.1 % in October 2014, continuing a decline of more than 2 years (European Central Bank 2014d, g; International Monetary Fund 2014b). Instead, the volume of negative yielding Eurozone government debt has swollen to € 1.2 trillion, equivalent to about a quarter of all outstanding Eurozone sovereign debt, as investors are sticking to a "core only" strategy to avoid any potential fallout on borrowing costs in periphery countries (Thompson 2015). Lastly, a broad QE package "is much less effective" in the euro area because European non-financial companies get most of their financing through banks and not capital markets like those in the United States, Mr. Asmussen said. "It could be a good thing, but I would warn against expecting the effects to be large," he added (Ewing and Appelbaum 2015; Jones 2015a).

The ECB's unconventional measures still face tremendous political obstacles from familiar quarters. The Merkel government still emphasizes compliance with the rules of the Stability and Growth Pact as indispensable for sustainable growth. An expansive monetary and fiscal policy would only exacerbate the problems in the distressed euro area member countries. Chancellor Merkel remains sceptical about a full-blown QE program in principle, fearing it will ease pressure on spendthrift member countries to reform their economies and bring their budgets under control. "One must prevent that the dealings of the ECB might appear in any way that the achievements in the fiscal and competitive field take a back seat," she warned. The ECB's decision on sovereign bond purchases should not distract from the fact "that real growth impulses" come from "prudent framework conditions" set by "politics." "Spain, Ireland, Portugal and partly also Greece prove the value of reforms and the return to growth," she said at the World Economic Forum. The four cases validate the positive causation between solid fiscal policy and economic growth. Recalcitrant governments should not be "tempted to buy time and avoid doing structural reforms."[46] Like the Chancellor, Mr. Schäuble sees an expansive monetary and fiscal policy as the basic cause for the economic problems in Europe. For him, compliance with the common rules of the Stability and Growth Pact is the only way out of the European national debt crisis. Sound budgetary management and structural reforms together with targeted public investments are the best guarantee for higher growth. In contrast to the IMF and Larry Summers he does not see a substantial increase in public infrastructure investment as "a free lunch" that will "reduce burdens on future generations."[47] "A renunciation of a policy without new

---

[46] Die Bundesregierung, *Rede vor Bundeskanzlerin Merkel zur Jahreseröffnung 2015 der Deutschen Börse*, Eschborn, January 19, 2015 (http://www.bundesregierung.de/Content/DE/Rede/2015/01/2015-01-20-merkel-dt-boerse.html); ibid., *Geldpolitik ersetzt keine Reformen*, Berlin, January 20, 2015 (http://www.bundesregierung.de/Content/DE/Artikel/2015/01/2015-01-20-merkel-deutsche-boerse.html); ibid., *Rede von Bundeskanzlerin Merkel anl. des Jahrestreffens 2015 des World Economic Forum*, Davos, January 22, 2015 (http://www.bundesregierung.de/Content/DE/Rede/2015/01/2015-01-22-merkel-wef.html).

[47] Lawrence Summers, Why public investment really is a free lunch, *Financial Times*, October 7, 2014; International Monetary Fund, *World Economic Outlook. Legacies, Clouds, Uncertainties*,

debt would destroy the slowly growing trust in Europe," he concluded (Deutscher Bundestag 2014). [48]

The Bundesbank remains a vocal opponent of large-scale purchases of sovereign bonds with respect to necessity, efficiency and risk. The ECB's extension of its mandate of strict monetary policy amounts to an undeserved bailout of undisciplined peripheral countries that will turn the monetary union into a debt union without prior consent of national parliaments. [49] Mr. Weidmann reminded the ECB that monetary policy, particular its bond buying program (QE) "cannot solve the structural problems in the euro area and financial stability risks may rise the longer the loose monetary policy lasts". There's no "Aladdin's Lamp" that can be rubbed vigorously to cure Europe's ills. Such purchases "might create new incentives to run up debt, besides adding to the reform fatigue in a number of countries." Market interventions such as the purchase of government bonds would undermine the disciplinary function of the market. But far-reaching adjustment processes are indispensable to increase the competitiveness of the crisis-hit countries and to reduce the levels of private public debt. The ECB should recognize "the limits of monetary policy" and comply with "principles that still hold today", in particular "the concept of an independent central bank clearly focused on price stability." Monetary policy should not be subjugated to fiscal policy in an attempt to increase growth in those countries that did not resolve their structural problems. He warned the ECB that "anticipating political union through the central bank's balance sheets is a dangerous path". Especially the purchase of lower-rated bonds would heighten "the fundamental risk of mutualizing sovereign liability risks via the central banks' balance sheet." Compliance with the fiscal policy rules in the Stability and Growth Pact is "not something which central banks can achieve on their own." Elected governments and parliaments should make such far-reaching decisions, not the European Central Bank. As euro area leaders have shied away from "common fiscal arrangements", they have to work with what they have got: "member state each remain responsible for their fiscal policies." Therefore, "the principle of national liability needs to be underscored."[50] Though Mr. Weidmann does not deny the risk

Washington, D.C., October 2014, pp. 20, 21–22 (http://www.imf.org/external/pubs/ft/weo/2014/02/pdf/c1.pdf).

[48] ibid., *Plenarprotokoll, 18/69*, Berlin, November 26, 2014, pp. 6504, 6505 (http://dip21.bundestag.de/dip21/btp/18/18069.pdf). Schäuble warnt EZB vor zu expansiver Geldpolitik, *Reuters*, December 5, 2014 [http://de.reuters.com/article/topNews/idDEKCN0JJ0S920141205].

[49] Jens Weidmann, *Stellungnahme gegenüber dem Bundesverfassungsgericht zu den Verfahren mit den Az 2BvR 1390/2, 2 BvR 1421/12, 2 BvR 6/12*, op. cit.; Bundesverfassungsgericht, *BVerfG, 2 BvR 1390/12 vom 17.12.2013*, op. cit.; ibid., *BVerfG, 2 BvR 2728/13 vom 14.01.2014, Absatz-Nr. (1–105)*, op. cit.; Q&A With German Bundesbank President Jens Weidmann, *Wall Street Journal*, October 7, 2014, op. cit.; Deutsche Bundesbank, *'Voraussetzungen für eine stabile Währungsunion'*, Speech of Dr Jens Weidmann, Bielefeld, October 13, 2014 (http://www.bundesbank.de/Redaktion/DE/Reden/2014/2014_10_13_weidmann.html?view=render).

[50] 'Ist er zu stark, bist du zu schwach', Interview mit Bundesbankpräsident Jens Weidmann, *Süddeutsche Zeitung*, May 22, 2014 (http://www.bundesbank.de/Redaktion/DE/Interviews/2014_05_22_weidmann_sz.html); Interview avec le Dr. Jens Weidmann, président de la Deutsche Bundesbank,

of deflation, he concludes that the impact of recent price data may be less serious than believed while those of a QE salvo could be more serious than assumed. "What we are currently seeing is a disinflationary process, not a deflationary spiral of decreasing wages and prices," he judged.[51] He summed up the three German messages to the European partners as follows: First, "price stability and growth, even in times of great monetary policy challenges, are not opposites but rather that price stability provides the basis for sustainable growth." Second, "rules only make sense if they are kept" by all at all times. Lastly, structural impediments to competition, innovation and productivity are the main barrier to growth, not monetary and fiscal policy.[52]

---

dans Le Monde du 13/08/2014 (http://www.bundesbank.de/Redaktion/DE/Interviews/2014_08_13_weidmann_le_monde_frz.html); 'The Euro Crisis Is Not Yet Behind us', Interview with Jens Weidmann, *Spiegel Online*, September 24, 2014 (http://www.spiegel.de/international/business/interview-with-bundesbank-head-jens-weidmann-on-euro-crisis-and-ecb-a-993409.html); Q&A With German Bundesbank President Jens Weidmann, *Wall Street Journal*, October 7, 2014 (http://blogs.wsj.com/economics/2014/10/07/qa-with-german-bundesbank-president-jens-weidmann/); International Monetary Fund, *Statement by the Hon. Jens Weidmann*, Governor's Statement No. 22, Washington, D.C., October 10, 2014, pp. 1–2 (https://www.imf.org/external/am/2014/speeches/pr22e.pdf); ibid., *Reforms for Recovery and Resilience*, Riga, October 17, 2014 (http://www.bundesbank.de/Redaktion/EN/Reden/2014/2014_10_17_weidmann.html); ibid., Weidmann:" Government bond purchases harbour major moral hazard", Passau, November 17, 2014 (http://www.bundesbank.de/Redaktion/EN/Topics/2014/2014_11_13_weidmann_passau.html); ibid., *Strengthening forces for growth – reforms geared towards boosting prosperity*, Speech at the economic summit of the Süddeutsche Zeitung, Berlin, November 28, 2014 (http://www.bundesbank.de/Redaktion/EN/Reden/2014/2014_11_28_weidmann.html); ibid., *Weidmann: 'Es gibt keinen einfachen und bequemen Weg'*, Frankfurt am Main, December 8, 2014 (http://www.bundesbank.de/Redaktion/DE/Themen/2014/2014_12_08_weidmann_zeit_deutsches_wirtschaftsforum.html?startpageId=Startseite-DE&startpageAreaId=Teaserbereich&startpageLinkName=2014_12_08_ weidmann_zeit_deutsches_wirtschaftsforum+324964); ibid., ‚*Special Responsibility*', op. cit.; ibid., ‚Staatsanleihekäufe sind kein Wundermittel, Frankfurt am Main, December 17, 2014 (http://www.bundesbank.de/Redaktion/DE/Themen/2014/2014_12_17_weidmann_icfw.html?startpageId=Startseite-DE&startpageAreaId=Teaserbereich&startpageLinkName=2014_12_17_weidmann_icfw+325406); ibid., *Heading for stability and prosperity – Bringing the euro area back on track*, Keynote speech by Dr. Jens Weidmann given at the City of London Corporation, London February 12, 2015 (http://www.bundesbank.de/Redaktion/EN/Reden/2015/2015_02_12_weidmann.html).

[51] Deutsche Bundesbank, *Heading for stability and prosperity*; op. cit.; ibid., '*Special Responsibility*', op. cit.; See also Claire Jones, Bundesbank president Jens Weidmann steps up criticism of QE, *Financial Times*, December 17, 2014; Gavyn Davies, Fault lines with the ECB, *Financial Times*, November 26, 2014 (http://blogs.ft.com/gavyndavies/2014/11/26/fault-lines-within-the-ecb/).

[52] Deutsche Bundesbank, *Weidmann: 'Es gibt keinen einfachen und bequemen Weg'*, December 8, 2014, op. cit.; Jack Ewing, Karl Otto Pöhl, Former President of the German Central Bank, Dies at 85, *New York Times*, December 11, 2014; David Henry, Karl Otto Poehl, Bundesbank Chief for Reunification, Dies, *Bloomberg News*, December 10, 2014 (http://www.bloomberg.com/news/2014-12-10/karl-otto-poehl-bundesbank-chief-for-reunification-dies-at-85.html); Deutsche Bundesbank, ‚Special Responsibility', op. cit.; ibid, '*Voraussetzungen für eine stabile Währungsunion*', op. cit.

German economic policy rests on two iron laws: the respect for law in general and the rules on fiscal and monetary stability in particular, plus frugal housekeeping and fiscal self-discipline as the key to boost economic growth. It is hard to see Germany ever giving up on of the two categorical imperatives of ordoliberalism (Bryant 2014; Taylor 2014; Barber 2014; Wagstyl 2014; Meyerson 2014; Norris 2014).[53] The self-righteousness with which the Merkel government stays its austere course risks becoming a bigger problem for the world economy. "The world cannot afford a European lost decade", Mr. Lew summed up the critique of German intransigence.[54] Berlin's penchant of prioritizing sound public finances and structural reforms highlights how far the German economic debate is removed from external demands to revive growth in the euro area by loosening the purse strings.

Germany's unchanged message to its euro area partners has the paradoxical consequence the Bundesbank so fervently opposes: given the lack of political resolve the ECB remains the only game in town and the sole actor with monetary arrows in its quiver that are of macroeconomic relevance. After months of pulling and hauling, Mr. Draghi reached for the last arrow in his quiver to breathing life into the flagging euro area economy and fending off the specter of deflation. On January 22, 2015 the ECB launched its long-awaited expanded asset purchases program. The central bank will buy € 60 billion of public and private sector securities from March 2015 until September 2016 across issuers from the various euro area countries on the basis of the ECB's capital key in the secondary markets.

The program will last as the ECB sees a "sustained adjustment" to the path of inflation consistent with its "aim of achieving inflation rated below, but close to 2 % over the medium term." Mr. Draghi admitted that "the prevailing degree of monetary accommodation was insufficient to adequately address heightened risks of too prolonged a period of low inflation." The resolute measures should underpin the ECB's determination to "strengthen demand, increase capacity utilization and support money and credit growth, and thereby contribute to a return of inflation rates towards two percent." In compliance with the preliminary verdict from the European Court of Justice on the OMT program that any bond purchases by the ECB must be limited to the extent necessary to maintain the existence of a functioning bond market, the QE program includes "two limits": the central bank "won't buy more than 25 % of each issue, and not more than 33 % of each issuer debt."[55]

The three points of the ECB's landmark decision are as follows: Members of the Governing Council were unanimous in their belief that "the asset purchase program is a pure monetary policy tool in a legal sense" and can therefore be used "in the

---

[53] You Kant do that, *The Economist*, September 15, 2014 (http://www.economist.com/news/europe/21616999-many-germans-fear-european-central-bank-not-their-side-you-kant-do).

[54] U.S. Department of the Treasury, *Remarks of Secretary Jacob J. Lew at the World Affairs Council*, op. cit.

[55] European Central Bank, *Introductory Statement by Mario Draghi to the press conference (with Q & A), Frankfurt am Main, January 22, 2015* (https://www.ecb.europa.eu/press/pressconf/2015/html/is150122.en.html).

right situations" "if and when required to deliver on its price stability mandate." The central bank has sent the unambiguous signal to the markets that it is both politically willing and institutionally able to do what it must to deliver price stability and keep inflation on target. Lastly, it has set a benchmark against which the conclusion of the QE program must be warranted. This gives the central bank the greatest possible discretion on when to terminate the program.[56]

But there are three limits Mr. Draghi conceded in his announcement. He relativized his emphasis on the "singleness of the monetary policy" by admitting that "we are not in a one-country setup. We are in a multi-country setup". He qualified "the principle of full risk sharing" by admitting that with regard to the QE program "there was a consensus on risk sharing set at 20 and 80 % on a no-risk-sharing base" while "the effectiveness" of the OMT program required "full risk sharing". Lastly, he acknowledged that monetary policy can only create the "the basis for growth". The ultimate success of "very expansionary monetary policies" depends on the Eurozone governments' readiness "to implement. . .structural reforms" and to undertake "a growth-friendly consolidation." The ECB's high political profile highlighted again by Mr. Draghi's bigger than expected QE move[57] comes at a political price.

- Mr. Draghi repeatedly emphasized that monetary policy alone is enough to pull the euro area economy out of its doldrums and to prevent lowflation from becoming a chronic condition. The ECB's expansionary monetary policy can succeed only in "combination" with governments engaging in growth-friendly fiscal policies and structural reforms as well as financial institutions lending more to the real economy. "What monetary policy can do is create the basis for growth. But for growth to pick up, you need investment; for investment, you need confidence; and for confidence, you need structural reforms." The QE decision was the last time that the ECB did buy euro zone governments more time to do the necessary work on the fiscal and structural components. As in the past, the ECB may find itself in the unenviable position to make up for the shortcomings of its fiscal and financial counterparts which do not recognize that

[56] European Central Bank, *Introductory Statement by Mario Draghi to the press conference on January 22, 2015*, op. cit.; Jack Ewing, E.C.B. Council Was Unanimous in Backing Legality, but not Timing, of Bond Purchases, *International New York Times*, February 20, 2015; Stephanie Flanders, Draghi has only done enough for now, *Financial Times*, January 23, 2015; Martin Wolf, Draghi's bold promise to do what it takes for as long as it takes, *Financial Times*, January 23, 2015; Wolfgang Münchau, Draghi's QE is an imperfect compromise for the eurozone, *Financial Times*, January 26, 2015.

[57] Some keen observers of the ECB expected that Draghi's QE salvo would be limited to € 500 billion. Jack Ewing and Binyamin Appelbaum, A Stress Test for Mario Draghi and the European Central Bank, Wolfgang Münchau, The ECB demigods and eurozone quantitative easing, *Financial Times*, December 8, 2014; ibid., Smart wrapping dignifies policy in Europe, *Financial Times*, December 29, 2014; John Plender, Oil fall adds to ECB's deflation worries, *Financial Times*, December 24, 2014; Coming soon? *The Economist*, January 3, 2015 (http://economist.com/news/finance-and-economics/21637422-ecb-might-unleash-its-long-awaited-programme-early-2015-coming-soon).

monetary accommodation, fiscal flexibility and structural reforms do reinforce each other, Mr. Draghi has repeatedly emphasized.[58]

- Mr. Draghi's timid advances to quantitative easing reflects pronounced disagreements within the ECB's Governing Council about the effectiveness of large-scale bond purchases[59] and profound differences on whether to begin QE soon and if so, how to make it work in Europe's fragmented bond market.[60] If the central bank could not even agree that it "intends" to expand its balance sheet—some members of the Executive Board favoured a more guarded language than "expected"—what will be the odds that policymakers will agree to buy sovereign bonds? Mr. Draghi's QE quandary is that "further measures" he deems necessary to promote the fulfilment of the ECB's mandate of price stability will exacerbate divisions within the euro area which bodes ill for the central bank's political ambition to use QE as "an instrument to create confidence, to unite Europe, not to divide Europe," Mr. Benoît Cœuré said.[61] The ECB's move down the QE road will test the ability of the euro area decision making system to build a consensus around such large-scale intervention among conflicting parties (Irwin 2014a).
- Even though the landmark decision has been adopted by "a large majority, so large we did not need to take a vote", Mr. Draghi said, the Governing Council approved a specific form of QE Mr. Weidmann had suggested in mid-December 2014: delegating the risk of buying bonds of less creditworthy countries with their relevant national central banks (Jones 2014c; Barkin 2015a; Davies

[58] European Central Bank, *Introductory statement by Mario Draghi to the press conference* on August 7, 2014, op. cit.; ibid., *Introductory remarks by Mario Draghi at the EP's Economic and Monetary Affairs Committee*, Brussels, September 22, 2014 (https://www.ecb.europa.eu/press/key/date/2014/html/sp140922.en.html); ibid., Speech by Mario Draghi, at the School of Economics and Business Studies "Federico Caffè" on *The economic policy of Federico Caffè in our times*, Rome, November 12, 2014 (https://www.ecb.europa.eu/press/key/date/2014/html/sp141112.en.html); ibid., *Interview by Mario Draghi with Handelsblatt*, op. cit.; ibid., European Central Bank, *Introductory Statement by Mario Draghi to the press conference on January 22, 2015*, op. cit.; Europe's deflation risk leaves no option but quantitative easing, *Financial Times*, January 10, 2015.

[59] Of the ECB's Governing Council 24 members, six voted against a decision in early December 2014 to increase thhe balance sheet by € 1 trillion. Claire Jones, Draghi's easing options hang on crucial court ruling, *Financial Times*, January 14, 2014.

[60] European Central Bank, Interview by Sabine Lautenschläger, Member of the Executive Board of the ECB, with Der Spiegel on January 7, 2015 and published on January 10, 2015 (https://www.ecb.europa.eu/press/inter/date/2015/html/sp150110.en.html); ibid., Interview de Benoît Cœuré, membre du directoire de la BCE, par Stéphanie Antoine, France 24, le 8 janvier 2015, diffusée le 10 janvier 2015 (https://www.ecb.europa.eu/press/inter/date/2015/html/sp150110_1.fr.html).

[61] Claire Jones, ECB poised to dash bond buying hopes, *Financial Times*, December 3, 2014; Claire Jones and Ferdinando Giugliano, ECB slashes Eurozone growth and inflation forecasts, *Financial Times*, December 5, 2014 (Ewing and Appelbaum 2015); Jack Ewing, Deep divide at E.C.B. on proposal to buy bonds, *International New York Times*, January 12, 2015; European Central Bank, Interview de Benoît Cœuré, par Stéphanie Antoine, op. cit.

2015).[62] "20 % of the additional asset purchases will be subject to a regime of risk sharing", while 80 % of purchases will fall on the balance sheets of national central banks which will assume most of the responsibility for losses from any default or restructuring of their national debt (European Central Bank 2015b). Breaking with the ECB's tradition set by previous sovereign bond-buying schemes, the limited mutualization of risk indicates that the ECB's freedom of manoeuvre is to a large degree dependent on the "mercy of realpolitik."[63] The ECB's QE quandary implies that the central bank has to strike a delicate balancing act between satisfying market expectation that it is determined to pursue its inflation target and to break the euro area stagnation, and schmoozing the main QE critics, namely the German government and the Bundesbank, that unleashing an aggressive bond buying program will not lessen the urgency for euro area governments to overhaul their economies and bring their budget under control.

- As ECB policies have become the headlights of German politics, Mr. Draghi moved cautiously forward to monetary easing, proportional to the rising problems of the euro area to convince the German government and a healthy majority in the ECB's Governing Council that using additional unconventional instruments are unavoidable to address prolonged demand weakness and persistent lowflation (Jones 2014a; Jolly 2014). Broad political consensus is essential for effective QE. "We don't need unanimity," Mr. Draghi said. But he added, "I believe it can be designed to have consensus."[64] But without the Chancellor's explicit tactical support as in the euro's darkest hour in 2012, the ECB's QE salvo "would resemble the halfhearted, and hence unsuccessful, interventions of the Bank of Japan in the 2000s." (Moghadam 2014; Münchau 2014; Barkin 2015a) She qualified her grudging acquiescence to Draghi's QE salvo[65] with the clear warning that "monetary policy does not replace reforms."[66] Given the

[62] Europe's deflation risk leaves no option but quantitative easing, *Financial Times*, January 10, 2015.

[63] Swaha Pattanaik, E.C.B.'s mission is often at mercy of realpolitik, *International New York Times*, November 3, 2014. Noah Barkin, Draghi risks losing allies in Germany, *International New York Times*, January 6, 2015. See also Anatole Kaletsky, The costs of political paralysis, *International New York Times*, November 7, 2014 Waiting for the European Central Bank, *International New York Times*, November 10, 2014 Anne Seith, Deep Divisions Emerge over ECB Quantitative Easing Plans, *Spiegel Online*, November 3, 2014 (http://www.spiegel.de/international/business/deep-divisions-emerge-over-ecb-quantitative-easing-plans-a-1000713.html).

[64] European Central Bank, *Introductory statement of Mario Draghi to the press conference (with Q&A)*, Frankfurt am Main, December 4, 2014, op. cit.; Transcript: interview with the ECB's chief economist, *Financial Times*, November 18, 2014 (http://ft.com/cms/s/0/2309e78c-6f2d-11e4-b060-00144feabdc0.html).

[65] She told British Prime Minister David Cameron in early January 2015 that QE was a "very, very bad idea." Claire Jones, Stefan Wagstyl and Chris Giles, How Europe's power couple split over QE, *Financial Times*, January 24/25, 2015.

[66] Die Bundesregierung, *Geldpolitik ersetzt keine Reformen*, Berlin, January 20, 2015 (http://www.bundesregierung.de/Content/DE/Artikel/2015/01/2015-01-20-merkel-deutsche-boerse.html); Jack

deep-seated aversion of German decision makers against the use of European institutions, i.e. the ECB, to sharing risks among member countries, Chancellor Merkel may take the same attitude of restraint to future bailouts and proposed changes to the euro area governance (Barkin 2015b; The Economist 2015).

- The ECB's compromise package trades off the bigger than expected scale of the bond purchases with a breach in the ECB's usual risk-sharing arrangements. Mr. Draghi emphasized that "the singleness of monetary policy remains in place." For him, the demutualization of risk is an economically irrelevant peculiarity that solved the politically sensitive problem to refute German objection about QE that it will lead to a redistribution of risks from the periphery to taxpayers in the core (Sandbu 2015). However, by delegating ultimate responsibility for bond purchases to the 19 euro area national central banks, the ECB "sends a signal that the Eurozone is not moving in the direction of greater mutualization of debt, something that will be necessary in the longer term for a successful single currency," one euro area finance minister told the Financial Times (Jones 2015b). "The more efficient (QE) is, and the more mutualization there is, the better," warned Christine Lagarde about the adoption of a hybrid approach—buying large-scale sovereign bonds, but sharing only some of the risk across the euro area. Watering down the QE program so that Berlin comes around may not only shatter the appearance of cross EU solidarity, a true union in all circumstances with the ECB acting as the lender of last resort. It may also dilute the effectiveness of the ECB's large sovereign bond buying program, exacerbate the doom-loop between banks and their weak sovereigns and raise questions about the independence of the central bank.[67] Constraining the ECB's modus operandi to what Berlins sees as best in its interests is "inconsistent with and violates the [EU] treaty," added Athanasios Orphanides, a former member of the ECB's Governing Council (Atkins and Jones 2015).
- Mr. Draghi's calculus that Berlin will acquiesce again to the ECB's unconventional measures as a last resort has put the Chancellor in a more precarious situation at home. Domestic veto players, including university professors, see

Ewing, Germany restrains its reaction to stimulus, *International New York Times*, January 24/25, 2015; Claire Jones, Stefan Wagstyl and Chris Giles, How Europe's power couple split over QE, *Financial Times*, January 26, 2015; Claire Jones and Stefan Wagstyl, The eurozone: a strained bond, *Financial Times*, January 19, 2015.

[67] Guntram B. Wolff and Silvia Merler, *The ECB has fired its bazooka*, Brussels: Bruegel, January 22, 2015 (http://www.bruegel.org/nc/blog/detail/article/1550-the-ecb-hs-fired-its-bazooka/). See also Neil Irwin, Timid, late and still the best hope for Europe, *International New Times*, January 23, 2015; Matt O'Brien, The ECB takes out the bazooka, *Washington Post*, January 22, 2015 (http://www.washingtonpost.com/blogs/wonkblog/wp/2015/01/22/the-ecb-takes-out-the-bazooka-itll-buy-over-1-trillion-euros-of-bonds-to-save-europes-economy/); Better late than never, *The Economist*, January 24, 2015 (htttp://www.economist.com/node/21603717/); Martin Wolf, Draghi's bold promise to do what it takes for as long as it takes, *Financial Times*, January 2/24, 2015; Gavyn Davies, Mr. Draghi finally delivers, *Financial Times*, January 23, 2015 (http://blogs.ft.com/gavyndavies/2015/01/23/qe-ecb-mr-draghi-finally-delivers/); Wolfgang Münchau, Why the ECB should not water down a QE programme, *Financial Times*, January 19, 2015; Claire Jones, ECB set to bow to German pressure over QE, *Financial Times*, January 17/18, 2015.

the ECB's QE move as another fatal step bending the strict monetary and fiscal rules that has to be encountered by legal actions. Hans-Werner Sinn, President of the Ifo Institute, denounced the ECB's initiative as "a fiscal bailout". With its decision to declare the ECB's OMT program "unlawful", the Bundesverfassungsgericht "has expressively prohibited the German government from sitting back while the ECB oversteps its mandate." If the Chancellor, like at the height of the euro crisis in summer 2012, acquiesced to Draghi's illegal overreach, "any German citizen can petition the court and force [her] to act."[68] Professor Joachim Starbatty, member of the European Parliament, announced that his parliamentarian group, the Alternative für Deutschland (AfD), declared to file a suit against the ECB's QE program on the ground that it would amount to a permanent and unconditional bailout guarantee (Plickert 2014). He is supported by the German lawmaker Peter Gauweiler already challenging the ECB's controversial OMT program in the European Court of Justice,[69] who had instructed a law professor to prepare a case against the ECB's QE program that would be—in his view—an illegal financing of spendthrift governments through the backdoor.[70] With the ECB's unconventional measures the Chancellor appears to have lost her freedom of action at home to concede to the central bank wide discretion to determine on its own what constitutes monetary policy.

In short, the Merkel government's overriding concern is the defense of the Maginot line of fiscal Disziplin by insisting on the consolidation of public budgets and the implementation of far-reaching structural reforms as the conditio sine qua non for substantial and sustainable growth. Consequently, German political decision makers chorus "Nein, Nein, Nein" to demands of a more expansionist approach via deficit spending and to any plea for fiscal leniency and debt restructuring. German Finance Minister Schäuble put the German economic thinking into a nutshell. "In my view, expansionary monetary policy and debt-financed fiscal policy are not the solution. On the contrary: I consider them to be one of the

---

[68] Hans-Werner Sinn, Merkel has a duty to stop Dragh's illegal fiscal meddling, *Financial Times*, September 30, 2014; ibid., Gefangen im Euro, op. cit., pp. 74, 87–88, 89–90, 108, 158;'300 Milliarden Euro Verlust durch Niedrigzinsen', Interview with Hans-Werner Sinn, *Frankfurter Allgemeine Zeitung*, December 5, 2014. See also Prof. Dr. Joachim Stabatty, *Ein offener Brief an die Kanzlerin*, Brussels, September 4, 2014 (http://www.alternativefuer.de/starbatty-ein-offener-brief-die-kanzlerin/); Prof. Dr. Heribert Dieter, *Kollateralschäden der EZB-Strategie*, Berlin: Stiftung Wissenschaft und Politik, SWP-Aktuell 2, January 2015, pp. 3–4, 8 (http://www.swp-berlin.org/fileadmin/contents/products/aktuell/2015A02_dtr.pdf.); Deutsche Bundesbank, *Heading for stability and prosperity*; op. cit.

[69] *Request for a preliminary ruling from the Bundesverfassungsgericht (Germany) lodged on 10 February 2014 – Peter Gauweiler and Others* (Case C-62/14) (2014/C 129/15), Official Journal of the European Union, April 28, 2014, C129/11-C129/13 (http://eur-lex.europa.eu/legal-content/EN/TXT/PDF/?uri=CELEX:62014CN0062&from=EN).

[70] Dr. Peter Gauweiler and Prof. Dr. Dietrich Murswiek, Presseerklärung: *Klage der Bundesregierung gegen das heute verkündete Anleihenkaufprogramm der EZB ist unvermeidlich*, Munich, January 22, 2015 (http://www.peter-gauweiler.de/pdf/pressemitteilungen/pm_2015-01-22b.pdf).

main causes of the financial and debt crises that have occurred in recent decades and of the weak growth that we are seeing." For him, the most important question for the euro area therefore is: "Can we adhere to the rules which prescribe fiscal consolidation and structural reforms in the Euro area?"[71] The German government is still more worried about the proper conditions of the economy in the tradition of the country's cherished ordoliberal economic model that disdains state intervention as a backdoor tool to avoid fiscal probity and structural reforms.

4.3 Message in the Bottle: Athenians, Pay Your Debt!

The euro crisis is back to where it started 6 years ago: in Greece. After the historical election victory of the Coalition of the Radical Left (Syriza) over its rival, the New Democracy (ND) of Prime Minister Antonis Samaras, by a wide margin on January 26, 2015.[72] The newly elected Prime Minister Alexis Tsirpas pledged a sharp turn from the Troika's bailout deals. "The Greek people gave a strong and clear mandate to immediately end austerity and change policies", he said in his inaugural address to the Greek parliament. He vowed to no longer abide by the terms of the bailout agreement. Instead, he would seek "a bridge agreement until June" that would provide the country a breathing space to negotiate "a stable and balanced arrangement" which "would not condemn us to further austerity" (Tsipras 2015; Kitsantonis 2015b; Hope 2015a; Bouras 2015). He proposed a European-wide debt conference similar to the conference that led to the London Debt Agreement of 1953 that settled the foreign debts of Germany.[73] Syriza's insistence to end austerity policies and not to seek an extension to the country's bailout program

[71] Bundesfinanzministerium, *Eurozone at a crossroads (again)*, Speech by Wolfgang Schäuble to open the Brookings Institution discussion entitled ‚Eurozone at a crossroads (again)', Washington, DC, April 16, 2015 (http://www.bundesfinanzministerium.de/Content/EN/Reden/2015/2015-04-17-brookings-washington.html). See also Deutscher Bundestag, *Plenarprotokoll 18/49*, Berlin, September 9, 2014, pp. 4460, 4464; 'Wir müssen mehr investieren und unsere Wettbewerbsfähigkeit verbessern', Bundesfinanzminister Dr. Wolfgang Schäuble im Interview mit *Welt am Sonntag*, October 19, 2014 (http://www.bundesfinanzministerium.de/Content/DE/Interviews/2014/2014-10-20-WamS.html).

[72] *Syriza* gained 36.34 % securing 149 out of 300 seats, while *ND* received 27.81 % which translates into 76 seats, a loss of 53 seats. The voter turnout was 63.87 %, 1.38 % more than in the last elections on June 17, 2012. Ministry of Interior, *Parliamentary Elections January 2015*, Athens, January 30, 2015 (http://ekloges.ypes.gr/current/v/public/index.html?lang=en&fullsite=1#{%22cls%22:%22main%22,%22params%22:{}}).

[73] Dean Andromidas and Paul Gallagher, Convene a European Debt Conference for 2015, *Executive Intelligence Review Economics*, January 23, 2015, p. 34 (http://www.larouchepub.com/eiw/public/2015/2015_1-9/2015-04/pdf/34-39_4204.pdf); Jürgen Kaiser, *One Made it Out of the Debt Trap. Lessons from the London Debt Agreement of 1953 for Current Debt Crises*, Berlin: Friedrich Ebert Foundation, June 2013 (http://library.fes.de/pdf-files/iez/10137.pdf). See also Alexis Tsirpas, Greece can balance its books without killing democracy, *Financial Times*, January 21, 2015; ibid., Open letter to *Handelsblatt*, January 13, 2015.

beyond its expiration date of February 28, 2015 put the new Greek government on a collision course with its international creditors.

If the Syriza government reneges on the country's part of the bailout agreement and confronts EU partners with unacceptable demands, the German government no longer excludes the option of a "Grexit". Berlin is confident that the euro area is better placed to survive a possible Grexit because various bailout systems, including the ESM, have been established since the height of the euro crisis that ensure that Greece's problems and its future are important for Greece alone.[74] The second reason why a Syriza-led government cannot play hardball on the country's debt load is the ECB's announcement on January 8, 2015 that it would suspend the special terms on which Greek banks enjoy access to ECB funds, especially the Emergency Liquidity Agreement (ELA), unless Athens seriously negotiated an extension of its current bailout program. "The continuation of the waiver...is also based on the assumption of a successful conclusion of the current review and agreement on a follow-up arrangement between the Greek authorities and the European Commission, in liaison with the ECB, and the IMF," an ECB spokesperson said.[75] A decision of the central bank to shut down emergency lending to Greece would send the unintended signal to the markets that "Greece is well on the road to exiting the euro." (Black and Chrysoloras 2015; Dixon 2015a; Barber 2015a; Ewing 2015) Taking Germany's liability concerns about the risks of a potential Greek default or a far-reaching restructuring of Greece's debt overhang ("haircut") on German taxpayers into account, the Governing Council set "some conditions" to the QE that in effect rule out purchases of Greek bonds in the immediate future. As long as Greece has to comply with the conditions of its bailout program, their bonds will not be eligible for purchases. In addition, the QE program has set an issuer limit of 33 %. Because of the ECB's existing holdings of Greek debt—the ECB bought Greek sovereign bonds as part of its Securities Market Program (SMP)—Athens will be eligible on this count in July the earliest.[76]

Lastly, Greece's debt load appears to be more sustainable as the simple "177 % of GDP" ratio would suggest. € 247 billion out of a total of € 315.5 billion is held by official creditors—€ 141.8 billion by the EFSF rescue fund, 52.9 billion by euro area member states in bilateral loans, € 27 billion bonds held by the ECB and € 25 billion on outstanding IMF loans. The repayment of Greek loans faces fewer financial risks in the near term than other euro area countries—Italy alone will need to sell € 308 billion in bonds in 2015—because they have a relatively long maturity of over 30 years—the last payment will be due in 2053—with interest rates

[74] Nilolaus Blome, Giorgos Christides, Christian Reiermann, Gregor Peter Schmitz, Germany Open to Possible Greek Euro Zone Exit, *Spiegel Online*, January 5, 2015 (http://www.spiegel.de/international/europe/merkel-and-germany-open-to-possible-greek-euro-zone-exit-a-1011277.html); Manfred Schäfers and Majid Sattar, Griechen, hört die Signale, *Frankfurter Allgemeine Zeitung*, January 5, 2015.

[75] ECB warns Greek funding access hinges on keeping bailout, *Reuters*, January 8, 2015 (http://www.reuters.com/article/2015/01/08/greece-banks-ecb-idUSL6N0UN19D20150108).

[76] European Central Bank, *Introductory Statement by Mario Draghi to the press conference on January 22, 2015*, op. cit.

substantially reduced. On its EFSF loans, Greece only pays 1 basis point over the rescue fund's borrowing costs or about 1.5 %.[77] Since official creditors have accepted a reduction of the interest rate on their loans to levels comparable to what an AAA-rated country would be charged, Greece must pay 2.4 % on average on its debts, 0.3 % less than Germany. Even though Greece's debt overhang is now much higher than before the crisis—in 2008, Greece's debt was 109 % of GDP—its interest payments are lower: 4.2 % of GDP in 2014 compared with 5 % in 2008. "Hence, further debt relief would not really change Greece's liquidity situation," Mr. Weidmann pointed out.[78] From these figures, the German weekly Der Spiegel concluded, "The situation is such that it would be difficult to find a majority in the German parliament for concessions to Greece."[79]

Hurdles remain, particularly over Greece's bridge financing proposal (Varoufakis 2015; Spiegel 2015g). The ECB is unwilling to approve the issuing of € 10 billion short-term Greek treasury bills as "bridge financing" for the next 3 months because they would be bought by Greek banks. Because of their heavy reliance on day-to-day liquidity funding from the ECB, central bank authorities are concerned that T-bill purchase via ELA loans would violate Article 123 of the EU treaties which prohibit the ECB from funding member states.[80] In addition, the ECB Governing Council decided in a split vote "to lift the waiver of minimum credit rating requirements for marketable instruments issued or guaranteed by the Hellenic Republic". By February 11, 2015 Greek banks can no longer use their large holdings of Greek sovereign bonds as collateral to borrow from the central bank at a cheap interest rate of 0.05 %.[81] The Council based its decision "on the fact that it is currently not possible to assume a successful conclusion of the program

[77] Lorenzo Bini Smaghi, Is Greece's debt really so unsustainable? *Financial Times*, January 12, 2015 (http://blogs.ft.com/the-exchange/2015/01/12/lorenzo-bini-smaghi-is greeces-debt-really-so unsustainable/); Nikolaos Chrysoloras, Greece Seeks Third Debt Restructuring: Who's on the Hook? *BloombergBusiness*, February 2, 2015 (http://www.bloomberg.com/news/articles/2015-02-02/greece-seeks-third-debt-restructuring-who-s-on-the-hook-).

[78] Deutsche Bundesbank, *Heading for stability and prosperity*, op. cit.

[79] Nilolaus Blome, Giorgos Christides, Christian Reiermann, Gregor Peter Schmitz, Germany Open to Possible Greek Euro Zone Exit, op. cit. See also Zoning out, *The Economist*, January 17, 2015 (http://www.economist.com/node/21639591/); Ferdinando Giugliano, Scepticism over claim debt pile is it really 'unsustainable', *Financial Times*, January 26, 2015.

[80] European Central Bank, *Introductory statement to the press conference (with Q&A) by Mario Draghi*, Nicosia, March 5, 2015, op. cit. See also European Central Bank, *Interview of Benoît Cœuré with Corriere della Sera*, January 27, 2015 (https://www.ecb.europa.eu/press/inter/date/2015/html/sp150129.en.html); ibid., *Interview of Benoît Cœuré with Politis*, March 8, 2015 (https://www.ecb.europa.eu/press/inter/date/2015/html/sp150308.en.html); Lisa Nienhaus and Thomas Gutschker, EZB will Tsirpas nicht noch mehr Geld verschaffen, *Frankfurter Allgemeine Zeitung*, March 7, 2015 (http://www.faz.net/aktuell/wirtschaft/eurokrise/griechenland/griechenland-krise-ezb-will-tsipras-nicht-noch-mehr-geld-verschaffen-13469664.html); Claire Jones and Stefan Wagstyl, ECB eweighs curbs on Greek banks's government debt purchases, *Financial Times*, March 20, 2015.

[81] The ECB has assisted Greek banks by exempting them from requirements on the collateral it accepts for access to funding. The waiver based on the technical extension of the EFSF program

review and is in line with existing Eurosystem rules."[82] Mr. Draghi declared that the central bank would be ready to reinstate the waiver "as soon as these conditions are in place."[83] EU officials pointed out that the reimbursement of the € 1.8 billion in profits on Greek bonds held by the ECB is tied to completion of the existing bailout program. The third source of the bridge financing—€ 10.9 billion left in Greece's bank recapitalization funds—is actually in the form of bonds no longer owned by Greece if the bailout expires. If Greece wanted to reach a "new contract" with its creditors, it still needed to submit an internationally supervised program of economic reforms, Mr. Schäuble said. [84]

In response to mounting strains within Greece's financial system, the ECB doubled its emergency funding to Greece since December 2014 to € 104 billion, equal to 65 % of its GDP. "In this sense, one can really say that the ECB is the central bank of Greece," Mr. Draghi pointed out.[85] The German central bank, however is deeply concerned that, like in the case of the Cyprus Popular Bank in 2012 (Thomas 2014a, b; Ewing and Thomas 2014; European Central Bank 2014f; European Central Bank. 2014),[86] the ECB's emergency funding would keep de facto Greek insolvent banks in business. In doing so, the ECB would violate its core rule that banks on the verge of failure should not be bailed out with additional loans. Emergency funding would thus amount to an illegal monetary financing of a

until the end of February 2015 and the existence of an IMF program involves suspending credit rating threshold on marketable instruments issued or guaranteed by the Greek sovereign.

[82] European Central Bank, *Eligibility of Greek bonds used as collateral in Eurosystem monetary policy operations*, Press Release, Frankfurt am Main, February 4, 2015 (http://www.ecb.europa.eu/press/pr/date/2015/html/pr150204.en.html); Jack Ewing and James Kanter, Greece Meets Setback in European Bailout Talks, *New York Times*, February 5, 2015; Claire Jones and Ferdinando Giugliano, ECB split points to sensitivity of Greek liquidity curbs, *Financial Times*, February 6, 2015.

[83] European Central Bank, *Introductory statement to the press conference (with Q&A) by Mario Draghi*, Nicosia, March 5, 2015; European Parliament, Committee: Economic and Monetary Affairs, *Greece should resume policy dialogue and agree on reforms, Draghi tells MEPs*, Brussels, March 23, 2015 (http://www.europarl.europa.eu/sides/getDoc.do?pubRef=-%2f%2fEP%2f%2fTEXT%2bIM-PRESS%2b20150320IPR36215%2b0%2bDOC%2bXML%2bV0%2f%2fEN&language=EN).

[84] Peter Spiegel, Final showdown approaches for EU and Greece, *Financial Times*, February 14/15, 2015; Schäuble über Tsirpas-Rede: 'Wir haben niemanden ein Hilfsprogramm aufgedrängt', *Spiegel Online*, February 9, 2015 (http://www.spiegel.de/video/suche/tag/Griechenland-Krise.html); Liz Alderman and Niki Kitsantonis, Greece Prepares Debt Compromise, *New York Times*, February 10, 2015.

[85] European Central Bank, *Introductory statement to the press conference (with Q&A) by Mario Draghi*, Nicosia, March 5, 2015; European Parliament, Committee: Economic and Monetary Affairs, *Greece should resume policy dialogue and agree on reforms, Draghi tells MEPs*, Brussels, March 23, 2015 (http://www.europarl.europa.eu/sides/getDoc.do?pubRef=-%2f%2fEP%2f%2fTEXT%2bIM-PRESS%2b20150320IPR36215%2b0%2bDOC%2bXML%2bV0%2f%2fEN&language=EN).

[86] ibid., *Introductory statement to the press conference (with Q&A)* by Mario Draghi, Frankfurt am Main, November 6, 2014 (http://www.ecb.europa.eu/press/pressconf/2014/html/is141106.en.html).

bankrupt state. "It was not the governing council's job to keep afloat banks that were awaiting recapitalization and were not currently solvent," warned Mr. Weidmann.[87]

The politics of debt relief for Greece remain formidable for Chancellor Merkel—not least because it would have been borne by euro area governments who have underwritten the EFSF and ESM bailout funds. She then has to explain to bailout-wary German voters why the loans to Greece will not be repaid in full as she had told them some years ago as the precondition for successive assistant programs. German taxpayers could be stuck with the bill if a country like Greece were to default on its debt. A debt restructuring agreement with Athens would impose direct losses on German taxpayer money—a reduction of Greece's public debt from 177 to 120 % of GDP or 90 % would cost German taxpayers € 23 respectively € 40 billion. Greece's inability to service its interest payments would amount to a total loss of up to € 84.815 billion or 2.9 % of GDP Germany has already contributed in bailout loans to Greece.[88] But a debt-write off and a dilution or cancellation of bailout conditions for Greece could open the floodgates for similar demands from Italy, Portugal, Spain, Ireland and even France (Plender 2014; Kitsantonis and Kanter 2014; Hope and Moore 2014; Smaghi 2015).

A scolding commentary in Bild, the Germany's largest selling tabloid, underlined Chancellor Merkel's limited room of manoeuvre in terms of easing conditions attached to the Greek bailout program. "What happens to a footballer who breaks the rules and does a crude foul? He leaves the pitch. He is sent off as a punishment. No Question. What happens with a country that does not keep the rules or implements agreements only reluctantly? It receives broad support and billions of aid—as we have seen so far in the case of Greece." Should Syriza government revoke Greece's bailout agreements, the German government will be well advised to show Athens like a wayward footballer "the red card" and "hustle" it out of the euro, "a long overdue move", Bild concluded (Schäfer 2015). Above all, the debtor countries need to remain on the hook for their profligate spending, at any cost. "The Greeks have to bear the consequences themselves," said Hans-Peter Friedrich, Deputy Whip of the CDU/CSU parliamentarian group. German taxpayers should not be asked to bear the fiscal burdens of others.[89] Lastly, the sinner countries need to be held accountable by the financial markets. "The so-called warm-water countries...only understand the tough language of the capital markets," as Anton

---

[87] Deutsche Bundesbank, *Monatsbericht, February 2015*, Frankfurt am Main, February 13, 2015, pp. 7–8 (http://www.bundesbank.de/Redaktion/DE/Downloads/Veroeffentlichungen/Monatsberichte/2015/2015_02_monatsbericht.pdf?__blob=publicationFile); Hans-Werner Sinn, Impose capital controls in Greece or repeat the mistake of Cyprus, *Financial Times*, February 17, 2015; Philip Plickert, Bundesbank ermahnt Athen, *Frankfurter Allgemeine Zeitung*, February 17, 2015.

[88] Es stehen Milliardenkredite auf dem Spiel, *Frankfurter Allgemeine Zeitung*, January 6, 2015; Martin Hock, Das würde der Grexit Kosten, *Frankfurter Allgemeine Zeitung*, March 18, 2015.

[89] Neue Griechen-Regierung steht schon! *Bild*, January 26, 2015 (http://www.bild.de/politik/ausland/griechenland-krise/linksrutsch-bei-der-wahl-in-griechenland-39488288.bild.html).

Börner, President of the Bundesverband Großhandel, Außenhandel und Dienstleistungen (BGA), put it (Wagstyl 2015b).

Professor Bernd Lucke, the AfD leader felt vindicated in his criticism that sinner countries were being rewarded for irresponsibly running up debts, while the virtuous countries were asked to foot the bill. He therefore "welcome[d] the belated insight from Ms. Merkel and from Schäuble that a Greek exit from the euro would be bearable (Wagstyl 2015a)." Events in Greece have reinforced the widespread concern within the German public that the stability-oriented approach of the revered Bundesbank has been replaced by an ECB policy which allows spendthrift countries to postpone needed spending and borrowing cuts while the German taxpayer is being asked to pay for their profligacy. In short, the German public is as deeply opposed to a risk-sharing sovereign bond buying program as it strongly supports showing Greece the "red card" in case the next government breaks the bailout rules.[90] Chancellor Merkel would risk a backlash of her voters were she to be seen to be too generous with the debtor countries. Center-right governments in Spain, Portugal and Ireland who have accepted painful bailout program face a similar challenge at home. They will not help their own re-election prospects if the Greek government manages to reverse the austerity imposed under the existing bailout program, thus giving "credence to the suggestion that there was or is an alternative way." (Whelan 2015; Kanter and Alderman 2015)

Greece should not expect taxpayers in Germany and other euro area countries to pick up the tab for its policy decisions, warned German Economics Minister Sigmar Gabriel, "If Greece wants to deviate from some of these measures, it must bear the cost itself rather than exporting this to other European countries via a debt cut or other such idea."[91] The threat of leaving the euro area as a bargaining chip in the negotiations with the troika would backfire because the rest of the euro area is no longer exposed to the danger of a Greek contagion. "That's why we can't be blackmailed and why we expect the Greece government, no matter who leads, to abide by the agreements made with the EU," Mr. Gabriel put it.[92] Finance Minister Schäuble added that Berlin was "prepared for discussions but would not be pressured by the Syriza government. "We are averse to blackmail," he said (Kitsantonis 2015a).

[90] According to an *ARD* television poll, 68 % of Germans oppose debt relief for Greece; 61 said that Greece should leave the monetary union if the country reneged on its international obligations. ARD DeutschlandTrend, *Eine Studie von infratest dimap im Auftrag für Tagesthemen*, January 8, 2015 (https://www.tagesschau.de/inland/deutschlandtrend-243.pdf). See also Forschungsgruppe Wahlen e.V., *Politbarometer Januar II 2015* (http://www.forschungsgruppe.de/Aktuelles/Politbarometer/); 62 Prozent wollen den Griechen den Euro lassen, *Bild*, February 5, 2015 (http://www.bild.de/geld/wirtschaft/griechenland-krise/62-prozent-der-deutschen-wollen-griechen-euro-lassen-39583062.bild.html).

[91] Greek markets hammered as fears grow over new government, *Financial Times*, January 29, 2015.

[92] Bundesministerium für Wirtschaft und Energie, *Gabriel: Wir erwarten Vertragstreue von Griechenland*, op. cit.

Mr. Gabriel denied that Berlin was making any contingency plans for a Grexit. "The goal of the German government, the EU and even the government in Athens itself is to keep Greece in the monetary union. There were no and there are no contrary plans," he said, noting that the common currency area had become more stable in recent years. Earlier Chancellor Merkel's spokesman, Steffen Seibert, declared the federal government expected Greece to continue to comply with its obligations. Stabilizing and strengthening the euro area "with all its members, including Greece" remained government policy.[93] Chancellor Merkel emphasized that her government has premised its policy to ensure "that Greece remains part of the euro zone." The principle "on the one hand Greece's own efforts and on the other solidarity" had worked well and should continue to be the "watchword".[94]

After 3 weeks of brinkmanship, the Eurogroup and Greece reached an eleventh-hour interim deal on February 20, 2015 that extends the bailout program for 4 months.[95] The agreement gives Athens a financial lifeline and helps ease concern of a Grexit from the euro area for a while. Contingent upon "the successful completion" of the "existing arrangement", a "strong commitment to a broader and deeper structural reform process", an "unequivocal commitment to honor [Greece's] financial obligations to all [its] creditors fully and timely", ensuring "the appropriate primary fiscal surpluses…in line with the November 2012 Eurogroup statement" and refraining "from any rollback of measures and unilateral changes to the policies and structural reforms that would negatively impact fiscal targets", the deal allows "any disbursement of the outstanding tranche of the current EFSF program" of € 7.2 billion and "the transfer of the 2014 SMP profits" of € 1.8 billion. In addition, the € 10.9 billion "funds, so far available in the [Hellenic Financial Stability Fund] HFSF" previously part-controlled by the Greece central bank, are being "held by the EFSF"; the funds is still be available "for bank recapitalization and resolution costs for the duration of the MFFA extension", but can "only be released on request by the ECB/SSM". Moreover, the arrangement offers the Syriza government some flexibility to ease the limits on public spending

[93] Gabriel erwartet Vertragstreue von Griechen, *Hannoversche Allgemeiene Zeitung*, January 5, 2015 (http://www.haz.de/Nachrichten/Politik/Deutschland-Welt/Sigmar-Gabriel-erwartet-Vertragstreue-von-Griechenland); Bundesministerium für Wirtschaft und Energie, *Gabriel: Wir erwarten Vertragstreue von Griechenland*, Berlin, January 5, 2015 (http://www.bmwi.de/DE/Themen/europa,did=677574.html); Bundesregierung, *Regierungspressekonferenz vom 5. Januar 2015*, Berlin, January 5, 2015 (http://www.bundesregierung.de/Content/DE/Mitschrift/Pressekonferenzen/2015/01/2015-01-05-regpk.html).

[94] The Federal Chancellor, *No change of course with regard to Greece*, London, January 8, 2015 (http://www.bundeskanzlerin.de/Content/EN/Artikel/2015/01_en/2015-01-08-griechenland_en.html); 'Wir wissen zu wenig über den Islam'. Interview mit Angela Merkel, *Frankfurter Allgemeine Zeitung*, January 16, 2015; Die Bundeskanzlerin, *Pressekonferenz von Bundeskanzlerin Merkel und dem italienischen Ministerpräsidenten Renzi*, Florence, January 23, 2015 (http://www.bundeskanzlerin.de/Content/DE/Mitschrift/Pressekonferenzen/2015/01/2015-01-23-merkel-renzi.html).

[95] Cécile Ducourtieux, La zone euro accorde une prolongation d'aide à la Grèce sous conditions, *Le Monde*, 21.02.2015 (http://www.lemonde.fr/europe/article/2015/02/20/a-bruxelles-optimisme-prudent-avant-une-enieme-reunion-de-l-eurogroupe_4580620_3214.html).

within the framework of the existing arrangement according to its "policy priorities" to improve "growth and employment prospects" and to enhance "social fairness". Greece's "first list of reform measures, based on the current arrangement," will be assessed by "the institutions" whether it is "sufficiently comprehensive to be a valid starting point for a successful conclusion of the review. . .by the end of April." Lastly, the institutions are prepared to view "the primary surplus target" in light of "the economic circumstances in 2015". Based on the "assessment" and "advice of the institutions" the euro zone member states will ratify "the extension of the current EFSF Master Financial Assistance Facility Agreement for up to 4 months by the EFSF Board of Directors" (European Council 2015a).

German Finance Minister Schäuble said after the conclusion of the talks, "As long as the program isn't successfully completed, there will be no payout." Referring to the false promises made by Mr. Tsirpas during the election campaign he pointedly told the Syriza government, "Being in government is a date with reality, and reality is often not as nice as a dream." He added, the Greek government "certainly will have a difficult time explaining the deal to their voters." The Chancellor welcomed the agreement which reinforced "the principle of quid pro quo" ("Leistung und Gegenleistung"). The starting point for negotiations was the list of economic reforms included in the current bailout program, the previous Greek government left unfinished. "The Greek government has the opportunity to pick up individual reforms that are still outstanding as of December 10[96] and replace them with other reforms if they. . .have the same effect and if they have been approved by the institution," Chancellor Merkel said.[97]

The Commission determined that the reform list, Mr. Varoufakis submitted to Mr. Dijsselbloem,[98] "is sufficiently comprehensive to be a valid starting point for a successful conclusion of the review." It added that "the key for a successful conclusion of the review" is the preparedness of the Greek government to "trans-

[96] The Chancellor referred to an inventory of incompelete reforms made by former Greek Finance Minister Gikas Hardouvelis on December 10, 2014 which became the focus of particular disdain for the *Syriza* party on the campaign trail. Prime Minister Tsirpas denied the existence of a"letter of Hardouvelis." Peter Spiegel, Greek bailout summit ends in disarray, *Financial Times*, March 21/22, 2015.

[97] European Council, *Extraordinary Eurogroup Meeting, National Briefing: Germany – Part 2 (Q&A)*, Brussels, February 20, 2015 (http://tvnewsroom.consilium.europa.eu/event/extraordinary-eurogroup-meeting-february-20151/national-briefing-germany-part-2-qa3174); Die Bundeskanzlerin, *Pressekonferenz von Bundeskanzlerin Merkel und dem schwedischen Ministerpräsidenten Löfven*, Berlin, February 25, 2015 (http://www.bundeskanzlerin.de/Content/DE/Mitschrift/Pressekonferenzen/2015/02/2015-02-25-pk-merkel-loefven.html); European Council, *National briefing: Germany – Part 2 (Q&A)*, Brussels, March 20, 2015 (http://tvnewsroom.consilium.europa.eu/video/national-briefing-germany-part-2-qa3179).

[98] Ministry of Finance, *Letter of Yanis Varoufakis to the President of the Eurorgroup*, Athens, February 23, 2015 (http://im.ft-static.com/content/images/e401fa8c-bc13-11e4-b6ec-00144feab7de.pdf).

form [its] general commitments into clear policy actions.[99] After consultation with the IMF and the ECB the Eurogroup approved the Greek proposals. It called on Greece "to further develop and broaden the list of reform measures." It agreed "to proceed with the national procedures with a view to reaching the final decision on the extension by up to 4 months of the current Master Financial Assistance Facility Agreement." (European Council 2015b) Both the ECB and the IMF concluded that that the list of reform measures "is a valid starting point for a successful conclusion of the review." But both institutions expressed reservations about the substance of the reform proposals. The ECB noted that Greek commitments "differ from existing program commitments in a number of areas". There would be a need to assess whether measures rejected by Greece were "replaced with measures of equal or better quality". The IMF bemoaned that in the most important areas, "there are neither clear commitments to design and implement the envisaged comprehensive pension and VAT policy reforms, nor unequivocal undertakings to continue already-agreed policies for opening up closed sectors, for administrative reforms, for privatization, and for labor market reforms." A successful completion of the review "cannot be confined within the policy perimeters outlined in the Government's list," the IMF concluded.[100] The statements of the institutions underline their determination to closely scrutinize the state of Greece's finances and to raise additional demands to achieve the objectives of the program before further financial assistance will be released to the Greek authorities.

A day before the European part of the Greece bailout was set to expire, the Bundestag voted overwhelmingly in favor of the 4-month extension of the Greek bailout.[101] 541 out of 587 lawmakers approved the extension, while 32 opposed it and 13 abstained.[102] It was the biggest majority for a euro area bailout with the unanimous support of both the SPD and the Greens; even Die Linke which had traditionally voted against bailouts backed an extension out of solidarity with the

---

[99] European Commission, *Letter by Vice-President Valdis Dombrovskis and Commissioner Pierre Moscovici to the President of the Eurorgroup, Jeroen Dijesselbloem, on the Greek government's reform proposal*, Statement/15/4488, Brussels, February 24, 2015 (http://europa.eu/rapid/press-releases_STATEMENT-15-4488_en.htm).

[100] International Monetary Fund, *Letter by IMF Managing Director Christine Lagarde to the President of the Euro Group on Greece,* Press Release No. 15/71, Washington, D.C., February 23, 2015 (http://www.imf.org/external/np/sec/pr/2015/pr1571.htm); European Central Bank, *Letter of Mario Draghi to the President of the Eurogroup*, Frankfurt am Main, February 24, 2015 (http://www.ecb.europa.eu/pub/pdf/other/20150224_letter-to-dijsselbloemen.pdf).

[101] Deutscher Bundestag, *Antrag des Bundesministeriums der Finanzen Finanzhilfen zugunsten Griechenlands; Verlängerung der Stabilitätshilfe*, Drucksache 18/4079, Berlin, February 23, 2015 (http://dip21.bundestag.de/dip21/btd/18/040/1804079.pdf); ibid., *Unterrichtung durch das Bundesministerium der Finanzen zu dem Antrag des Bundesministeriums der Finanzen vom 23. Februar 2015 – Drucksache 18/4079 – Finanzhilfen zugunsten Griechenlands; Verlängerung der Stabilitätshilfe*, Drucksache 18/4093, Berlin, February 24, 2015 (http://dip21.bundestag.de/dip21/btd/18/040/1804093.pdf).

[102] Deutscher Bundestag, *Plenarprotokoll 18/89, Endgültiges Ergebnis*, Berlin, February 27, 2015, pp. 8434–8436 (http://dipbt.bundestag.de/doc/btp/18/18089.pdf).

left-wing Syriza government. But a record number of dissenters from Chancellor Merkel's conservative bloc—29 of the 32 defectors came from the CDU/CSU—underscored their growing misgivings as to whether the Syriza government could be trusted to deliver on its reform pledges. The scale of the dissent indicated the difficulties that lie ahead when the Merkel government has to convince its own conservative bloc that a new bailout for Greece is in Germany's own best interest. As Mr. Schäuble told the Bundestag ahead of the vote, "In the 70 years since the German catastrophe, we—this applies to us Germans more than for all the others—will only have a future in the twenty-first century if European unity succeeds and we hold Europe together." This assumes that "all are aware about their responsibility for a common currency and meet it." Germany would continue to help Greece "to a very exceptional degree". But German "solidarity" is premised on "reliability, solidity and mutual consideration" and not on the ability "to blackmail each other." The bailout programs for Greece "rest on the principle help for self-help. We are ready, but Greece must take on responsibility on its own."[103]

What looked like a game of chicken turned out to be a highly predetermined game of poker. The reported rapid outflow of bank deposits together with a significant shortfall of tax revenues until mid-February (Spiegel 2015c, e; Kanter 2015a; Moore 2015a) not only weakened Greece's financial system but also Athens' ability to resist its European partners any longer. The dire situation left the Syriza government no choice but to accept a deal in which the German government succeeded in all tactical and substantive matters. Convinced that the currency union is now strong enough to cope with a Grexit, Berlin advanced a combined strategy that aimed to "wait Greece out". A renewed rejection of the Eurogroup's proposal for an extension of the bailout program might have caused a banking collapse within days. It would have forced Athens to impose capital controls to prop up its troubled financial institutions, leading to economic disarray and inciting public outcry. A default and ultimately a Grexit with its dire political, economic and financial consequences for Greece's economy and its people could only be averted by "accommodating Europe" (Thomas and Ewing 2015; Münchau 2015b; Spiegel 2015b; Kanter and Kitsantonis 2015).

The Syriza government made some painful concessions. It accepted an extension of the current bailout program and not a bridging loan, separate from the existing bailout program, the fiscal targets set within the framework of the existing arrangement—the Memorandum of Economic and Financial Policies (MEFP), the Memorandum of Understanding and on Specific Economic Policy Conditionality (MoU) and the Technical Memorandum of Understanding (TMU).[104] The institutions—the IMF, the ECB and the European Commission—remain in firm control of evaluating

[103] Deutscher Bundestag, *Plenarprotokoll 18/89*, Berlin, February 27, 2015, pp. 8408, 8409.

[104] European Commission, Directorate-General for Economic and Financial Affairs, *The Second Economic Adjustment Programme for Greece. Third Review*, Occasional Papers 159, Brussels, July 2013, pp. 105–222.

Greece's economic reform measures and the disbursement of bailout funds[105]—the two-page statement uses the word "institutions" ten times. The release of bailout money is linked to the "strong commitment" of the Greek government "to a broader and deeper structural reform process". Only if the institutions are satisfied after an initial view, will the extension be submitted to several Eurozone national parliaments to give the deal final approval.[106] "Any disbursement of the € 7.2 billion in remaining bailout aid is contingent upon "approval of the conclusion of the review" which will not happen until "the end of April." There was no suggestion in the extension agreement that a € 15 billion limit on Treasury bill issuance imposed by the troika on the Greek government might be lifted to ease the budgetary constraints, including declining tax revenues, the Syriza government has to cope with in the next few weeks.

In fact, the bailout extension does not offer any new financial aid, let alone address Greece's weighty debt overhang problem. "We're not talking about new billions for Greece, we're not talking about any changes to this program—rather it's about providing or granting extra time to successfully end this program," emphasized Mr. Schäuble.[107] That means no fresh money will arrive in time to pay off the € 4 billion in debt service to international creditors falling due until May. The ambiguity on where the interim funding for Greece will come from gives Greece's creditors an additional lever "to keep pressure on Athens". But "it begs the question where Greece will secure funding from in the intervening period, should that be necessary", wrote Mujtaba Rahman, head of European analysis at the Eurasia Group. "If that were the Grexit trigger, we're just where we were before," concluded Martin Sandbu.[108] In essence, the Syriza government has agreed to comply with the tough bailout limits on public spending and to let the "institutions" continue to monitor its reform efforts. Within the parameters of the existing bailout program, Athens snatched some flexibility to propose its own list of reform measures which are still subject to the institutions' approval. And it gained some

[105] Mr. Varoufakis, in his letter to the President of the Eurogroup, wrote that "the Greek government committed to working in close agreement with the European partners and institutions, as well as with the International Monetary Fund." Ministry of Finance, *Letter of Yanis Varoufakis to the President of the Eurorgroup*, op. cit.

[106] The extension of the bailout program required the approval of lawmakers in Austria, Estonia, Finland, Germany, Greece, The Netherlands and Slovakia by the end of February 2015.

[107] Deutscher Bundestag, *Plenarprotokoll 18/89*, Berlin, February 27, 2015, p. 8407. See also Bundesministerium der Finanzen, '*Es liegt in den Händen der Verantwortlichen in Athen*'. Interview mit Bundesfinanzminister Dr. Wolfgang Schäuble im „Bericht aus Berlin"der ARD, Berlin, March 1, 2015 (http://www.bundesfinanzministerium.de/Content/DE/Interviews/2015/2015-03-01-bericht-aus-berlin-textfassung.html).

[108] Peter Spiegel, Eurogroup conference call raises hopes for Greek bailout extension, *Financial Times*, February 24, 2015; Martin Sandbu, Free lunch: Four misperceptions about Greece, *Financial Times*, February 23, 2015 (http://www.ft.com/intl/cms/s/0/75fc65fa-bb40-11e4-b95c-00144fea7de.html); Outgamed, *The Economist*, February 21, 2015 (http://www.economist.com/node/21644592/).

budgetary flexibility with regard to the 2015 primary surplus target as assessed by the institutions.[109]

Negotiations between Syriza government and the Eurogroup have since then grown increasingly acrimonious. The Eurogroup considered the seven of reforms included in Athens "first list" of reforms insufficient.[110] On April 1 Athens submitted a revised reform program to the institutions with "the larger purpose. . .to unlock short-term financing that will permit the Greek government to meet its immediate obligations."[111] The new proposal did not close the gap between Athens expressed hope to conclude a final debt deal as quickly as possible to overcome its looming liquidity crisis and creditors 'expectations to see some meaningful actions before they release more bailout money to Greece. The measures fell short of addressing several issues, including an overhaul of the Greek pension system and greater labor market liberalization.[112] (Spiegel 2015a; Dixon 2015c) At the Eurogroup meeting in Riga on April 24 both sides remained divided. Mr. Dijesselbloem said there were still "wide differences" between Athens and its international creditors on significant issues, especially a reform of the Greek pension system, a budget with a high primary surplus and intrusive inspections by bailout monitors. He stressed that the remaining bailout funds could be unlocked only if the Greek government made "significantly more progress" on economic plans. But "we are still far from that," he summed up the contentious meeting. Mr. Draghi warned that "time is running out" for resolving the Greek standoff. The central bank's ELA funding for Greek banks should continue as long as they were "solvent and have adequate collateral." But "a change in the environment" could force the central bank to change the favourable conditions for Greek banks' access to emergency funding, he added.[113]

---

[109] Jennifer Rankin and Helena Smith, Eurozone chiefs strike deal to extend Greek bailout for four months, *The Guardian*, February 20, 2015 (http://www.theguardian.com/business/2015/feb/20/eurozone-chiefs-meet-for-last-ditch-talks-to-avert-greece-cash-crunch); Matt O'Brien, Greece and Europe agree to a compromise, avoiding financial catastrophe, *Washington Post*, February 20, 2015 (http://www.washingtonpost.com/blogs/wonkblog/wp/2015/02/20/greece-and-europe-agree-to-a-compromise-avoiding-financial-catastrophe/); Liz Alderman and James Kanter, Longer Lifeline on Greek Aid, With Caveats, New York Times, February 21, 2015; Peter Spiegel, Greece and Eurozone agree bailout extension, *Financial Times*, February 21, 2015; Outgamed, *The Economist*, February 21, 2015 (http://www.economist.com/node/21644592/); A scrappy deal keeps Greece from the wolves, February 23, 2015.

[110] Ministry of Finance, *Letter of the Minister to the President of the Eurogroup*, Athens, February 23, 2015 (http://im.ft-static.com/content/images/4e4b2122-c40f-11e4-a02e-00144feab7de.pdf); Peter Spiegel, Greece warned to start reforms to gain cash, *Financial Times*, March 2, 2015; ibid., Greek talks with creditors finally to start, *Financial Times*, March 10, 2015.

[111] *Greek Reforms in the context of the 20/02/2015 EUROGROUP Agreement*, Athens, March 2015, p. 2 (http://im.ft-static.com/content/images/55b27a7e-d87c411e4-ba53-00144feab7de.pdf).

[112] Peter Spiegel, Greece submits new list of reforms to eurozone, *Financial Times*, April 2, 2015; Greece falling short of final debt deal, *Financial Times*, April 7, 2015; Hugo Dixon, Greece must walk the talk – and soon, *International New York Times*, April 7, 2015

[113] European Council of the European Union, *Remarks by Jeroen Dijsselbloem at the press conference following the Eurogroup meeting*, Riga, April 24, 2015 (http://www.consilium.europa.eu/en/press/press-releases/2015/04/24-eurogroup-dijsselbloem-remarks/); European

As the crisis drags on, few palatable options remain open for the Syriza government to avert a debt default. Without the release of the remaining bailout funding, the Syriza government faces the stark choice between honoring its debt to international creditors and its domestic commitments, including an obligation to continue paying civil servants, pensioners and suppliers unless it does present a credible reform program that meets central concerns of its Eurozone partners. In a five-page letter to Chancellor Merkel and other European leaders, Prime Minister Tsirpas warned "that the ECB's special restrictions when combined with disbursement delays would make it impossible for any government to service its debt." (Spiegel 2015h; Smale 2015; Hope 2015b) In an informal meeting with Christine Lagarde, the Greek Finance Minister, Yanis Varoufakis, assured that the € 450 million payment to the Fund would be forthcoming on April 9. Both "noted that continuing uncertainty is not in Greece's interest."[114] Missing payment to the IMF would have far-reaching consequences for Athens. The IMF part of the € 7.2 billion in remaining bailout aid would be automatically locked; the ECB would then have no other choice but to suspend emergency liquidity assistance for the Greek financial sector creditors. Even the prospect of a cutoff could spark a bank run among Greek depositors that would further aggravate the already fragile health of the Greek banking system and the public finances.

Although Athens raised € 1.14 billion in an auction of 6-month Treasury bills on April 8 which helped it to pay its dues of € 450 million to the IMF a day later (Lewin and Platt 2015), it is widely expected that given the parlous state of Greece's public finances and the rapid outflow of bank deposits the matter will come to a head within the next weeks when larger redemptions to the IMF and the ECB are due. "We coped in February and March thanks to improved inflows and payment delays," said Yannis Dragasakis, Deputy Prime Minister. But the situation can't continue—it will trigger recession, and society can't handle more recession, more unemployment and more austerity." (Spiegel et al. 2015) The Eurogroup gave Athens until late June to present more ambitious proposals that would permit the EU-IMF lenders to release the next allocation of bailout money. But the Greek government still insists that the "red lines"—a reform of the pension system and a higher primary budget surplus—cannot be crossed. As in the past, negotiations to reach a deal could drag on until the very last day. "There is a negotiation where you have 30 days to reach a deal with someone. Why do it on the 20th day when you can continue and push for something better on the 21st? Or the 22nd? You can keep going until the 30th," Greek Finance Minister Varoufakis revealingly stated after the Riga meeting (Kanter 2015b).

Council of the European Union, *Questions and answers during the press conference that followed the Eurogroup meeting*, Riga, April 24, 2015 (http://tvnewsroom.consilium.europa.eu/event/eurogroup-meeting-april-2015/press-conference-part-5-qa2189); James Kanter, Eurozone Officials' Frustation With Greek Leadership is Boiling Over, *New York Times*, April 25, 2015.

[114] International Monetary Fund, *Statement by IMF Managing Director Christine Lagarde on Greece*, Press Release No. 15/162, Washington, D.C., April 5, 2015 (http://www.imf.org/external/np/sec/pr/2015/pr15162.htm).

With every day that passes without a new comprehensive arrangement between Greece and its European creditors in sight, while the liquidity problems become more pressing for Athens, the specter of Grexit from the currency bloc nobody really wants to precipitate becomes ever likelier.[115] Opening of the Pandora Box that is Grexit[116] would inevitably trigger destabilizing speculation whether this was the exit moment for the next country in the row. As the Financial Times pointedly put it, "the sight of a country leaving would render conceivable what had hitherto been impossible to imagine."[117] Such a scenario would revive doubts about the future integrity and viability of the monetary union. "The Eurozone is more than a fixed-rate system. . .It's a single currency and the single currency has to be perpetual for all its members, and as soon as one leaves, the question is, who's next? And that's not the way things must go, "warned Pierre Moscovici (Higgins and Kanter 2015; Giles 2015). A Grexit would show that the monetary union is very much reversible. It would lead financial markets to reinterpret the monetary union "a souped-up fixed exchange rate system" (Münchau 2010; Wolf 2015b; Krugman 2015; Fleming 2015) rather than as an irrevocable common currency union.

Moreover, the German government's optimistic assumption that the currency union may be better equipped to deal with a full-blown crisis in Greece might quickly change. The euro area is "better equipped" to manage the risks of contagion from a flare-up in Greece, said Mr. Draghi. However he added: "Having said that, we are certainly entering unchartered waters if the crisis were to precipitate, and it is very premature to make any speculation about it."[118] It is the second-order problems that worry American officials. If a Greek default does occur, it could create a rash of nasty logistical and legal surprises resembling the sequel to the Lehman Brothers debacle in September 2008. Even a careful analysis of risks does not preclude unintended consequences and nasty surprises. While financial exposure to

---

[115] Greece slides towards the euro trapdoor, *Financial Times*, March 21/22, 2015; Brinkmanship in the Eurozone, *International New York Times*, March 23, 2015; Ferdinando Giugliano, Spectre of Grexit back as cash runs out, *Financial Times*, April 8, 2015; Kerin Hope, Athens scrapes together cash for April but default looms in May, *Financial Times*, April 8, 2015.

[116] Paul Krugman, Europe's Greek Test, *International New York Times*, January, 31/February 1, 2015; Matt O'Brien, Greece really might leave the euro, *Washington Post*, January 30, 2015 (http://www.washingtonpost.com/blogs/wonkblog/wp/2015/01/30/greece-really-might-leave-the-euro/); Anne-Sylvaine Chassany and Peter Spiegel, Eurozone alarm grows over Greek bailout brinkmanship, *Financial Times*, February 2, 2015; Ferdinando Giugliano, Varoufakis faces challenge of turning games theory into winning strategy, *Financial Times*, February 14/15, 2015.

[117] Greek exit from the euro is not a risk worth taking, *Financial Times*, March 18, 2015. See also Moody's Investors Service, *Stable credit outlook for euro area sovereigns, but Grexit and deflation present downside risks*, London, March 17, 2015 (https://www.moodys.com/research/Moodys-Stable-credit-outlook-for-euro-area-sovereigns-but-Grexit--PR_320619);
FitchRatings, *Grexit' Still Possible; Systemic Crisis Unlikely*, London, March 6, 2015 (https://www.fitchratings.com/creditdesk/press_releases/detail.cfm?pr_id=980861&cm_sp=homepage-_-Featured_Content_Archive-_-%27Grexit%27%20Remains%20Possible,%20But%20Systemic%20Crisis%20Unlikely).

[118] International Monetary Fund, *Press Conference: ECB President Mario Draghi*, Washington, DC, April 17 2015 (http://www.imf.org/external/mmedia/view.aspx?vid=4181350682001).

Greece had changed significantly since the height of the crisis in summer 2012, US Treasury Secretary Jack Lew, like Mr. Draghi, concluded that a Greek default would place a cloud of uncertainty und unpredictability over the European and global economies. "I do not think anyone can predict how markets will respond to dramatic changes in circumstances."[119] Suggestions by the German government that a wider fallout of a Greek default would be manageable could prove a pipedream.

Greece's looming liquidity crisis reveals once more the paradoxes of Chancellor Merkels's euro crisis management. Her central concern is that a "Greccident" will inflict serious damage to the currency union and the European project, notably the Single European Market (SEM) whose greatest beneficiary is Germany. She reassured her Eurozone partners to work for a new loan agreement knowing full well what is a stake, "I have always said, if the euro fails, then Europe fails."[120] However, the logic of her minimalist policy makes the German public purse an ever bigger stakeholder in the euro crisis but never willing "to devote enough resources to ensure they were effective." (Wren-Lewis 2013) Because of its staunch refusal to agree to a "haircut" for public holders of Greece's debt the Merkel government is trapped into providing new bailout assistance if Athens proves unable to service its maturing debt or to cover its fiscal imbalances—it is widely expected that Greece would need a third bailout package of € 30–50 billion to cover its financing needs.[121]

---

[119] International Monetary Fund, *IMFC Statement by Jacob J. Lew, Secretary of the Treasury, United States,* Washington, DC, April 18, 2015 (http://www.imf.org/External/spring/2015/imfc/statement/eng/usa.pdf), Sam Fleming, Lew urges Greece to speed up reforms, *Financial Times*, April 18, 2015; Gillian Tett, America fears a European sequel to Lehman, *Financial Times*, April 24, 2015.

[120] Deutscher Bundestag, *Plenarprotokoll, 18/94*, Berlin, March 19, 2015, p. 8885 (http://dipbt.bundestag.de/doc/btp/18/18094.pdf); The Federal Chancellor, *Mastering crises in line with the European spirit*, Berlin, March 19, 2015 (http://www.bundeskanzlerin.de/Content/EN/Artikel/2015/03_en/2015-03-19-regierungserklaerung_en.html); Die Bundeskanzlerin, *Pressekonferenz von Bundeskanzlerin Merkel zum Europäischen Rat am 20. März 2015*, Brussels, March 20, 2015.

[121] Aaron Eglitis, Greece May Need Third Rescue, EU's Dombrovskis Says, Bloomberg, March 2, 2015 (http://www.bloomberg.com/news/articles/2015-03-02/greece-may-need-third-rescue-eu-s-dombrovskis-says). See also Tobias Buck, Greece in talks for third bailout of up to € 50bn, Spain says, Financial Times, March 3, 2015; Peter Spiegel, Greece likely to need extra € 38 bn this year, Financial Times, February 12, 2015; 'Angst macht mir das nicht'. Interview mit ESM-Chef Klaus Regling, *Handelsblatt*, October 4, 2013 (http://www.esm.europa.eu/press/interviews/2012-2013.htm); Schäuble: Griechenland braucht drittes Hilfsprogramm, *Frankfurter Allgemeine Zeitung*, August 21, 2013; Bundesbank rechnet 2014 mit neuem Hilfspaket für Griechen, *Spiegel Online*, August 11, 2013 (http://www.spiegel.de/wirtschaft/soziales/bundesbank-rechnet-mit-neuem-hilfspaket-fuer-griechenland-a-915900.html); European Commission, *The Second Adjustment Programme for Greece Fourth Review*, Brussels, April 2014, p. 72 (http://ec.europa.eu/economy_finance/publications/occasional_paper/2014/pdf/ocp192_en.pdf).

The categorical rejection of "another haircut"[122] and the insistence that Athens should comply with the rules accompanying its rescue loans underline German continuity in the management of Greece's debt overhang through a politically convenient policy of extend-and-pretend: lengthening the maturity with reduced interest rates paid on public debt and pretending that all public debt will eventually be paid (Münchau 2015a; Irwin 2014b). Despite substantial bailout assistance of € 240 billion, the sustainability of Greece's gargantuan debt remains a formidable challenge. What is needed is a reliable and effective solution to prevent miscalculation in this dangerous standoff and misstep at the precipice. To avoid the worst case of a Grexit, Europe would be well advised to pursue a multi-pronged bailout strategy.

- Substantive actions by Athens should be limited to few significant reforms that Athens can and should pass in weeks like the modernization of its administrative system or a reform of the pension system. Prioritizing urgently needed reform actions would account for Athens' capacity to implement meaningful reforms and test its seriousness to produce a plausible plan to reform essential parts of the Greek state in the near future (Moghadam 2015).
- European institutions and national governments accept lower interest rates and an extension of the maturities on Greece's debt. A zero spread instead of 50 basis points on bilateral loans, a 10-year maturity extension of bilateral loans and a 10-year extension of EFSF loans would amount to a net present value benefit of € 31.7 billion or 17 % of Greece's 2015 GDP (Plender 2014; Darvas and Hüttl 2015; Moore and Hope 2015).
- Debt repayment obligations should be linked to healthy growth of the Greek economy. A "menu of debt swaps" of outstanding debt for new growth-linked bonds, could include two types of new bonds. The first type, indexed to nominal GDP growth, would replace European rescue loans, while a "perpetual bonds" would swap ECB holdings of Greek bonds into zero coupon bonds pegged to a robust recovery (Allen et al. 2014; Maghadam 2015; Corsetti et al. 2015; Lubben 2015). That way, the Syriza government could pump more money swiftly into the country's depressed economy while the European partners could say Athens can spend more because it is reforming more (Barber 2015b; Münchau 2015b; Wolf 2015c; Moore 2015b; Lawson-Remer 2015).[123]

[122] Die Bundeskanzlerin, *Merkel gegen Schuldenschnitt für Griechenland*, Berlin, January 31, 2015 (http://www.bundeskanzlerin.de/Content/DE/Artikel/2015/01/2015-01-31-merkel-griechenland.html); ibid., *Pressekonferenz von Bundeskanzlerin Merkel und US-Präsident Obama*, Washington D.C., February 9, 2015 (http://www.bundeskanzlerin.de/Content/DE/Mitschrift/Pressekonferenzen/2015/02/2015-02-09-merkel-obama.html).

[123] Jens Weidmann, *Stellungnahme gegenüber dem Bundesverfassungsgericht zu den Verfahren mit den Az 2BvR 1390/2, 2 BvR 1421/12, 2 BvR 6/12*, op. cit.; Bundesverfassungsgericht, *BVerfG, 2 BvR 1390/12 vom 17.12.2013*, op. cit.; ibid., *BVerfG, 2 BvR 2728/13 vom 14.01.2014, Absatz-Nr. (1–105)*, op. cit.; Q&A With German Bundesbank President Jens Weidmann, *Wall Street Journal*, October 7, 2014, op. cit.; Deutsche Bundesbank, '*Voraussetzungen für eine stabile*

- Greece primary budget surplus target laid down in the current Troika bailout program could be lowered from 3 % of economic output this year and 4.5 % in 2016 and 2017 to 1.5 %. The difference of up to 3 % would give Athens more fiscal leeway of about € 15 billion over the next 3 years to spur economic growth.[124]
- Reducing fixed interest charges is not sufficient to brighten the outlook of the Greek economy. This requires a "substantial" write down of Greece's debt—halving its debt and halving the required fiscal balance—in exchange for structural reforms of the political, tax administrative and economic system. Since both the IMF and ECB are prohibited by their statutes to agree to a voluntary haircut, only one source is left to be restructured: bailout loans of about € 195 billion from the euro area. A substantial debt relief would be consistent with "debt substantially below 110 % of GDP by 2022," which the IMF pushed for and the Eurogroup agreed to on November 27, 2012.[125]

The central challenge is whether all actors involved are ready to find a mutually acceptable compromise. If membership in the euro bloc is "effectively irreversible" (Eichengreen 2007)[126] as the European Commission asserted in early January 2015,[127] its member countries need to answer two questions which are crucial to find a road map to resolving the venomous standoff. What costs are European leaders willing to bear to keep Greece in the currency bloc? The issue remains whether euro area governments are prepared to make meaningful financial sacrifices, including a substantial write down of Greece's debt even though they know full well that facilitating a positive outcome in the tug-of-war with Greece will not promise them electoral rewards at home (Whelan 2015). Secondly, the new Syriza government needs to convince their European partners it is serious about

Währungsunion', Speech of Dr Jens Weidmann, Bielefeld, October 13, 2014. (http://www.bundesbank.de/Redaktion/DE/Reden/2014/2014_10_13_weidmann.html?view=render).

[124] International Monetary Fund, *Greece, IMF Country Report No. 14/151*, Washington, D.C., June 2014, p. 45 (http://www.imf.org/external/pubs/ft/scr/2014/cr14151.pdf); Zsolt Darvas, *A major step towards a Greek compromise*, Brussels: Bruegel, February 3, 2015 (http://www.bruegel.org/nc/blog/detail/article/1561-a-major-step-towards-a-greek-compromise/); Peter Spiegel, Greece likely to need extra € 38 bn this year, *Financial Times*, February 12, 2015.

[125] International Monetary Fund, *Ex Post Evaluation of Exceptional Access under the 2010 Stand-by-Arrangement,* op. cit., pp. 26–28; ibid., *IMF Completes Fifth Review Under Extended Fund Facility Arrangement for Greece and Approves €3.41 Billion Disbursement*, Press Release No.14/254, Washington, D.C., May 30, 2014 (https://www.imf.org/external/np/sec/pr/2014/pr14254.htm); European Union, *Eurogroup statement on Greece*, Brussels, November 27, 2012 (http://www.eurozone.europa.eu/media/367646/eurogroup_statement_greece_27_november_2012.pdf).

[126] ibid., *The Euro: love it or leave it*, London: Centre for European Policy Studies, May 4, 2010 (http://www.voxeu.org/article/eurozone-breakup-would-trigger-mother-all-financial-crises).

[127] "The euro is here to stay," said Annika Breidthardt, the Coordinating Spokesperson for Economic and Financial Affairs of the European Commission. Liz Alderman, Countries Take Tough LineToward Greece, *New York Times*, January 6, 2015.

implementing further structural reform of the state and private sector.[128] Like his European partners, Mr. Tsirpas faces the same quandary at home. He has to convince his party's far-left faction, the Left Platform that a deal with the country's European creditors and the IMF is in the country's best interest, even though the basic logic of assistance in return for economic reform would remain unchanged—contrary to the pledges Syriza made in its election campaign (Barker et al. 2015; Hope and Barber 2015; Dixon 2015b; Spiegel and Hope 2015; Barber 2015c; Barber and Hope 2015; Spiegel 2015d).

In sum, the politics of the bailout extension for Greece underscores how the management of the euro crisis remains a work in progress. The outcome of the Greek liquidity crisis "has as much to do with domestic politics as it does with euro-wide economics." (Whelan 2015) Just as Syriza has to overcome the suspicion to any kind of market reforms, Greece's European partners, especially Germany, have to overcome their dogmatic resistance against substantial debt relief (Maghadam 2015; Wolf 2015b; Privitera 2015; Meyerson 2015; Fratzscher 2015; Stephens 2015). Even though Greece is a force négligeable within the Eurozone economy, its destiny remains tightly interwoven with the euro's long-term survival. "Creating the Eurozone is the second-worst monetary idea its members are ever likely to have. Breaking it up is the worst," argued Martin Wolf.[129] Doing whatever it takes to keep the Pandora Box of a Grexit closed will be the crucial test for policy decision makers in the euro area, not central bankers in Frankfurt. Taking the right decision at the right time requires some form of risk sharing that is essential to the survival of the currency union.[130] The moment of truth is rapidly approaching.

---

[128] International Monetary Fund, *Greece – IMF Country Report No. 14/151*, Washington, D.C., June 10, 2014 (http://www.imf.org/external/pubs/ft/scr/2014/cr14151.pdf); Martin Wolf, Greek debt and a default of statesmanship, *Financial Times*, January 28, 2015.

[129] Martin Wolf, Greek debt and a default of statesmanship, *Financial Times*, January 28, 2015. See also Grexit would shock eurozone, says Trichet, *Financial Times*, February 24, 2015 (http://video.ft.com/4077618535001/Grexit-would-shock-eurozone-says-Trichet/Markets?ftcamp=published_links%2Frss%2Fhome_europe%2Ffeed%2F%2Fproduct); French EU Commissioner Moscovici: 'A Grexit Would Be a Catastrophe', *Spiegel Online*, March 13, 2015 (http://www.spiegel.de/international/europe/eu-commissioner-moscovici-discusses-efforts-to-rescue-greece-a-1023449.html).

[130] European Central Bank, *Stability and Prosperity in Monetary Union*, Speech by Mario Draghi, at the University of Helsinki, Helsinki, November 27, 2014 (https://www.ecb.europa.eu/press/key/date/2014/html/sp141127_1.en.html); ibid., *Stability and Prosperity in Monetary Union*, Opinion piece by Mario Draghi for Project Syndicate, Frankfurt am Main, January 2, 2015 (http://www.ecb.europa.eu/press/key/date/2015/html/sp150102.en.html); ibid., *Introductory Statement to the European Parliament on the ECB Annual Report 2013*, Brussels, February 25, 2015 (https://www.ecb.europa.eu/press/key/date/2015/html/sp150225.en.html).

References

Alderman, L. (2014, August 21). France acknowledges economic Malaise, Blaming Austerity. *New York Times*.

Allen, P., Eichengreen, B., & Evans, G. (2014, February 28). *Debt-for-equity swaps offer Greece a better way*. London: Center for European Policy Studies. http://www.voxeu.org/article/debt-equity-swaps-offer-greece-better-way

Atkins, R., & Jones, C. (2015, January 21). Ex-central banker hits at ECB for conceding to Germany on QE. *Financial Times*.

Barber, T. (2014, October 3). Germany is no EU 'odd man out' despite stance on fiscal rigour. *Financial Times*.

Barber, T. (2015a, January 13). Greece and Europe must compromise to avoid Grexit. *Financial Times*.

Barber, T. (2015b, February 3). Greece finance minister reveals plan to end debt stand-off. *Financial Times*.

Barber, T. (2015c, April 15). Don't bank on Greek premier ditching his Syriza diehards. *Financial Times*.

Barber, T., & Hope, K. (2015, April 18–19). Greece: Decision time. *Financial Times*.

Barker, A., Hope, K., & Wagstyl, S. (2015, February 16). Gap still yawns between Greece and its creditors. *Financial Times*.

Barkin, N. (2015a, January 6). Draghi risks losing allies in Germany. *International New York Times*.

Barkin, N. (2015b, January 24). Draghi risks losing allies in Germany. *International New York Times*, January 6, 2015.

Black, J., & Chrysoloras, N. (2015, January 13). The politics behind the ECB's threat to cut Greece funding. *Bloomberg*. http://www.bloomberg.com/news/2015-01-13/ecb-warning-to-greece-deploys-tactic-honed-in-crisis.html

Bouras, S. (2015, February 9). *Greek leader Tsipras Pledges to press ahead on undoing austerity measures*. http://www.wsj.com/articles/greek-leader-tsipras-pledges-to-press-ahead-on-undoing-austerity-measures-1423426204

Bryant, C. (2014, September 10). Berlin rejects spending splurge to boost eurozone recovery. *Financial Times*.

Carnegy, H. (2014a, February 12). France risks "serious blow" to financial credibility. *Financial Times*.

Carnegy, H. (2014b, October 6). France tells Europe it must focus on growth rather than deficits. *Financial Times*.

Carnegy, H., & Chassany, A.-S. (2014, November 19). France warns EU investment fund will flop without 'real money'. *Financial Times*.

Corsetti, G., et al. (2015, March). *A new start for the Eurozone: Dealing with Debt*, London: Centre for Economic Policy Research (pp. 5–14, 27–30, 38–40). http://www.voxeu.org/sites/default/files/Monitoring%20the%20Eurozone.pdf

Darvas, Z., & Hüttl, P. (2015, January 9). *How to reduce the Greek debt burden?* Brussels: Bruegel. http://www.bruegel.org/nc/blog/detail/article/1533-how-to-reduce-the-greek-debt-burden/

Davies, G. (2015, January 7). A critical few weeks for the eurozone. *Financial Times*. http://blogs.ft.com/gavyndavies/2015/01/07/Gavyn-davies-a-critical-few-weeks-for-the-eurozone

Deutscher Bundestag (2014, November 25). *Plenarprotokoll 18/68* (p. 6421), Berlin. http://dip21.bundestag.de/dip21/btp/18/18068.pdf

Dinmore, G. (2014, March 14). Italy's tax-cutting plan fuel debt worries. *Financial Times*.

Dinmore, G., & Segreti, G. (2014, June 27). Business association warns of Italy's weak growth. *Financial Times*.

Dixon, H. (2015a, January 12). After vote, Greece will race against time. *International New York Times*.

Dixon, H. (2015b, March 30). Greeks need their leader to be tough. *International New York Times*.
Dixon, H. (2015c, April 7). Greece must walk the talk – and soon. *International New York Times*.
Eichengreen, B. (2007, September). *The breakup of the Euro*. Cambridge, MA: National Bureau of Economic Research, Paper No 13393. http://www.nber.org/papers/w13393.pdf
European Central Bank. (2014a, March). *Monthly bulletin March 2014*, Frankfurt am Main. http://www.ecb.europa.eu/pub/pdf/mobu/mb201403en.pdf
European Central Bank. (2014b, June 5). *Introductory statement by Mario Draghi to the press conference (with Q&A)*, Frankfurt am Main. http://www.ecb.europa.eu/press/pressconf/2014/html/is140605.en.html
European Central Bank. (2015a, January 2). *Liquidity analysis*, Frankfurt am Main. https://www.ecb.europa.eu/mopo/liq/html/index.en.html#portfolios
European Central Bank. (2015b, January 22). *Introductory statement by Mario Draghi to the press conference (with Q & A)*. https://www.ecb.europa.eu/press/pressconf/2015/html/is150122.en.html.
European Central Bank. (2014c, August 7). *Introductory statement by Mario Draghi to the press conference (with Q&A)*, Frankfurt am Main. http://www.ecb.europa.eu/press/pressconf/2014/html/is140807.en.html
European Central Bank. (2014d, September 4). *Introductory statement by Mario Draghi to the press conference (with Q&A)*, Frankfurt am Main. http://www.ecb.europa.eu/press/pressconf/2014/html/is140904.en.html
European Central Bank. (2014e, October 17). *Statement on New York Times articles*, Press Release. http://www.ecb.europa.eu/press/pr/date/2014/html/pr141017_1.en.html
European Central Bank. (2014f, November 21). *Opening keynote speech by Mario Draghi at the Frankfurt European Banking Congress*, Frankfurt am Main. https://www.ecb.europa.eu/press/key/date/2014/html/sp141121.en.html
European Central Bank. (2014g, November 27). *Monetary developments in the Euro area*, Frankfurt am Main (pp. 1–S3). http://www.ecb.europa.eu/press/pdf/md/md1410.pdf
European Commission. (2011). *Alert mechanism report 2015* (prepared in accordance with Articles 3 and 4 of Regulations (EU) No 1176/2011 on the prevention and correction of macroeconomic imbalances).
European Commission. (2014a, October 28). *Statement by vice-president Katainen on the Draft Budgetary Plans*, Brussels. http://europa.eu/rapid/press-release_STATEMENT-14-343_en.htm?locale=de
European Commission. (2014b, November 2014). Directorate general economic and financial affairs. *Italy – Review of progress on policy measures relevant for the correction of macroeconomic imbalances*, Brussels (pp. 3–8). http://ec.europa.eu/economy_finance/economic_governance/documents/2014-11-07_italy_mip_specific_monitoring_report_to_epc_en.pdf
European Commission. (2015a, January 13). *Stability and growth pact: Commission issues guidance to encourage structural reforms and investment*, Strasbourg. http://europa.eu/rapid/press-release_IP-15-3220_en.htm
European Commission. (2015b, February 26). *2015 European semester: Assessment of growth challenges, prevention and correction of macroeconomic imbalances, and results of in-depth reviews under regulation (EU) No 1176/2011* (pp. 4–8, 14–15). Brussels. http://ec.europa.eu/europe2020/pdf/csr2015/cr2015_comm_en.pdf
European Council. (2015a, February 20). *Eurogroup statement on Greece*, Brussels. http://www.consilium.europa.eu/en/press/press-releases/2015/02/150220-eurogroup-statement-greece/
European Council. (2015b, February 24). *Eurogroup statement on Greece*, Statement 73/15, Brussels. http://www.consilium.europa.eu/en/press/press-releases/2015/02/140224-eurogroup-statement-greece/
Ewing, J. (2014, December 5). Europe's top banker again hints at more stimulus in future. *New York Times*.
Ewing, J. (2015, February 19). E.C.B. could be power broker in solving Greek Debt crisis. *New York Times*.

Ewing, J., & Appelbaum, B. (2015, January 3). A stress test for Mario Draghi and the European Central Bank. *International New York Times*.

Ewing, J., & Thomas, L. (2014, October 18). Checkup time at Europe's Banks. *New York Times*.

Fleming, S. (2015, April 18–19). Lew urges Greece to respond to speed up reforms. *Financial Times*.

Fratzscher, M. (2013, November 19). Investment, not the surplus, is Germany's big problem. *Financial Times*.

Fratzscher, M. (2014, August 28). The German locomotive has become Europe's liability. *Financial Times*.

Fratzscher, M. (2015, January 28). Germany should recall its time in Europe's sick bay. *Financial Times*.

Giles, C. (2015, April 18–19). Moscovici warns Greece to agree to reforms or face default. *Financial Times*.

Greetham, T. (2014, August 21). Time to dust off old euro crisis strategies. *Financial Times*.

Hadas, E. (2014, August 26). Fixing Italy by winning Germany's trust. *International New York Times*.

Harris, F. (2014, October 18–19). Germany fails to take the hints. *International New York Times*.

Higgins, A., & Kanter, J. (2015, March 20). Europe's leaders keep Greece on sidelines. *International New York Times*.

Hope, K. (2015a, February 9). No extension to Greeek bailout, says Tsirpas. *Financial Times*.

Hope, K. (2015b, March 25). Peter Spiegel and Claire Jones, Athens raids public health coffers in hunt for cash. *Financial Times*.

Hope, K., & Barber, T. (2015, April 22). Faces behind Greece's radical government. *Financial Times*.

Hope, K., & Moore, E. (2014, December 30). Fears for a fresh Greek crisis after poll called. *Financial Times*.

Horobin, W. (2014, June 17). France's state auditor Warns on deficit target. *Wall Street Journal Online*. http://online.wsj.com/articles/frances-state-auditor-warns-on-deficit-target-1403014483

International Monetary Fund. (2014a, June). *2014 article IV consultation with the Euro area concluding statement of the IMF mission*, Washington, DC (section 6). http://www.imf.org/external/np/ms/2014/061914.htm

International Monetary Fund. (2014b, June 25). *Euro Area Policies*, IMF Country Report No. 14/198, Washington, D.C. (pp. 5–6). http://www.imf.org/external/pubs/ft/scr/2014/cr14198.pdf

Irwin, N. (2014a, October 27). E.C.B. split with Berlin may decide Europe's fate. *International New York Times*.

Irwin, N. (2014b, December 29). Why Greece's new crisis isn't spreading to the rest of Europe. *International New York Times*.

Joffe, J. (2015, January 13). No exit for Greece. *International New York Times*.

Jolly, D. (2014, November 22/23). Central Bank seeks to jolt E.U. growth back to life. *International New York Times*.

Jones, C. (2014c, December 17). Bundesbank president Jens Weidmann steps up criticism. *Financial Times*.

Jones, C. (2014a, September 3). Eurozone: Draghi's new deal. *Financial Times*.

Jones, C. (2014b, December 3). ECB poised to dash bond-buying hopes. *Financial Times*.

Jones, C. (2015a, January 5). Economists call for political action on eurozone. *Financial Times*.

Jones, C. (2015b, January 23). European Central Bank unleashes quantitative easing. *Financial Times*.

Jones, C., & Wagstyl, S. (2014, November 13). Eurozone policy makers brand for weak growth figures. *Financial Times*.

Kanter, J. (2014a, July 3). Italy's leader to use E.U. perch to press his case of debt. *International New York Times*.

Kanter, J. (2014b, October 30). Budget approval for France and Italy comes With Asterisk. *New York Times*.
Kanter, J. (2015a, February 17). Meeting over Greek debt ends in acrimony. *International New York Times*.
Kanter, J. (2015b, April 25). Eurozone Officials' Frustation with Greek leadership is boiling over. *New York Times*.
Kanter, J., & Alderman, L. (2015, February 16). Greek view on austerity worries those who cut back. *International New York Times*.
Kanter, J., & Kitsantonis, N. (2015, February 23). Greece seeks last-minute changes to avoid default. *International New York Times*.
Kitsantonis, N. (2015a, January 31). Greece says it won't cooperate with Bailout auditors. *New York Times*.
Kitsantonis, N. (2015b, February 9). Prime Minister of Greece will not Prolong Bailout. *New York Times*.
Kitsantonis, N., & Kanter, J. (2014, December 30). Europe braces for economic fallout as Greece heads to early elections. *International New York Times*.
Krugman, P. (2015, February 6). A game of chicken. *New York Times*.
Lawson-Remer, T. (2015, February 4). A deal Europe can't refuse. *International New York Times*.
Lewin, J., & Platt, E. (2015, April 9). Greece sells short-term bills and raises € 1bn. *Financial Times*.
Lubben, S. J. (2015, February 6). The Pitfalls in the Greek Debt proposal. *New York Times*. http://dealbook.nytimes.com/2015/02/06/the-pitfalls-in-the-greek-debt-proposal/
Mackintosh, J. (2014, December 12). The short view. *Financial Times*.
Maghadam, R. (2015, January 27). Halve Greek debt and keep the Eurozone together. *Financial Times*.
Meyerson, H. (2014). Economically, Germany is a threat to itself. *Washington Post*, October 15, 2014. http://www.washingtonpost.com/opinions/harold-meyerson-germany-poses-a-threat-to-its-own-economy/2014/10/15/38eeac6e-5497-11e4-892e-602188e70e9c_story.html
Meyerson, H. (2015, January 28). In Greek crisis, Germany should learn from its fiscal past. *Washington Post*. http://www.washingtonpost.com/opinions/harold-meyerson-in-greek-crisis-germany-should-learn-from-its-fiscal-past/2015/01/28/2d25bbd4-a721-11e4-a7c2-03d37af98440_story.html
Moghadam, R. (2014, December 11). Europe's guardians of monetary orthodoxy need not fear the printing press. *Financial Times*.
Moghadam, R. (2015, April 9). A dose of sanity to break the perilous deadlock over Greece. *Financial Times*.
Moore, E. (2015a, February 3). Greek debt offer sounds appetising but details could be bitter. *Financial Times*.
Moore, E. (2015b, February 4). Greek debt offer sounds appetising but details could be bitter. *Financial Times*.
Moore, E., & Hope, K. (2015, January 14). Size of Greek Debt mountain limits scope for solutions. *Financial Times*.
Münchau, W. (2010, March 22). Gaps in the Eurozone 'football league'. *Financial Times*.
Münchau, W. (2014, December 8). The ECB, demigods and eurozone quantitative easing. *Financial Times*.
Münchau, W. (2015a, January 5). Political extremists may be the eurozone's saviours. *Financial Times*.
Münchau, W. (2015b, February 23). The skirmish is over – let the Greek debt battle begin. *Financial Times*.
Norris, F. (2014, October 18–19). Germany fails to take the hints. *International New York Times*.
Öttinger, G. (2014, November 21). Europe's economic future depends on French reforms. *Financial Times*.
Plender, J. (2014, December 30). Forgive the debt or earn the wrath of its victims. *Financial Times*.

Plickert, P. (2014, December 23). Deutsche Politiker attackieren die ECB. *Frankfurter Allgemeine Zeitung*.
Politi, J. (2014, October 16). Budget will push Italy to the edge of EU deficit rules. *Financial Times*.
Portes, R., & Weil, P. (2014, August 21). Draghi has to do, as well as say, whatever it takes. *Financial Times*.
Praet, P. (2014, December 19). Is the ECB doing enough? *Project Syndicate*. http://www.project-syndicate.org/commentary/ecb-monetary-policy-targets-by-peter-praet-2014-12
Privitera, A. (2015, January 27). *Merkel's double challenge. Syriza and QE*, Washington, DC: American Institute for Contemporary German Studies. http://www.aicgs.org/issue/merkels-double-challenge/
Roger, P. (2014, February 11). Dépense publique: "La France est dans une zone dangereuse". *Le Monde*. http://www.lemonde.fr/politique/article/2014/02/11/depenses-la-cour-des-comptes-s-impatiente_4364027_823448.html
Roger, P. (2015). *l'Etat dépensera moins d'argent qu'en 2014*. http://www.lemonde.fr/politique/article/2014/10/01/sapin-en-2015-l-etat-depensera-moins-d-argent-qu-en-2014_4498239_823448.html
Sandbu, M. (2015, January 23). Three deft tricks that earned Draghi his 'Super Mario' nickname. *Financial Times*.
Sapin, M. (2014, August 15). Pourquoi il faut réorienter les politiques économiques européennes. *Le Monde*.
Schaeffer, F. (2014, November 28). La lettre de Manuel Valls adressée à Bruxelles. *Les Echos*. http://www.lesechos.fr/economie-france/budget-fiscalite/0203974513597-la-lettre-de-manuel-valls-adressee-a-bruxelles-1069319.php
Schäfer, J. W. (2015, January 4). Rote Karte für Athen! *Bild*. http://www.bild.de/news/standards/griechenland/rote-karte-fuer-athen-39195568.bild.html
Smaghi, L. B. (2014, October 28). Here's why Germany needs to start spending. *Financial Times*.
Smaghi, L. B. (2015, January 5). Until it is resolved, the Greek problem will undermine the whole eurozone. *Financial Times*. http://blogs.ft.com/the-exchange/2015/01/05/lorenzo-bini-smaghi-until-it-is-resolved-the-greek-problem-will-undermine-the-whole-eurozone/
Smale, A. (2015, March 24). Berlin talks relieve some strain, if not Greek debt. *International New York Times*.
Smale, A., & Alderman, L. (2014, October 8). Europe's resistance to austerity grows, *International New York Times*.
Spiegel, P. (2014a, November 27). Juncker interview: the annotated transcript. *Financial Times*.
Spiegel, P. (2014b, December 9). Brussels urged to refocus on Eurozone. *Financial Times*.
Spiegel, P. (2014c, October 22). EU to warn France and Italy on budget plans. *Financial Times*.
Spiegel, P. (2015a, January 24–25). Radical or realist? *Financial Times*.
Spiegel, P. (2015b, February 17). Greece bailout talks collapse in acrimony. *Financial Times*.
Spiegel, P. (2015c, February 19). Kerin Hope and Alex Barker, Athens outlines bailout extension plans. *Financial Times*.
Spiegel, P. (2015d, February 23). Athens lacks wiggle room as wrangling rumbles. *Financial Times*.
Spiegel, P. (2015e, March 2). How Jeroen Dijsselbloem did the deal to extend the Greece bailout. *Financial Times*.
Spiegel, P. (2015f, March 10). Coeuré calls for more respect for EU budget rules. *Financial Times*.
Spiegel, P. (2015g, March 23). Greece's leader warns Merkel of 'impossible' debt repayments. *Financial Times*.
Spiegel, P. (2015h, April 2). Greece submits new list of reforms to eurozone. *Financial Times*.
Spiegel, P., & Hope, K. (2015, April 6). Frustrated officials want Greek premier to ditch Syriza far left. *Financial Times*.
Spiegel, P., Hope, K., & Barker, A. (2015, April 27). Eurozone officials look beyond Varoufakis to spur Greek talks. *Financial Times*.
Stephens, P. (2015, January 30). The stand-off that may sink the euro. *Financial Times*.

Storbeck, O. (2015, April 17). Germany pushes budget discipline too far. *International New York Times.*

Taylor, P. (2014, September 30). Germany resists pleas for stimulus. *International New York Times.*

The Economist. (2015, January 24). Charlemagne: Berlin v Frankfurt, http://www.economist.com/node/21640360

Thomas, L. (2014a, October 18). Before a Bailout, E.C.B. minutes showed doubts over keeping a Cyprus bank Afloat. *New York Times.*

Thomas, L. (2014b, November 19). Europe's Central Bank defies its own rules in Cyprus Bailout. *New York Times.*

Thomas, L., & Ewing, J. (2015, February 13). As Greece maneuvers, who's calling who's bluff. *International New York Times.*

Thompson, C. (2015, January 9). Investors put € 1.2tn into negative havens. *Financial Times.*

Thomson, A. (2014a, April 24). France to slow deficit reduction plan. *Financial Times.*

Thomson, A. (2014b, April 25). French finance minister vows to stick to spending cuts. *Financial Times.*

Thomson, A. (2014c, August 15). France warns on budget deficit target. *Financial Times.*

Tsipras, A. (2015, February 8). *Speech during the programmatic statement of the government.* http://www.primeminister.gov.gr/english/2015/02/08/primeministers-a-tsipras-speech-during-the-programmtic-statements-of-thegovernment/

Varoufakis, Y. (2015, February 17). No time for games in Europe. *International New York Times.*

Wagstyl, S. (2014, October 8). Berlin holds firm on fiscal rigour despite recession risk. *Financial Times.*

Wagstyl, S. (2015a, January 5). Berlin insists it expects Greece to remain in eurozone. *Financial Times.*

Wagstyl, S. (2015b, January 20). German media attack Eurozone QE plans. *Financial Times.*

Wagstyl, S. (2015c, February 20). Schäuble sets the stage for showdown with Athens. *Financial Times.*

Whelan, N. (2015, February 13). Centre–right governments have no interest in seeing this new left-wing Greek government succeed. *Irish Times.* http://www.irishtimes.com/opinion/centre-right-governments-have-no-interest-in-seeing-this-new-left-wing-greek-government-succeed-1.2101957

Wolf, M. (2014, May 14). Time for Draghi to open the sluice. *Financial Times.*

Wolf, M. (2015a, January 21). Bolder steps from Europe's central bankers. *Financial Times.*

Wolf, M. (2015b, January 28). Greek debt and a default of statesmanship. *Financial Times.*

Wolf, M. (2015c, February 4). A deal to bring modernity to Greece. *Financial Times.*

Wren-Lewis, S. (2013, June 13). *How a Greek drama became a global tragedy*, Oxford University. http://mainlymacro.blogspot.de/2013/06/how-greek-drama-became-global-tragedy.html

Chapter 5
Germany's Role in the Euro Crisis Management

The divisive debate over Germany's role in the euro crisis management and what it means for its European partners raises three interrelated questions: First, did Germany's strategy of expansionary fiscal contraction and internal devaluation address the root causes of the euro crisis? Second, has the Berlin Republic as Europe's undisputed economic and political powerhouse yielded to the temptation of an imperial power? Lastly, does the euro crisis mark a tectonic shift from the reflexive commitment of a Europeanized Germany to a Germanized Europe?

5.1 The Grapes of Wrath

For more than 5 years, the German strategy of expansionary fiscal contraction and internal devaluation has produced no success story. The economic outlook for the Eurozone economy is still biased towards the "downside",[1] with deep divisions between core and periphery. Since the start of the crisis in 2008 until the end of 2014, Greece's gross domestic product contracted by 26 %, Italy's by 9.5 %, Portugal's by 6.9, and Spain's by 5.8 %.[2] The data for the first three quarters of 2014 confirmed that the recovery in the euro area has stalled.[3] With feeble growth no longer confined to the ailing peripheral economies, concern is shifting to the core. Italy's economy shrank again by 0.1 % in the third quarter. The growth forecast of 0.8 % has been revised downwards to 0.2 % by the end of the year. The third-largest euro area economy appears to be stuck in a permanent recession.[4]

---

[1] European Central Bank (2014a), International Monetary Fund (2014a, p. 7), Center for Economic Policy Research (2014).

[2] Eurostat (2014a).

[3] Eurostat (2014b, c, d).

[4] Sanderson and Segreti (2014), Ewing and Pianigiani (2014), Financial Times (2014a).

F.-J. Meiers, *Germany's Role in the Euro Crisis*,
DOI 10.1007/978-3-319-20514-4_5

The French economy still remains in reverse gear; it expanded by 0.3 % for the first time in 2014 after it had no growth for the first two quarters.[5] In light of the consistently weak economic data the French government lowered its forecast for GDP growth in 2014 to 0.4 % (previously 1.0 %).[6]

Spring of 2015 has brought a fresh breeze for the Eurozone economy. A dramatic decline of energy prices, a weaker euro and intervention by the ECB are brightening the outlook for the euro area economy. Seasonally adjusted GDP rose by 0.3 % in the euro area during the fourth quarter of 2014; over the whole year, the euro area economy rose by 0.9 %. Germany's economy grew 0.7 % in the last quarter of 2014, the strongest performance since the economy grew by 0.8 % in the first quarter of 2013; this resulted in a 1.6 % increase (adjusted for calendar effects) for the whole of 2014. The stronger-than-expected growth data is powered by rising real wages, the windfall gains from lower oil prices and a strong labor market which have turned domestic demand into the key growth driver.[7] Germany's growth figure was matched by Spain's whose economy grew by 1.4 % last year; Portugal's economy has ported another quarter of 0.5 % growth which translates into a gain of 0.9 % for the whole year. However, the picture is not consistently positive. Greece's nascent recovery turned into a 0.4 % contraction. The Italian economy was still stagnant, it contracted 0.4 % in 2014 while the French economy only managed to eke out growth of 0.1 %, or 0.4 % annualized.[8] The European Commission said in its Winter Economic Forecast that growth this year will rise moderately to 1.3 %. The euro economy is set to expand 1.9 % in 2016. Economic growth is "broad-based". For the first time in 8 years, all euro member countries' economies are expected to grow. But "the divergence in economic performance" across the euro area will "likely continue". For France and Italy, the projected growth rate for 2015 remains a meagre 1 % respectively 0.6 %; both economies should expand by 1.8 % and 1.3 % in 2016.[9] The ECB expects the economic recovery "to broaden and strengthen gradually." In view of the lower oil prices, progress made in fiscal consolidation and structural reforms and ongoing improvements in financial conditions and price competitivness, the ECB raised its forecast for growth this year from 1 to 1.5 % and increased its estimate for 2016 from 1.5 to 1.9 %.[10] In its Interim Economic Assessment, the OECD increased its forecast for the Eurozone economy by 0.3–1.4 % in 2015 and 2 % the next year. Lower oil prices and the effects of quantitative easing by the ECB would "constitute important new positive growth factors."[11]

---

[5] Jones and Wagstyl (2014).

[6] Carnegy (2014), Jones and Thomson (2014), Le Monde (2014), Elysee (2014).

[7] Federal Statistical Office (2015).

[8] Eurostat (2015a), German Federal Statistical Office (2015), Charrel (2015), Jolly (2015).

[9] European Commission (2015, pp. 1–2).

[10] European Central Bank (2015a).

[11] Organization for Economic Cooperation and Development (2015a, pp. 1, 4).

The Commission conceded in a previous report that the euro zone economy was not only "particularly weak" but was also underperforming "historic examples of post-crisis recoveries". The main causes behind the subdued pace of recovery, now in its seventh year, "are set to fade only very gradually."[12] The IMF warned that growth should "strengthen more gradually and unevenly as the crisis-legacy brakes ease only slowly." Notwithstanding the positive effects of the ECB's action, "high real debt burdens, impaired balance sheets, high unemployment, and investor pessimism about prospects for a robust recovery", together with "deep-seated obstacles on productivity and competitiveness" will continue to weigh on "demand" and "the region's medium-term growth potential."[13] The OECD concluded that, "even in our positive scenarios we're not getting back to historical averages."[14] Projected growth rates would remain "too low to fully repair and activate labor markets". In addition, the OECD pointed to the "abnormally low inflation and interest rates" which would create "a growing risk of financial instability with risk-taking and leverage driven by liquidity rather than fundamentals." Instead, "a more balanced approach to policy" would be required "with fiscal and, especially, structural policies providing synergistic support to monetary policy."[15] The more positive economic outlook could be "dampened by the necessary balance sheet adjustments in various sectors and the rather slow pace of implementation of structural reforms," acknowledged Mr. Draghi.[16] In short, formidable challenges still lie ahead to recover the dramatic output losses the ailing euro area economies have suffered since the onset of the crisis in 2008. At present, the most challenging reality is chronic weakness of private sector demand in the euro area that Martin Wolf termed "chronic demand deficiency syndrome." For the next few years, there is no task more important than restoring buoyant demand.[17]

The feeble overall growth is insufficient to have a meaningful impact on the depression-level joblessness in the currency area's misery belt. Unemployment is stuck stubbornly above 11 % since April 2013 while the distressed euro area economies are still mired in depressingly high levels: 25.7 % in Greece, 23.0 % in Spain, 13.5 % in Portugal, 13.0 % in Italy, 10.6 % in France and 9.8 % in Ireland in March 2015. Youth unemployment remains at scarcely believable levels in many countries of the euro periphery: more than 50 % in Greece and Spain, around 40 % in Italy and Portugal and close to 30 % in Ireland.[18] ECB economists forecast a fall

---

[12] European Commission (2014a, pp. 1, 2, 7–8, 12–19, 30, 38, 39).

[13] International Monetary Fund (2014a, pp. 8, 24), International Monetary Fund (2015, p. 50), Group of Twenty (2014a, pp. 3–5), Group of Twenty (2014b, pp. 2, 9).

[14] Organization for Economic Cooperation and Development (2014a). See also Organization for Economic Cooperation and Development (2014c, p. 8), Organization for Economic Cooperation and Development (2014b, pp. 4, 5, 10).

[15] Organization for Economic Cooperation and Development (2014c, pp. 1–2, 4), Organization for Economic Cooperation and Development (2015b).

[16] European Central Bank (2014b, 2015a), European Central Bank (2014c, p. 2), European Central Bank (2014d, pp. 1, 4, 6, 11).

[17] Charrel (2015), Wolf (2015a), Financial Times (2015a).

[18] Eurostat (2015b).

of the unemployment rate from 11.6 % in 2014 to 9.9 % in 2017. One in ten workers in the euro area will remain unemployed by the time when the central bank expects the full effects of its bond-buying program have rippled through the Eurozone economy. The persistent high levels of joblessness underline not only structural flaws in region's biggest labor markets, where governments like in Italy and France keep labor markets in a "calcified state". They also highlight the severeness of the euro crisis which has critically constrained the economy's capacity to create jobs, even when demand rebounds.[19]

Consumer prices in the currency area reached a standstill in April 2015, slightly up from the −0.1 % in March, after a record low of −0.6 % in January and −0.3 % in February. The inflation rate expected over 5 years starting in 5 years ("five year-five year" inflation-linked swap rate) has dropped from 2.1 % in July 2014 below 1.5 % in mid-January 2015. The core inflation which excludes energy and food prices, remained at 0.6 %, the lowest rate since Eurostat began measuring it in 1997, signaling that weak demand within the euro area continue to weigh on price pressures.[20] The "ogre"[21] of deflation looms largest in the crisis-hit economies—Greece: −1.9 %; Spain: −0.8 %, Ireland: −0.3 %, Italy: 0 % and Portugal: 0.3 % in March 2015.[22] The European Commission forecasts an inflation rate in the euro area of −0.1 % in 2015 before climbing to 1.3 % the next year. The ECB concluded that longer-term inflation expectations had started to recover; inflation is expected to remain very low in the months ahead before increasing to 1.5 % next year and to 1.8 % in 2017.[23]

The sharp decline of commodity prices are a stimulus program for free that supports households' disposable income and corporate profitability, Mr. Weidmann argued,[24] but it could be a severe blow to the credibility of the Central Bank. Despite the more promising economic outlook and the receding risk of a severe bout of deflation, the ECB will not approach its inflation target of below, but close to, 2 % until 2017 at the earliest. In unusually direct terms, Mr. Draghi warned about the risk that the euro area could become trapped in a "classic deflationary cycle" if lowflation were to last for "a prolonged period of time." Lowflation provides a "fertile ground for a pernicious negative spiral, which then also affects expectations," he noted.[25] With an inflation rate entrenched far below 1 %, the euro area faces the highly troubling situation that caused Japan's "lost decade": a

---

[19] European Central Bank (2015b, p. 5), European Central Bank (2015c, p. 11). See also Jones (2015a); Financial Times (2015a).

[20] Eurostat (2015c), J.P. Morgan Asset Management (2015).

[21] Laggard (2014), World Economic Forum (2014), International Monetary Fund (2014b), Organization for Economic Cooperation and Development (2014c, p. 4).

[22] Eurostat (2015d).

[23] European Commission (2015), European Central Bank (2015a), European Central Bank (2015c, pp. 5, 11, 12).

[24] Deutsche Bundesbank (2014), Plender (2014).

[25] European Central Bank (2014e, f).

protracted period of across-the-board decline in general price levels known as deflation at a time when the region is already suffering the ill-effects of weak demand.[26] Deflation can propel a self-reinforcing downward spiral particularly in the euro area's stressed economies with staggering debts: they would have even more difficulties in meeting their obligations, because economic output and tax receipts would further shrink, while an increasing proportion of their national budgets are consumed on debt servicing.[27]

Government debt as a proportion of GDP rose across the euro area from 66 % in 2007 to 95 % at the end of 2013. The debts of the misery belt have increased by an average of 26 % since 2010 to 131 % of GDP, or 120 % excluding Greece.[28] By 2015, Spanish general government debt (Maastricht definition) will be 101.4 %, of GDP; Irish, 121.1 %; Portuguese, 131.8 %; Italian, 134.5 %; and Greek, 177.2 %.[29] Even if the bond yields stay at record low level for years to come, nominal GDP must grow on average by 3 % a year just to keep the public debt ratio stable; the misery belt economies need to grow by 5 % indefinitely, to lower their debt burden to the 60 % Maastricht debt criteria. Since the mid-1970s there have been just three countries—Norway, Singapore and Belgium—who had managed to run primary surpluses as large as 5 % for as long as 10 years. A fall in nominal GDP will increase the debt-to-GDP even when the country does not incur any new debt.[30] The disappointing results of the deleveraging policies underscore the "difficulty of reducing debt-to-income-ratios sharply through austerity policies." Instead, deleveraging of the public sector through austerity measures lays open "a poisonous combination. . .between high and higher debt/GDP and slow and slowing GDP growth."[31] The weak economic outlook makes the euro area's debt problems more intractable, thus raising, once again, concerns about the sustainability of sovereign debts. The implication is that the euro area's strategy to rely on large and sustained primary budget surpluses to solve its debt problem is both economically and politically unfeasible.[32]

Lastly, one regretful legacy of the euro crisis has been a weakening of the relationship between rulers and ruled. The same dynamics of political economy that caused unrest in Greece could be felt more widely in the euro area.[33] From Rome to Lisbon, public tolerance of rigid fiscal and monetary policy "has reached

[26] Bernanke (1995, pp. 1–28), Fisher (1933), The Economist (2014b, pp. 21–22, 24).

[27] Calvo (2014), de Grauwe (2014), Moghadam et al. (2014), Wolf (2014a, b), Evans-Pritchard (2014), The Economist (2014a).

[28] Eurostat (2014e), European Commission (2014a, pp. 36–38), European Commission (2014b, pp. 64–67, 70–71).

[29] Organization for Economic Cooperation and Development (2014d, pp. 109, 139, 173, 148, 182), International Monetary Fund (2014a, p. 34).

[30] Wolf (2014c), Münchau (2014), Eichengreen and Panizza (2014), Eichengreen (2014).

[31] Buttiglione et al. (2014, pp. 63, 79).

[32] Eichengreen and Panizza (2014).

[33] The Economist (2015a), Irwin (2014), Rachman (2014). See also Münchau (2015), Hope and Moore (2014), Kitsantonis and Kanter (2014), Alderman (2014).

its limits"[34] The gravity of the economic and financial crisis and inadequate economic policies to address depression-high levels of unemployment in the euro area's misery belt together with a widespread feeling of a loss of national democratic control and grave concern with immigration, have fed public disillusion about the European integration project which millions of voters associate with hardship and failure.[35] Fringe parties especially on the right flank made sweeping gains in the elections to the European Parliament on (2014, May 25)—the French Front National (FN), the United Kingdom Independence Party (UKIP) and the Dansk Folkeparti (DF) lead the anti-EU surge. The outcome disclosed a deep cleavage between euro area countries' need for further economic integration and European voters' rejection of further and faster European integration. After 6 years of deep economic crisis, the greatest challenge to the European project is economic stagnation and, above all, political apathy and repulsion.[36] The rise of anti-system parties notably in the crisis-stricken countries jeopardizes the euro project because it premises on the preservation of a consensus amongst its member countries on how to keep the single currency together. If that consensus is shattered, "the whole delicate house of cards of debt, bailouts and austerity begins to wobble."[37] The euro area's economic and political crisis will intensify if there is no boost to substantial and sustainable economic growth soon.

In the depth of an economic depression, Greek voters decisively rejected the medicine of punishing economic austerity that has demanded continuing sacrifice to meet the demands of creditors[38] without delivering economic growth, more jobs and lower debt. Syriza became the first party to take power in a euro area country which had campaigned on a platform to roll back painful austerity measures and renegotiate the bailout terms with the country's creditors. "The verdict of the Greek people ends, beyond any doubt, the vicious circle of austerity in our country," Alexis Tsirpas, Syriza's charismatic young leader, declared in his victory speech, "The verdict of the Greek people, your verdict, annuls today in an indisputable fashion the bailout agreements of austerity and disaster." Syriza's unequivocal win may inspire populist anti-austerity parties on the left and right from Spain (Podemos—We Can) to Italy (MoVimento Cinque Stelle—Five Star Movement and Lega Nord per l'indipendenza della Padania—Northern League) to France

[34] European Commission (2013a).

[35] Stokes and Bell (2013), Stokes and Oates (2014), European Commission (2013b, p. 10), European Commission (2014c, pp. T26, T28, T30, T33).

[36] European Parliament (2014), The Economist (2014c), Taylor (2014), International Monetary Fund (2014a, p. 4).

[37] Rachman (2014).

[38] The bailout programs for Greece, in effect, rescued creditor-country banks which would have been the amongst the biggest losers if Greece had defaulted on its debt. "Just 11 percent of the loans directly financed government activities. Another 16 percent went on interest payments. The rest went on capital operations of various kinds: the money came in and flowed out again. A more honest policy would have been to bail lenders out directly. But this would have been too embarrassing." Wolf (2015b). See also Krugman (2015a).

(Front National) where continuing economic weakness has stirred a populist backlash against austerity policies that brought them nothing but staggering joblessness and widespread social misery. Syriza's victory demonstrates that the old order can be toppled and the salvation lies in radical alternatives. The lesson of the post crisis years has been that enforced austerity can go only so far as the ballot box allows. The longer the economic slump continues, the more voters join the burgeoning ranks of the populist parties on the left and right who staunchly oppose a continuation of austerity policies Berlin still sees as the right medicine to bring about a strong and sustainable recovery of the euro area economy.[39] The populist backlash against austerity policies underscores a growing divide between national democratic accountability and European rules and obligations to ensure that euro area member countries follow sound fiscal and monetary policies. From Greece to France, countries defy any infringement on their sovereignty and refuse to act in a way that is consistent with a more "rigid partnership" envisaged by the Maastricht Treaty.[40] If new elected governments are unwilling to keep up with the commitments of previous governments and instead prioritize the political, economic, and social preferences of their electorate, then the European Union, notably the Eurogroup, will have a hard time to consistently functioning in line with the requirements of a monetary union. Greece's Prime Minister Tsirpas put The Union's quandary in a nutshell when he said, "We are committed to restoring our national and popular sovereignty, together with the support of Greek people, who will be the ultimate judge of our actions." Podemos, like Syriza in Greece, sees itself as the voice of and for the people. Spanish voters share the idea that the country needs "to restore its sovereignty and escape economic diktats from Brussels and Berlin", points out Carolina Bescansa, a founding member of the party.[41]

The alarming new evidence underlines the sober reality that the euro area growth plan is not working. By prohibiting governments reflating their economies, the Stability and Growth Pact amounts to an "institutionalized austerity" that is prolonging the euro area's economic travails: growth is meagre or non-existent, debt and joblessness have risen constantly in the peripheral countries, and the risk of pervasive and persistent lowflation continues to grow.[42] The very tentative pace of the recovery leads to the sober conclusion that the euro area will remain economically depressed for a long time to come, politically indecisive and vulnerable to social and political upheavals. The German strategy of expansionary fiscal contraction and internal devaluation exacerbates the twin problems of feeble demand and lowflation, especially in the weak euro area economies. The German model of fiscal rectitude and monetary stability leaves the central question unanswered: how can governments deleverage from high private and public debts

[39] Witte (2015), Yardley and Alderman (2015), The Economist (2015b), Mazower (2015), Blome et al. (2015), Taylor (2015).

[40] Mayer (2015). See also Stark (2015).

[41] Financial Times (2015b), Buck (2015).

[42] Jones (2015b), Coppola (2015), Samuelson (2015), Financial Times (2014b), Krugman (2015b).

without driving their economies back into a far bigger slump and falling into a deflation trap?

5.2 Stress-Testing the Leadership of Europe's Powerhouse

There is still a misapprehension about German power and leadership. Some observers argue that Germany took advantage of the euro and the asymmetric rules of the bailout programs for selfish national purposes. Hysterical charges have been made against the German government, especially Chancellor Merkel, that she is "a closet Hitler" using the euro as "the first Panzer Division of the Fourth Reich"[43] to establish an imperial German leadership role. The "German question"—about the role of a country "too big for Europe and too small for the world" Henry Kissinger once phrased it—is back on the agenda.

Although Germany is the most important country for overcoming the euro area's problems, its capacities to project its power at the European level are substantially confined. If Germany had vetoed a bailout program at the height of the euro crisis in spring 2010 and summer 2012, it would have triggered a systemic crisis that could unravel not only the monetary union, but also the central achievement of the European integration project,—the common market. Thus, the Merkel government was in a bind to defray the costs of conditional and targeted financial assistance to assure the survival of the monetary union as a whole. As the largest economy in the European Union, Germany is liable for approximately 27 % of the ESM rescue program. But the costs to bail out countries like Spain or Italy go far beyond the firepower of the euro area's creditor–in-chief. To prevent a disintegration of the currency union, Berlin is critically dependent on the material support of other euro zone member countries, European institutions, especially the ECB, and the financial markets. Germany is only one voice among the 28 EU member countries. Every nation, including the misery belt, has to agree on treaty changes Germany deems necessary to prevent future disasters. Past experiences with far-reaching reform projects suggest that any attempt to establish a common economic and fiscal order to the German ordoliberal image would imply protracted negotiations which can only be successfully concluded by compromise, not by the imposition of a German Diktat. And the "German Diktat" must be approved by all 28 national parliaments and, in some cases, by a referendum. The EU's abandoned constitution and its successor, the Lisbon Treaty of 2009, were together rejected in three out of six referendums.[44] Germany is Europe's economic powerhouse, but it is not all-powerful. It is still only 1 of 28. That means that "Berlin must show a willingness to compromise, just like everyone else," observed EU Commissioner Günther Öttinger.[45] And the German government has to walk a fine line to sooth its domestic

[43] MacDonough (2013).

[44] Schwarzer and Land (2012).

[45] Blome et al. (2014).

audience—the Bundesbank, the Bundesverfassungsgericht, the bailout-weary coalition parties, and the entrenched euro-sceptic majority of the German electorate—that the rules of the Stability and Growth Pact apply equally to all euro member countries and that Germany's public purse will not be put at risk while convincing the financial markets and her European partners that Germany is firmly committed to the long-term stability of the euro area and to preservation of the grand bargain with France on which the durability of the monetary union critically depends.[46]

Merkel's euro crisis playbook with a clear-cut preference for domestic needs exposed a widening rift between the two traditional drivers of European political and economic integration about the governance and character of the monetary union. While Berlin seeks maximum control and minimal costs, Paris prefers maximum fire power and minimal control. Berlin is demanding monetary stability, fiscal rigour, no move to mutualized debt obligations and no direct access to rescue funds to bail-out troubled banks, fearful that Germany will become the lender of last resort saddled with failing loans. Paris advocates rapid access to shared European resources in the name of European solidarity to promote economic growth and employment and to inject capital directly into failing banks.[47] The second major cabinet reshuffle in France in late August exposed not only widening divisions within the French government with the socialist left becoming more vocal in its opposition to the President's supply-side economic reform program. It also heightened a growing rift between Paris and Berlin over whether austerity measures were sufficient to restore the euro area's declining economic fortunes.[48] Because of the growing economic imbalance between both countries French governments find themselves in the uncomfortable position to follow the German playbook. "Berlin and Paris are no longer playing in the same league. This imbalance is at the very heart of the Franco-German malaise," observed Dominique Moïsi, senior adviser at the Institut Français des Relations Internationales (IFRI) in Paris.[49] Two decades of feebleness of the French economy have washed out the founding bargain of the European project: le balance between German economic strength and French political leadership. Le déséquilibre is threatening to undermine the foundations of the grand bargain between France and Germany. The widening divisions between Berlin and Paris on monetary and fiscal issues cast doubts about the ability of the Franco-German engine to maintain its traditional role of moving the European integration process into new directions.[50]

---

[46] Stephens (2013), Cohen (2013).

[47] Peel and Carnegy (2012, 2013), Barber (2014), Pew Research Global Attitudes Project (2013, pp. 3, 34–35), German Marshall Fund of the United States (2014, pp. 7, 28–32).

[48] Bilfesky and Alderman (2014).

[49] Barkin (2014), Smale and Alderman (2014).

[50] Kauffmann and Uterwedde (2010, pp. 13–19), Glomb (2011), Deubner (2011), Goulard (2012), Schwarzer (2012, pp. 112–122), Schild (2013, pp. 24–47), The Economist (2013a), Errera and Ischinger (2014), Stephens (2014a), Peet and La Guardia (2014, pp. XII, XIV, 96–104).

The German classe politique has a profound uneasiness to get along on foreign and security issues where indifference to action isn't an option anymore. Former Polish Foreign Minister Radek Sikorski saw "inactivity" of "Europe's indispensable nation" as the biggest threat Germany poses to its neighbours.[51] In response to growing allied uneasiness about German military restraint on the world stage the German president Joachim Gauck, Foreign Minister Frank-Walter Steinmeier and Defense Minister Ursula von der Leyen urged a more active German foreign policy, taking responsibility commensurate with the country's economic weight.[52] But only 37 % of the German public support a more active German foreign policy with 60 % against; 86 % back a stronger German engagement in humanitarian missions, while 82 % oppose a stronger engagement of the Bundeswehr in out-of-area missions.[53]

Germany's hesitant response to Russia's relapse into the great power politics of the nineteenth and twentieth centuries reveals again Berlin's predicament "that a serious foreign policy imposes the sort of choices it has sought to avoid."[54] Merkel's awe inspiring shuttle diplomacy in urgent search for a resolution of the Ukraine crisis underscores Berlin's determination to take President Gauck's demand seriously to play a vital leadership role on the world's diplomatic stage. German policy makers have demonstrated that German leadership is for them no longer a matter of debate, but of necessity. But the unresolved question remains what German crisis management will do when actors like Russia do not abide by "a reliable, rules-based international order", especially the postwar principle that no borders can be altered by force, and appear unwilling to provide "predictable circumstances far beyond our borders" and "to strengthen the building blocks of international order", as German Foreign Minister Frank-Walter Steinmeier summarized the distinctive elements of German foreign policy in the twenty-first century. How can the "peaceful structures of order" be defended "where they are flagrantly infringed"?[55]

The Ukrainian case, like the still unsettled Iranian nuclear issue, underscores the Berlin Republic's pronounced preference for institutionalized cooperation in multilateral fora that includes a readiness to impose ever tougher economic sanctions on those actors who do not play by the rules. But German foreign and security policy is profoundly sceptical about the appropriateness and usefulness of military forces as a tool in international crisis management. Forces can only be used in tightly defined circumstances, preferably in stabilization and reconstruction missions, as a last resort,[56] and under clearly defined rules, i.e. under a mandate of the

[51] Ministry of Foreign Affairs of the Republic of Poland (2011, p. 9).

[52] Der Bundespräsident (2014), Deutschlandradio (2014), Bundesministerium der Verteidigung (2014a), Auswärtiges Amt (2014).

[53] Körber Stiftung (2014, pp. 3, 5), Wanner and Bulmahn (2013, pp. 18, 19, 34, 44, 48).

[54] Stephens (2014b, c), Wergin (2014), Wagstyl (2014), Peel (2014), Smale (2014), Sierakowski (2014).

[55] Auswärtiges Amt (2015a, b), Steinmeier (2015).

[56] One exception was Berlin's decision in late August 2014 to provide the Kurds with defensive lethal arms, including a train-and-equip program, in their battle against the *Islamic State* (IS) in Northern Iraq. Bundesministerium der Verteidigung (2014b).

UN Security Council. Like the building of the Berlin Wall, Merkel's Ukraine crisis management diplomacy is based on the assumption that the West should play a long game by which Ukraine will eventually emerge as a prosperous and democratic state. In a speech at the University of Helsinki Chancellor Merkel summarized the German approach to the settlement of the conflict in the Donbas region as follows, "We want to resolve the Ukraine crisis—but with political means. . . .we should be under no illusions. It is going to be a long haul."[57]

The main goal of Merkel's "twin-track strategy" of political dialogue and economic sanctions, if deemed necessary, has been to bring Russia and Ukraine from the battlefield to the bargaining table. In its political efforts to defuse the conflict, the German government is determined to avoid any military move that might be conceived as a provocation by Russia. At the NATO Wales summit meeting in September 2014, Chancellor Merkel blocked demands by eastern European allies to deploy allied troops and heavy weapons in former Soviet bloc countries on a permanent basis. She argued that a permanent deployment of NATO forces on the territory of Eastern member countries would be perceived by the Russian government as a hostile move that would lead to the termination of the NATO-Russia Founding Act of 1997 which set out a road map for building "a stable, peaceful and undivided Europe, whole and free, to the benefit of all its peoples.cooperation between the two sides".[58] Instead, she put her weight behind an alternative proposal: the formation-of a new multinational brigade of up to 5000 troops—the Very High Readiness Joint Task Force (VJTF)—based at the first German-Netherlands Corps Headquarters in Münster (Germany). The new unit should respond "to challenges that arise, particularly at the periphery of NATO's territory" and "to act as a potential deterrent to further escalation."[59] The Chancellor also assured German contributions to other alliance resurance measures, like the upgrading of the multinational headquarters of the Danish, Polish and German brigades in Szczecin (Poland) and more air policing on NATO's eastern border.

Chancellor Merkel is also deeply opposed to providing lethal defensive military assistance to the beleaguered Ukrainian army to counter Russia's military assistance to the rebels in the eastern provinces of Donesk and Luhansk arguing that doing so would only add fuel to the fire. She told the Munich Security Conference that nobody expected the West to mount a military attack to bring the Berlin Wall down. East Germany held out 28 years in "dictatorship and unfreedom" until the wall came down in November 1989. Drawing on parallels through her personal experience in the German Democratic Republic and the containment policy during the cold war she concluded, "the progress Ukraine needs cannot be achieved by more weapons. I don't see a military solution to this conflict." The only viable option on the table is to "continue to pursue a diplomatic solution, although we have

[57] The Federal Chancellor (2015a).

[58] Die Bundeskanzlerin (2014, 2015), NATO (1997).

[59] NATO (2014), Headquarters 1 (German/Netherlands) Corps (2014).

suffered a lot of setbacks," she conceded.[60] But U.S. President Barack Obama left the option of lethal assistance to Ukraine pointedly on the table to change President Putin's cost-risk calculus[61] of Russia's role in the Ukrainian conflict. "What I've asked my team to do is look at all options. . .and the possibility of lethal defensive weapons is one of those options that's being examined," he said after a meeting with Chancellor Merkel at the White House.[62]

As Russian President Vladimir Putin shows no inclination to resolve the conflict for the foreseeable future, Merkel's long game approach raises two questions. How can her commitment to resist aggression be credible in the eyes of the Kremlin if she safely concentrates on the diplomatic and economic rather than the military instruments[63] of containment, as George F. Kennan's "strongpoint" concept did in contrast to the "perimeter defense" approach of Paul H. Nitze?[64] Secondly, do the German Chancellor and Germany's European and transatlantic partners have the "patience and resolve" to undo Russia's game plan in what Russian President Vladimir Putin is calling Novorossiya (Новороссия) or New Russia to establish an alternative project to the Western conception of representative democracy and civil society perceived as a Western ruse to impose its geopolitical interests at the expense of the Russian nation? In other words, are Germany and its European partners prepared to set the Ukraine crisis in the context of President Putin's "bigger geopolitical goal to tear up the continent's post-communist settlement"[65] U.S. President George H.W. Bush termed "a continent that is diverse yet whole [and free]"?[66]

Germans are deeply ambivalent about their growing role in Europe and generally uncomfortable talking about leadership. The shadows of history weigh on Germany more heavily than on any other big European country. The country's two attempts at projecting power since its unification in 1871 by the Kaiser Reich and the Dritte Reich in particular ended in disaster and catastrophe.[67] Just mentioning the German

---

[60] The Federal Chancellor (2015b), Smale (2015). See also Auswärtiges Amt (2015a), Bundesministerium der Verteidigung (2015).

[61] For a fundamentally different assessment see Hill and Gaddy (2015), Mearsheimer (2015), Sanders (2015).

[62] The White House (2015), Jaffe (2015), Davis and Higgins (2015), Schmemann (2015).

[63] Former Secretary of Defense Leon Panetta put it this way: ". . .when you are dealing with somebody like Putin, the only thing he understands is hard power. . . .At some point, we are going to draw a line." Former U.S. Permanent Representative to NATO, Ivo Daalder, concluded, "Mr. Putin will settle only when the costs of continuing the war are too high. Supplying arms to Ukraine will ease the costs to Russia, increasing the likelihood that a real settlement can be negotiated." 'You Have To Deal with Russians from Strength', *Spiegel Online*, February 14, 2015 [http://www.spiegel.de/international/world/former-us-defense-secretary-leon-panetta-discusses-putin-crisis-a-1018325.html]; Daalder (2015).

[64] Gaddis (1982, pp. 83, 85, 86, 88, 89–109).

[65] Stephens (2015a, b), Rachman (2015a), Snyder (2015), Nekrasov (2015).

[66] U.S. Diplomatic Mission in Germany (1989).

[67] Winkler (2006, 2007).

word Hegemon, let alone the taboo word Führer (leader), and German politicians' blood runs cold. They prefer to talk about "responsibility" rather than "power", about "Europe, peace, multilateralism and cooperation" rather than national interests or power politics. Chancellor Merkel described the concept of hegemony as "totally foreign to me".[68] Defense Minister von der Leyen concluded that the Berlin Republic needs to exercise leadership that "represents [its] political culture in the 21st century: It is leadership from the centre." But the necessity to lead from the centre is relativized by the lesson "our people have learned" from the "painful history in the 20th century" that has become part of "our DNA": "to think twice".[69] Leading from the centre, Berlin wants to engage "earlier, more decisively, and more substantively" by using "our diplomatric toolbox…for productive initiatives."[70] Leadership from the centre underlines the self-image of Germany's preferred role in international affairs as a "civilian power" who actively promotes the "civilizing" of international relations, yet is highly wary about the logic of power politics in international relations and highly reluctant about the use of armed force as a basic tool of foreign policy,[71] as the current diplomatic engagement of Chancellor Merkel and Foreign Minister Steinmeier in negotiating a ceasefire agreement in Ukraine or the talks about constraining Iran's nuclear program underline.

If Berlin resorts to military tools like currently in North Iraq, its role is limited to that of an enabler that provides the Kurds lethal defensive military assistance in their fight against the Islamic State (IS). But unlike France, Germany does not consider the dispatch of warplanes a useful option to defeat the IS or to join a multifront campaign in the Sahel against terror networks.[72] In short, Chancellor Merkel, like all her predecessors, painstakingly avoids any impression of German hyperpuissance or Überpower.[73] The Berlin Republic has become Europe's economic powerhouse, but it lacks "both the broad political base and the cultural or 'soft' dimensions of power"[74] necessary to assume a confident and self-assured leadership role in and outside of Europe. Berlin's allies and partners should therefore "not expect too much too soon" from the central power still being held captive by "a culture of atonement".[75]

The glaring gap between what Germany should do and what it is willing to do unveils the structural problem German decision makers are confronted with since the end of the cold war. The weight of the new realities confronts the Berlin

[68] Thurau (2013), Beddoes (2013).

[69] Bundesministerium der Verteidigung (2015).

[70] Auswärtiges Amt (2014, 2015b), Auswärtiges Amt (2015c, pp. 5–13, 43–47).

[71] Kirste and Maull (1996, pp. 297, 300–301), Maull and Harnisch (2001, pp. 3–5).

[72] Barluet (2015), Schmitt (2015).

[73] The term "hyperpusissance" had been introduced by former French Foreign Minister Hubert Védrine to characterize the pre-eminent role of the United States in the international system after the end of the Cold War. Védrine (2000). See also Joffe (2006).

[74] Markovits and Reich (1997, p. 3).

[75] The Economist (2015c).

Republic with new responsibilities which the Bonn Republic did not have to care about. Gone are the days when simply being rather than doing was the essence of Germany's membership in NATO. As result of the fundamentally changed security environment and its different demands posed on German security and defence policy, the two core elements of Germany's foreign and security policy—multilateral cooperation and the culture of reticence—no longer complement and reinforce each other.[76] The Berlin Republic is in an "unenviable predicament": it "is caught between the Scylla of collective memory which will not permit it to exercise power in a normal manner, and the Charybdis of contemporary exigencies, which demand German acceptance of its responsibilities in Europe and maybe even in the world."[77] When it comes to geopolitics, Germany prefers the opposite role of a "reluctant hegemon", "strategic slumber" or "benign geopolitical power" with a penchant for soft power and a visceral aversion to the use of military force as an instrument of foreign and security policy.[78] The danger is no longer from German tanks and guns but "from the insistent effort to abstain from the exercise of power." Germans prefer an ideal international role for the Berlin Republic that remains loyal to the basic tenet of the Bonn Republic: a Switzerland writ large.[79] Germany's structural power emanates from the size and strength of its economy and resulting patterns of commerce. The Deutschmark became the symbol of successful reconstruction, political and moral rehabilitation, German probity, industriousness and economic success. This structural power involves the capacity to set agendas and to use the country's resources to guide Europe according to the ordoliberal principles that had served Germany so well since its founding in 1949.[80]

In sum, the cautious and reluctant exercise of military power, together with the assertive use of economic power to urge others to emulate the German economic model or else meet with German disapproval, are the two sides of German exceptionalism. But the modus operandi of how military and economic power is exercised differs. The shining city upon the hill seeks to avoid involvement in actions that include the use of military force particularly in heavy ground-combat operations (Germany as a reluctant power), but is assertive when it comes to enforcing the country's culture of stability on its European partners whose economic policies the German public, and especially the Bundesbank distrusted (Germany as an assertive power). The Berlin Republic has established itself as Europe's economic powerhouse, but it resists the temptation of a would-be "geo-economic semi-hegemon" to use its economic leverage to advance strategic interests even

---

[76] Meiers (2006, p. 359), Meiers (2007, pp. 623–644), Meiers (2008a, pp. 99–114), Meiers (2008b).

[77] Markovits and Reich (1997, p. 7).

[78] Techau (2013a, b), The Economist (2013b), Paterson (2011, p. 74), Kundnani (2011, p. 43), Kundnani (2012), Freedland (2012), Speck (2012, p. 4), Bittner (2013), Grant (2014), Winkler (2014).

[79] Markovits and Reich (1997, p. 6). See also Berger (1998), Duffield (1998), Banchoff (1999), Longhurst (2004), Nielsen (2006).

[80] Hanrieder (1989, pp. 224, 228). See also Baker et al. (1981), Rohrlich (1987, pp. 61–93).

with the risk of a disastrous conflict with its European partners. There is no sign that Germany's leadership-by-default is determined to use its "economic means in a way that seems more Clausewitzian than Kantian" which effectively replaces "the network structure" of the EU by "a kind of hub-and-spoke relational structure."[81] Berlin's new influence in Europe is limited to the economic realm. Even in its domaine réserve, Europe's leading power depends on the collaboration of its European partners to preserve the achievements of the European project and to deepen the Union further. "Germany must convince rather than dictate. It is just as dependent on Europe as Greece", the German daily Süddeutsche Zeitung succinctly put it.[82]

5.3 Germany's Changing European Vocation

Lastly, a narrative has been cultivated that the central power is moving away from the country's traditional European vocation. Contrary to the predictions of the neorealist school of international relations that Germany would undergo a pronounced change characterised by much greater autonomy and unilateralism, even to the extent that the German government would acquire nuclear weapons,[83] Germany's foreign and security policy has been marked by a high degree of continuity. The Berlin Republic remains committed to, and embedded in, a dense web of multinational institutions, namely NATO and the EU. European integration, the transatlantic link, and the commitment to multilateral cooperation continue to be the guiding principles of the foreign and security policy of the Berlin Republic. Germany's unequivocal commitment to the European integration process was anchored in the constitution when Article 23 of the Basic Law was amended to include commitments to developments of the European Union and "the realisation of a united Europe". The European Union will remain the "major reference frame"[84] of the foreign policy of the Berlin Republic.

While the thrust of Germany's foreign policy has not changed, its role within the European Union did change. Former Foreign Minister Hans-Dietrich Genscher often cited Thomas Mann's famous phrase that a European Germany is preferable to a German Europe. However, as Germany's resources grew, so did its ability to "Germanize Europe". Since unification Germany's Europe policy became more "British",[85] that is a more forceful articulation of German interests and a more assertive German leadership role to use the greater power resources as leverage to

[81] Kundnani (2014, pp. 104, 111), Feldstein (1997).

[82] Quoted in Crossland (2012).

[83] See, for example, Mearsheimer (2001, pp. 393–395).

[84] Bagger (2015, p. 32). See also Steinmeier (2015).

[85] The term "British" has been introduced by Hans-Friedrich von Ploetz, former State Secretary within the Foreign Office. See Hort (1997).

push for preferred German policy outcomes.[86] The Merkel government saw the euro crisis as a political opportunity to rectify the shortcomings of EMU's institutional architecture in accordance with the core principles of the German ordoliberal economic model. Her pragmatic compliance with orderliberal principles reveals one of the fundamental problems of Merkel's euro crisis management. Since its founding, Germany has had two overriding strategic objectives: sound money and European integration. The euro crisis brought these two twin imperatives into conflict with each other.[87] The necessity to choose between the two bedrock principles of Germany's foreign policy confronted German decision makers with unenviable predicament whether they give priority to the country's "reflexive commitment to institution building"[88] or the "ingrained" beliefs and convictions of Germany's culture of stability. In cases where core principles of Germany's ordoliberal economic model were challenged, Merkel stood up and stubbornly insisted on the abidance of the red lines set by the German ordoliberal economic model. Only when confronted with the imminent threat of the euro going over the cliffs in spring 2010 and summer 2012, she deviated from ordoliberal orthodoxy in favour of an incremental policy which acquiesced to the urgent need of common actions for the weak southern tier economies, but only under the condition of solidity in return for solidarity. However, her minimalist approach has been a day late and a euro short. The ECB's OMT program did not solve the crisis; it only provided the euro member countries some time to address the structural problems the crisis laid open.

Lastly, the euro crisis caused a sweeping change of one central feature of Germany's Europe policy. Unlike her onetime mentor Helmut Kohl[89] and her Finance Minister Wolfgang Schäuble,[90] Merkel does not see herself as the guardian of a federalist Europe with a European Commission transcending into a European government, a Eurozone economic governance behind a budget chief and a "Eurozone parliament". In her world, there is a central role of national governments and intergouvernmentalism.[91] Merkel is protective of Germany's freedom of action; unwilling to sacrifice national sovereignty to collective action, wary of risk-sharing elements and staunchly opposed to anything that smells of a transfer union. Her "politics of small, incremental steps" strives for increasing coordination at the intergovernmental level, not centralizing decision making in the European Commission or the ECB. When Merkel talks about "more Europe", she means "tackling the causes of the crisis", not the adoption of "communitization" measures

---

[86] Dyson (1994, p. 149), Crawford (2007, pp. 15, 175, 176, 186).

[87] Wolf (2010), Mayer (2015).

[88] Anderson and Goodman (1993, pp. 60, 62).

[89] For Kohl's scathing critique of Germany's foreign policy in general and Merkel's handling of the euro crisis in particular see his interview (Internationale Politik 2011, pp. 10–17).

[90] Schäuble and Lamers (1994, pp. 271–280), Schäuble (2012, 2014a, b, c).

[91] Bundeskanzlerin (2011).

which in her opinion are not "doable" under the German constitution.[92] In short, the member states should remain in firm control when it comes to the next major steps toward a closer economic and monetary union.

Merkel's pivot away from Germany's traditional policy on Europe can easily be misunderstood. Germany's dominant role in the euro crisis management is not another sign of "a creeping de-Westernization" of the Berlin Republic, not a metamorphosis of Germany's "long road west" from an "imperative" to "a choice", as Hans Kundnani argues.[93] Chancellor Merkel is still strongly committed to the preservation of the European integration process and the monetary union, but with one qualified reservation: on German terms. Her game plan aims at a return to a refurbished Maastricht treaty, not a push forward to a fiscal union.[94] "More Europe" that ensures national decision-making control is her categorical imperative. Another driving force of Merkel's behavior during the euro crisis is the German creed which coalesced into a single policy. "What is good for Germany is good for Europe", the Chancellor revealingly said in a speech to the Bundestag on (2014, September 11). All European partners will gain if they emulate the German social market economy model seen as the beacon to the world. In short, there are ideational, not "realist"[95] factors which best explain Germany's policy in Europe. To understand fully the course and consequences of German policy in Europe it is thus indispensable "to examine the domestic political dynamics of the country", particularly the culture of stability deeply engrained within the German economic policy establishment.[96] There are deep cultural differences the euro crisis has brought to light once again, as Jürgen Stark rightly observed. But if "others were living beyond their means, [while] Germany avoided excesses", one begins to wonder how these "cultural peculiarities" can be adjusted in such a way that the German view of a reformed euro area as a Disziplin union is accepted everywhere as the only way forward.[97] Stark's observation together with Merkel's preference for intergovernmental cooperation along the lines of a refurbished Maastricht Treaty have two simple flaws: there is no consensus among the member countries to act in a way that is consistent with the needs of a monetary union. The call for a "central fiscal stabiliser" with "central intervention and control rights" is as a contentious within the Union as the call for "common fiscal arrangements".[98] The federal government, together with the critical domestic veto players do not agree to a genuine "transfer union" as "the great leap forward" because they suspect that the spendthrift cultures of the warm-water countries Portugal, Italy, Greece and Spain,

---

[92] Deutscher Bundestag (2012a, p. 22225), Deutscher Bundestag (2012b, p. 21863).

[93] Kundnani (2014, p. 114).

[94] Kirkegaard (2013), Davies (2013), The Economist (2013c), Barker (2013), Münchau (2013).

[95] Kundnani (2014, p. 6).

[96] Nielsen (2006, p. 3). See also Meiers (2006, pp. 352–353, 355–356).

[97] Stark (2015).

[98] Deutsche Bundesbank (2015), Bank of England (2015). See also European Central Bank (2014g, 2015d).

the so-called PIGS, are incompatible with Germany's culture of stability.[99] Secondly, Merkel's incremental policymaking prevented the currency union from collapsing, but failed to put it on a sound and sustainable basis. Her preference for national decision-making control has reinforced the root cause of the euro crisis: the fundamental contradiction between a supranational currency and the preservation of the prerogatives of the nation state in economic, fiscal and social policies within a highly heterogeous political and economic environment that generated a multitude of unintended consequences with unforeseen costs.[100]

References

Alderman, L. (2014, December 18). European markets eye on austerity weary Greece. *New York Times*.

Auswärtiges Amt (2014, February 1). Speech by Federal Minister of Foreign Affairs, Dr. Frank-Walter Steinmeier, at the occasion of the 50th Munich Security Conference, Munich. http://www.auswaertiges-amt.de/EN/Infoservice/Presse/Reden/2014/140201-BM_M%C3%BCSiKo.html

Auswärtiges Amt (2015a, February 8). Speech by Federal Foreign Minister Frank-Walter Steinmeier at the 51st Munich Security, Munich. http://www.auswaertiges-amt.de/EN/Infoservice/Presse/Reden/2015/150208_MueSiKo.html

Auswärtiges Amt (2015b, February 25). Speech by Foreign Minister Frank-Walter Steinmeier at the closing event of 'Review 2014 – A Fresh Look at German Foreign Policy', Berlin. http://www.auswaertiges-amt.de/EN/Infoservice/Presse/Reden/2015/150225-BM_Review_Abschlussveranstaltung.html?nn=699270

Auswärtiges Amt (2015c, February). Review 2014 – Crisis order Europe. Berlin. http://www.auswaertiges-amt.de/cae/servlet/contentblob/699442/publicationFile/202977/Schlussbericht.pdf

Anderson, J. J., & Goodman, J. B. (1993). Mars or minerva? A United Germany, in a post-cold war Europe. In R. O. Keohane, J. S. Nye, & S. Hoffmann (Eds.), *After the cold war. International institutions and state strategies in Europe, 1989–1991*. Cambridge, MA: Harvard University Press.

Bagger, T. (2015). The German moment in a fragile world. *The Washington Quarterly, 37*(4), 25–35.

Baker, K., Dalton, R. J., & Hildebrandt, K. (1981). *Germany transformed*. Cambridge, MA: Harvard University Press.

Banchoff, T. (1999). *The German problem transformed. Institutions, politics and foreign policy, 1945–1995*. Ann Arbor, MI: University of Michigan Press.

Bank of England. (2015, January 28). *Fortune favours the bold*. Speech given by Mark Carney, Governor of the Bank of England, Lecture to honour the memory of The Honourable James Michael Flaherty, P.C., Dublin. http://www.bankofengland.co.uk/publications/Documents/speeches/2015/speech794.pdf

Barber, T. (2014, September 12). The gulf in budget discipline between Paris and Berlin. *Financial Times*.

Barker, T. (2013, October 24). Imperial life in the Merkel republic. *The National Interest*. http://nationalinterest.org/commentary/imperial-life-the-merkel-republic-9297

[99] Rachman (2015b), Mayer (2015).

[100] Enderlein (2015, pp. 31, 34, 39), Enderlein and Fritz-Vannahme (2014, pp. 14–20).

Barkin, N. (2014, May 13). Partnership in peril, even with a smile. *International New York Times*.
Barluet, A. (2015, February 23). La France engage le porte-avions «Charles-de-Gaulle» contre l'État islamique. *Le Figaro*. http://www.lefigaro.fr/flash-actu/2015/02/23/97001-20150223FILWWW00042-la-france-engage-le-porte-avions-charles-de-gaulle-contre-l-etat-islamique.php
Beddoes, Z. M. (2013, June 15). Europe's reluctant hegemon. *The Economist*. http://www.economist.com/node/21579140
Berger, T. U. (1998). *Cultures of antimilitarism. National security in Germany and Japan*. Baltimore, MD: The Johns Hopkins University Press.
Bernanke, B. (1995). The macroeconomics of the great depression: A comparative approach. *Journal of Money, Credit, and Banking, 27*(1), 1–28.
Bilfesky, D., & Alderman, L. (2014, August 26). French cabinet is dissolved, a victim of austerity. *New York Times*.
Bittner, J. (2013, November 4). Rethinking German pacifism. *New York Times*.
Blome, N., Müller, P., Reiermann, C., Schmitz, G. P., & Schult, C. (2014, January 2). Merkel clashes with EU commission. *Spiegel Online*. http://www.spiegel.de/international/europe/relations-worsen-between-angela-merkel-and-european-commission-a-941243.html
Spiegel Staff (2015, January 30). Could Tsirpas' win upset balance of power in Europe? *Spiegel Online*. http://www.spiegel.de/international/europe/greek-election-makes-euro-zone-exit-real-possibility-a-1015907.html
Buck, T. (2015, February 20). Spanish politics: Podemos' populist surge. *Financial Times*.
Bundeskanzlerin. (2011, November 2). Merkel's speech at the occasion of the 61st academic year of the College of Europe in Bruges. http://m.bundeskanzlerin.de/ContentArchiv/DE/Archiv17/Reden/2010/11/2010-11-02-merkel-bruegge.html?nn=819844
Bundesministerium der Verteidigung. (2014a, January 31). Speech by Federal Minister of Defense, Dr. Urusla von der Leyen, at the occasion of the 50th Munich Security Conference, Munich. https://www.securityconference.de/fileadmin/MSC_/2014/Reden/2014-01-31_Rede_BMin_von_der_Leyen_MSC_2014.pdf
Bundesministerium der Verteidigung. (2014b, August 31). *Pressestatements der Bundesministerin der Verteidigung und des Bundesaußenministers im Bendlerblock*. Berlin http://www.bmvg.de/portal/a/bmvg/
Bundesministerium der Verteidigung. (2015, February 6). Speech by the Federal Minister of Defense, Dr. Ursula von der Leyen, on the Occasion of the 51st Munich Security Conference, Munich. http://www.bmvg.de/portal/a/bmvg
Buttiglione, L., Lane, P., Reichlin, L., & Reinhart, V. (2014, September 29). *Deleveraging, what deleveraging? The 16th Geneva report on the world economy*. Geneva: International Center for Monetary and Banking Studies (ICMB). http://www.voxeu.org/sites/default/files/image/FromMay2014/Geneva16.pdf
Calvo, G. (2014, January 13). On the road to double-dipped recession or deflation? *The Economist*. http://www.economnist.com/node/21593574
Carnegy, H. (2014, July 25). François Hollande mood frays over stalled economy. *Financial Times*.
Center for Economic Policy Research. (2014, June 16). *Euro area business cycle dating: Euro area mired in recession pause*. London. http://www.cepr.org/sites/default/files/EABCD%2020140611%20Findings.pdf
Charrel, M. (2015, February 14). La zone euro n'a pas retrouvé son PIB d'avant la crise, *Le Monde*. http://www.lemonde.fr/economie/article/2015/02/14/la-zone-euro-n-a-pas-retrouve-son-pib-d-avant-crise_4576626_3234.html#hY0oOvzqcT2zMo73.99
Cohen, R. (2013, September 24). Merkel the great. *New York Times*.
Coppola, F. (2015, January 8). Why QE won't resolve the eurozone's fundamental money problem. *Financial Times*. http://blog.ft.com/the-exchange/2015/01/08/why-qe-wont-resolve-eurozones-fundamental-money-problem/?

Crawford, B. (2007). *Power and German foreign policy: Embedded hegemony in Europe*. Basingstoke: Palgrave Macmillan.
Crossland, D. (2012, February 1). Germany's power 'Is causing fear' in Europe. *Spiegel Online*. http://www.spiegel.de/international/europe/the-world-from-berlin-germany-s-power-is-causing-fear-in-europe-a-812715.html
Daalder, I. (2015, January 28). Arms Ukraine and show Russia that conflict has a cost. *Financial Times*.
Davies, G. (2013, September 16). Angela Merkel – lame duck or savior of the euro? *Financial Times*.
Davis, J. H., & Higgins, A. (2015, February 10). U.S. leaves option of arming Kiev on the table. *International New York Times*.
de Grauwe, P. (2014, January 16). Should we worry about deflation? *The Economist*. http://economist.com/node/21593980
Der Bundespräsident. (2014, January 31). *Germany's role in the world: reflection on responsibility, norms, and alliances*. Federal President Joachim Gauck to open the 50th Munich Security Conference, Munich. http://www.bundespraesident.de/SharedDocs/Reden/EN/JoachimGauck/Reden/2014/140131-Munich-Security-Conference.html;jsessionid=F8849BDED7E7AB5E4B885ECBAC69EC8F.2_cid293?nn=1891680
Deubner, C. (2011, April). *Der deutsche und französische Weg aus der Finanzkrise*. DGAP-Analyse No. 2. Berlin: Deutsche Gesellschaft für Auswärtige Politik.
Deutsche Bundesbank. (2014, December 28). *'Am Ende haften wir alle für die Verluste'*, Interview mit Bundesbankpräsident Jens Weidmann mit der Frankfurter Allgemeinen Sonntagszeitung. http://www.bundesbank.de/Redaktion/DE/Interviews/2014_12_28_weidmann_fas.html
Deutsche Bundesbank. (2015, February 12). *Heading for stability and prosperity – Bringing the euro area back on track*. Keynote speech by Dr. Jens Weidmann given at the City of London Corporation, London. http://www.bundesbank.de/Redaktion/EN/Reden/2015/2015_02_12_weidmann.html
Deutscher Bundestag. (2012a, June 27). *Plenarprotokoll 17/186*. Berlin. p. 22225. http://dipbt.bundestag.de/dip21/btp/17/17186.pdf
Deutscher Bundestag. (2012b, June 14). *Plenarprotokoll 17/184*. p. 21863.
Deutschlandradio. (2014, June 14). 'Deutschland steht an der Seite der Unterdrückten', Joachim Gauck talks with Joachim Wiese. *Deutschlandradio Kultur*. http://www.deutschlandradiokultur.de/norwegen-reise-deutschland-steht-an-der-seite-der.1008.de.html?dram:article_id=289135
Die Bundeskanzlerin. (2014, July 2). *Pressekonferenz von Bundeskanzlerin Merkel und dem Nato-Generalsekretär Rasmussen*. Berlin. http://www.bundeskanzlerin.de/Content/DE/Mitschrift/Pressekonferenzen/2014/07/2014-07-02-pk-merkel-rasmussen.html
Die Bundeskanzlerin. (2015, September 5). *Pressekonferenz von Bundeskanzlerin Merkel, Bundesaußenminister Steinmeier und Bundesverteidigungsministerin von der Leyen zur Teilnahme am NATO-Gipfeltreffen*. Newport/Wales. http://www.bundeskanzlerin.de/Content/DE/Mitschrift/Pressekonferenzen/2014/09/2014-09-05-pk-nato.html
Duffield, J. S. (1998). *World power forsaken. Political culture, international institutions, and German security policy after unification*. Stanford: Stanford University Press.
Dyson, K. (1994). *Elusive union: The process of economic and monetary union in Europe*. Harrow: Longman.
Eichengreen, B. (2014, November 18). A dance for the European debt burden will not last forever. *Financial Times*.
Eichengreen, B., & Panizza, U. (2014, July 30). *Can large primary surpluses solve Europe's debt problem?* London: Centre for Economic Policy Research. http://www.voxeu.org/article/can-large-primary-surpluses-solve-europe-s-debt-problem
Elysee. (2014, August 20). Interview de François Hollande accordée au Monde. [http://www.elysee.fr/interviews/article/interview-de-francois-hollande-accordee-au-monde

Enderlein, H. (2015). The Euro as a showcase for explanatory governance. In Hertie School of Governance (Ed.), *The governance report. Eurozone crisis, economic governance, institutional dilemmas, constitutionalism, indicators*. Oxford: Oxford University Press.

Enderlein, H., & Fritz-Vannahme, J. (2014). *Repair and prepare: Strengthening Europe's economies after the crisis*. Gütersloh: Bertelsmann Stiftung & Jacques Delors Institut – Berlin. https://www.bertelsmann-stiftung.de/fileadmin/files/user_upload/Pilot_Study_Repair_and_Prepare.pdf

Errera, G., & Ischinger, W. (2014, April 22). France and Germany must rebuild their relationship, for the good of Europe. *The Guardian*. http://www.theguardian.com/commentisfree/2014/apr/22/france-germany-rebuild-relationship-good-europe

European Central Bank. (2014a, May 8). *Introductory statement to the press conference by Mario Draghi*. Frankfurt am Main. http://www.ecb.europa.eu/press/pressconf/2014/html/is140508.en.html

European Central Bank. (2014b, September 22). *Introductory remarks by Mario Draghi at the EP's Economic and Monetary Affairs Committee*. Brussels. https://www.ecb.europa.eu/press/key/date/2014/html/sp140922.en.html

European Central Bank. (2014c, October 24). *Mario Draghi: Economic situation in the euro area*. Brussels. https://www.ecb.europa.eu/press/key/date/2014/html/sp141024_1.en.pdf?3ce4091c3fa5a2cf312d4895e1f52dd8

European Central Bank. (2014d, December). *December 2014 eurosystem staff macroeconomic projections of the euro area*. Frankfurt am Main. http://www.ecb.europa.eu/pub/pdf/other/eurosystemstaffprojections201412.en.pdf

European Central Bank. (2014e, May 26). *Monetary policy in a prolonged period of low inflation*. Speech by Mario Draghi, President of the ECB; at the ECB Forum on Central Banking, Sintra. http://www.ecb.europa.eu/press/key/date/2014/html/sp140526.en.html

European Central Bank. (2014f, August 22). Speech by Mario Draghi, president of the ECB, symposium in Jackson Hole. http://www.ecb.europa.eu/press/key/date/2014/html/sp140822.en.html

European Central Bank. (2014g, November 27). *Stability and prosperity in monetary union*. Speech by Mario Draghi, at the University of Helsinki, Helsinki. https://www.ecb.europa.eu/press/key/date/2014/html/sp141127_1.en.html

European Central Bank. (2015a, March 5). *Introductory statement to the press conference (with Q&A) by Mario Draghi*. Nicosia.

European Central Bank. (2015b, March). *March 2015 ECB staff macroeconomic projections for the euro area*. Frankfurt am Main. https://www.ecb.europa.eu/pub/pdf/other/ecbstaffprojections201503.en.pdf?7385bf4f8a3f4021928e832362e3da8e

European Central Bank. (2015c, April 14). *Economic bulletin 3/2015*. Frankfurt am Main. https://www.ecb.europa.eu/pub/pdf/ecbu/eb201503.en.pdf?3c926e02bc581974264bf28bcfb74f50

European Central Bank. (2015d, February 25). *Introductory statement to the European Parliament on the ECB annual report 2013*. Brussels. https://www.ecb.europa.eu/press/key/date/2015/html/sp150225.en.html

European Commission. (2013a, April 23). *Austerity growth debate: What President Barroso actually said at the Brussels think tank dialogue*. Brussels. http://europa.eu/rapid/press-release_MEMO-13-368_en.htm

European Commission. (2013b, May). Public opinion in the European Union, Standard Eurobarometer 79, Brussels. http://ec.europa.eu/public_opinion/archives/eb/eb79/eb79_first_en.pdf

European Commission. (2014a, November 4). *European economic forecast autumn 2014*. Brussels. http://ec.europa.eu/economy_finance/publications/european_economy/2014/pdf/ee7_en.pdf

European Commission. (2014b, February). *European economic forecast, winter 2014*. Brussels. http://ec.europa.eu/economy_finance/publications/european_economy/2014/pdf/ee2_en.pdf

European Commission. (2014c, March). *Special Eurobarometer 415, tables of results*. Brussels. http://ec.europa.eu/public_opinion/archives/ebs/ebs_415_data_en.pdf

European Commission. (2015, February 5). *Winter economic forecast: Outlook improved but risks remain*. Brussels. http://europa.eu/rapid/press-release_IP-15-4085_en.htm
European Parliament. (2014, May 27). *Results of the 2014 European elections*. http://www.results-elections2014.eu/en/election-results-2014.html
Eurostat. (2014a, December 8). *GDP and main components-volumes*. Luxembourg. http://appsso.eurostat.ec.europa.eu/nui/show.do?dataset=nama_gdp_k
Eurostat. (2014b, May 15). *Euro area GDP up by 0.2%, EU28 up by 0.3%*. Press Release 76/2014, Luxembourg. http://epp.eurostat.ec.europa.eu/cache/ITY_PUBLIC/2-15052014-AP/EN/2-15052014-AP-EN.PDF
Eurostat. (2014c, August 14). *GDP stable in the euro area and up by 0.2% in the EU28*. Press Release 125/2014, Luxembourg. http://epp.eurostat.ec.europa.eu/cache/ITY_PUBLIC/2-14082014-AP/EN/2-14082014-AP-EN.PDF
Eurostat. (2014d, November 14). *BIP im Euroraum um 0,2% und in der EU28 um 0,3% gestiegen*. Press Release 171/2014, Luxembourg. http://epp.eurostat.ec.europa.eu/cache/ITY_PUBLIC/2-14112014-AP/DE/2-14112014-AP-DE.PDF
Eurostat. (2014e, April 23). *Euro area and EU28 government deficit at 3.0% and 3.3% of GDP respectively*. News Release 64/2014, Luxembourg. http://epp.eurostat.ec.europa.eu/cache/ITY_PUBLIC/2-23042014-AP/EN/2-23042014-AP-EN.PDF
Eurostat. (2015a, March 6). *GDP up by 0.3% in the euro area and by 0.4% in the EU28*. Press Release 42/2015, Luxembourg. http://ec.europa.eu/eurostat/documents/2995521/6730965/2-06032015-AP-EN.pdf/27a0c028-e297-4350-b41d-2b5af66cdaf5
Eurostat. (2015b, April 30). *Euro area unemploymentrate at 11.3%, EU28 at 9.8%*. Press Release 76/2015, Luxembourg. http://ec.europa.eu/eurostat/documents/2995521/6807651/3-30042015-AP-EN.pdf/c619bed7-7d9d-4992-95c3-f84e91bfcc1d
Eurostat. (2015c, January 30). *Euro area annual inflation rate down to -0.6 percent*. Press Release 21/2015, Luxembourg. http://ec.europa.eu/eurostat/documents/2995521/6581740/2-30012015-BP-EN.pdf/d776fbcc-89b2-4bae-beb0-ad30fa709244
Eurostat. (2015d, April 30). *Inflation in the euro area*. Luxembourg. http://ec.europa.eu/eurostat/statistics-explained/index.php/Inflation_in_the_euro_area
Evans-Pritchard, A. (2014, June 9). ECB's deflation paralysis drives Italy, France and Spain into debt traps. *The Telegraph*. http://www.telegraph.co.uk/finance/comment/ambroseevans_pritchard/10740593/ECBs-deflation-paralysis-drives-Italy-France-and-Spain-into-debt-traps.html
Ewing, J., & Pianigiani, G. (2014, August 7). Slowdown in Italy adds to fears over Ukraine. *International New York Times*.
Federal Statistical Office. (2015, February 24). *Detailed gross domestic product results for the 4th quarter of 2014*. Press Release 061/2015-02-24, Wiesbaden. https://www.destatis.de/EN/PressServices/Press/pr/2015/02/PE15_61_811.html
Feldstein, M. (1997). EMU and international conflict. *Foreign Affairs, 76*(6), 60–76.
Financial Times. (2014a, August 9/10). Editorial: The end of Matteo Renzi's Italian honeymoon. *Financial Times*.
Financial Times. (2014b, December 30). A new deal for the euro must go far beyond QE. *Financial Times*.
Financial Times. (2015a, March 25). Europe is a waiting room thronging with the sick. *Financial Times*.
Financial Times. (2015b, February 21). Greek prime minister's statement. *Financial Times*. http://www.ft.com/intl/cms/s/0/a8dab1de-b9e2-11e4-933f-00144feab7de.html
Fisher, I. (1933). *The debt deflation theory of great depressions*. http://fraser.stlouisfed.org/docs/Meltzer/fisdeb33.pdf
Freedland, J. (2012, March 16). Germany, Europe's reluctant Goliath, is hiding its true strength. *The Guardian*. http://www.theguardian.com/commentisfree/2012/mar/16/germany-reluctant-goliath-eurozone-shadow
Gaddis, J. L. (1982). *Strategies of containment. A critical appraisal of postwar American national security policy*. New York: Oxford University Press.

German Federal Statistical Office. (2015, February 13). *Gross domestic product increased considerably in 4th quarter of 2014*. Press Release 048/2015-02-13. https://www.destatis.de/EN/PressServices/Press/pr/2015/02/PE15_048_811.html;jsessionid=3434C401A88197BE8679CA532FE6A16E.cae3

German Marshall Fund of the United States. (2014, September). *Transatlantic trends. Key findings*. Washington, DC. http://trends.gmfus.org/files/2012/09/Trends_2014_complete.pdf

Glomb, W. (2011). *Le tandem franco-allemand face à la crise de l' Euro*. Paris: Foundation pour l' Innovation Politique.

Goulard, S. (2012, May). *Frankreich und Deutschland angesichts der Euro-Krise*. DGAP-Analyse No. 6. Berlin: Deutsche Gesellschaft für Auswärtige Politik.

Grant, C. (2014, May 6). *What is wrong with German foreign policy?* Centre for European Studies, London. http://www.cer.org.uk/insights/what-wrong-german-foreign-policy

Group of Twenty. (2014a, September 20). *Global prospects and policy challenges*. G20 Finance Ministers and Central Bank Governors Meeting, Cairns, Australia. http://www.imf.org/external/np/g20/pdf/2014/091714.pdf

Group of Twenty. (2014b, October). *World economic outlook. Legacies, clouds, uncertainties*. Washington, DC. http://www.imf.org/external/pubs/ft/weo/2014/02/pdf/c1.pdf

Hanrieder, W. F. (1989). *Germany, America, Europe: Forty years of German foreign policy*. New Haven, CT: Yale University Press.

Headquarters 1 (German/Netherlands) Corps. (2014, December 18). *1 (GE/NL) corps ready For NRF 15*. Münster. http://1gnc.org/archive/news/singleview/eintrag/496/

Hill, F., & Gaddy, C. (2015, February 5). How aiding the Ukrainian military could push Putin into a regional war. *Washington Post*. http://www.washingtonpost.com/opinions/giving-weapons-to-ukraine-could-goad-putin-into-a-regional-war/2015/02/05/ec2e9680-abf5-11e4-ad71-7b9eba0f87d6_story.html

Hope, K., & Moore, E. (2014, December 30). Fears for Greek crisis after poll called. *Financial Times*.

Hort, P. (1997, October 30). Die deutsche Europapolitik wird "britischer". Bonn stellt das Integrationsmodell in Frage und orientiert sich mehr und mehr an Kosten und Nutzen. *Frankfurter Allgemeine Zeitung*.

International Monetary Fund. (2014a, June 25). *Euro area policies*. IMF Country Report No. 14/198, Washington, DC. http://www.imf.org/external/pubs/ft/scr/2014/cr14198.pdf

International Monetary Fund. (2014b, January 21). *Transcript of a conference call on world economic outlook update*. Washington, DC. http://www.imf.org/external/np/tr/2014/tr012114.htm

International Monetary Fund. (2015, April 14). *World economic outlook. Uneven growth: Short- and long-term factors*. Washington, DC. http://www.imf.org/external/pubs/ft/weo/2015/01/pdf/c2.pdf

Irwin, N. (2014, December 30). Why Greece's new crisis isn't spreading to the rest of Europe. *International New York Times*.

J.P. Morgan Asset Management. (2015, January 19). *Weekly strategy report*. London. http://insights.jpmorgan.co.uk/adviser/commentary-and-analysis/weekly-strategy-report-19-january-2015/

Jaffe, G. (2015, February 9). Obama makes clear he is in no rush to push U.S. deeper into Ukraine conflict. *Washington Post*. http://www.washingtonpost.com/politics/obama-makes-clear-he-is-in-no-rush-to-push-us-deeper-into-ukraine-conflict/2015/02/09/44b228aa-b063-11e4-886b-c22184f27c35_story.html

Joffe, J. (2006). *Überpower. The imperial temptation of America*. New York: W.W. Norton.

Jolly, D. (2015, February 14). Eurozone growth exceeds expectations, led by strength in Germany. *New York Times*.

Jones, C. (2015a, March 24). Double digit unemployment predicted even if the eurozone recovers. *Financial Times*.

Jones, C. (2015b, January 5). Economists call for political action on eurozone. *Financial Times*.

Jones, C., & Thomson, A. (2014, August 15). Germany contracts and France stagnates second quarter. *Financial Times*.

Jones, C., & Wagstyl, S. (2014, November 15/16). Eurozone's return to growth fails to soothe concern. *Financial Times*.

Kauffmann, P., & Uterwedde, H. (2010, October 25). Verlorene Konvergenz? Deutschland und Frankreich und die Euro-Krise. *Aus Politik und Zeitgeschichte*, No. 43.

Kirkegaard, J. F. (2013, September 13). *Germany's sleepy but significant elections*. Peterson Institute for International Economics, Washington, DC. http://blogs.piie.com/realtime/?p=3996

Kirste, K., & Maull, H. W. (1996). Zivilmacht und Rollentheorie. *Zeitschrift für Internationale Beziehungen, 3*(2), 297. 300–301.

Kitsantonis, N., & Kanter, J. (2014, December 30). Europe braces for economic fallout as Greece heads to early elections. *International New York Times*.

Körber Stiftung (2014, May). *Einmischen oder Zurückhalten?* Ergebnisse einer repräsentativen Umfrage von TNS Infratest Politikforschung zur Sicht der Deutschen auf die Außenpolitik, Berlin. http://www.koerber-stiftung.de/umfrage-aussenpolitik

Internationale Politik. (2011). "Wir müssen wieder Zuversicht geben". Helmut Kohl über eine Außenpolitik, der es an Verläßlichkeit mangelt. *Internationale Politik, 66*(5), 10–17.

Krugman, P. (2015a, January 30). Europe's Greek test. *New York Times*.

Krugman, P. (2015b, February 9). Nobody understands debt. *New York Times*.

Kundnani, H. (2011). Germany as a geo-economic power. *Washington Quarterly, 34*(3), 31–45.

Kundnani, H. (2012, May 4). What hegemon? Germany's self-centeredness and short-term thinking disqualify it as a hegemon. *Internationale Politik*. https://ip-journal.dgap.org/en/ip-journal/topics/what-hegemon

Kundnani, H. (2014). *The paradox of German power*. London: C. Hurst.

Laggard, C. (2014, January 15). *The global economy in 2014, national press club*. Washington, DC. http://www.imf.org/external/np/speeches/2014/011514.htm

Le Monde. (2014, August 15). Croissance zéro en France au deuxième trimestre. *Le Monde*.

Longhurst, K. (2004). *Germany and the use of force*. Manchester: Manchester University Press.

MacDonough, G. (2013, June 25). What happened in Europe? *New York Times*.

Markovits, A. S., & Reich, S. (1997). *The German predicament. Memory and power in the New Europe*. Ithaca, NY: Cornell University Press.

Maull, H. W., & Harnisch, S. (2001). Introduction. In S. Harnisch & H. W. Maull (Eds.), *Germany as civilian power? The foreign policy of the Berlin Republic*. Manchester: Manchester University Press.

Mayer, T. (2015, January 30). Carney is wrong about how to solve Europe's problems. *Financial Times*.

Mazower, M. (2015, January 31/February 1). European democracy enters dangerous times. *Financial Times*.

Mearsheimer, J. J. (2001). *The tragedy of great power politics*. New York: W.W. Norton.

Mearsheimer, J. J. (2015, February 9). Don't arm Ukraine. *International New York Times*.

Meiers, F.-J. (2006). *Zu neuen Ufern. Die deutsche Sicherheits- und Verteidigungspolitik in einer Welt des Wandels 1990–2000*. Paderborn: Schöningh.

Meiers, F.-J. (2007). The German predicament: The red lines of the security and defence policy of the Berlin Republic. *International Politics, 44*(5), 623–644.

Meiers, F.-J. (2008a). La politique allemande de sécurité et de défense. Equilibrer durablement les attentes extérieures et les contraintes intérieures. In C. Demesmay & H. Stark (Eds.), *Radioscopies de l'Allemagne 2008*. Paris: Institut français des relations internationales.

Meiers, F.-J. (2008b, June). *Crossing the red lines? The grand coalition and the paradox of German foreign policy*. Washington, DC: The Johns Hopkins University/American Institute for Contemporary German Studies, Policy Report No. 32.

Ministry of Foreign Affairs of the Republic of Poland. (2011, November 28). *Poland and the future of the European Union*. Speech of Mr. Radek Sikorski, Foreign Minister of Poland, to the German Council on Foreign Relations, Berlin. http://www.mfa.gov.pl/resource/33ce6061-ec12-4da1-a145-01e2995c6302:JCR

Moghadam, R., Teja, R., & Berkmen, P. (2014, January 16). *Euro- area – "deflation" versus lowflation*. Posted by IMFdirect. http://blog-imfdirect.imf.org/2014/03/04/euro-area-deflation-versus-lowflation/

Münchau, W. (2013, December 1). Germany's coalition will have to break promises. *Financial Times*.

Münchau, W. (2014, September 22). Italy debt burden is a problem for us all. *Financial Times*.

Münchau, W. (2015, January 5). Political extremists may be the eurozone's saviours. *Financial Times*.

NATO. (1997, May 27). *Founding act on mutual relations, cooperation and security between NATO and the Russian Federation signed in Paris, France*. Brussels. http://www.nato.int/cps/en/natohq/official_texts_25468.htm

NATO. (2014, September). *Wales summit declaration*. Newport, Wales, § 8. http://www.nato.int/cps/en/natohq/official_texts_112964.htm?mode=pressrelease

Nekrasov, A. (2015, March 30). Russia looks to its history in search of a new ideology. *Financial Times*.

Nielsen, A.-D. (2006). *Germany, pacifism and peace enforcement*. Manchester: Manchester University Press.

Organization for Economic Cooperation and Development. (2014a, November 25). *Putting the euro area on a road to recovery*. Presentation of the OECD Economic Outlook by Catherine L. Mann, OECD Chief Economist, Paris. http://www.oecd.org/eco/outlook/economicoutlook.html

Organization for Economic Cooperation and Development. (2014b, November 6). *Advance G-20 release: OECD economic report*. Paris. http://www.oecd.org/eco/outlook/G20-economic-projections-handout.pdf

Organization for Economic Cooperation and Development. (2014c, September 15). *Interim economic assessment*. Paris. http://www.oecd.org/eco/outlook/Interim-Assessment-Handout-Sep-2014.pdf

Organization for Economic Cooperation and Development. (2014d, May 6). *OECD economic outlook* (Vol. 2014, Issue 1). Paris. http://www.oecd-ilibrary.org/economics/oecd-economic-outlook-volume-2014-issue-1_eco_outlook-v2014-1-en

Organization for Economic Cooperation and Development. (2015a, March 18). *Interim economic assessment*. Paris. http://www.oecd.org/eco/outlook/Interim-Assessment-Handout-Mar-2015.pdf

Organization for Economic Cooperation and Development. (2015b, March 18). *Interim economic outlook press conference with Catherine L. Mann, OECD Chief Economist*. Paris. http://www.oecd.org/economy/outlook/economicoutlook.htm

Patterson, W. E. (2011). The reluctant hegemon. *Journal of Common Market Studies, 49*, 74.

Peel, Q. (2014, August 12). Merkel wants a stable world and is willing to pay a price. *Financial Times*.

Peel, Q., & Carnegy, H. (2012, October 17). Rifts emerge as Berlin puts fiscal union centre stage. *Financial Times*.

Peel, Q., & Carnegy, H. (2013, January 20). Europe: an uneven entente. *Financial Times*.

Peet, J., & La Guardia, A. (2014). *Unhappy union: How the Euro crisis – and Europe – can be fixed*. London: Profile Books Ltd.

Pew Research Global Attitudes Project. (2013, May 13). *The new sick man of Europe: The European Union*. Washington, DC. http://www.pewglobal.org/2013/05/13/the-new-sick-man-of-europe-the-european-union/

Plender, J. (2014, December 24). Oil fall adds to ECB's deflation worries. *Financial Times*.

Rachman, G. (2014, December 30). Eurozone's weakest link is the voters. *Financial Times*.

Rachman, G. (2015a, March 3). Vladimir Putin's survival strategy is lies and violence. *Financial Times.*
Rachman, G. (2015b, February 24). A Greek deal cannot fix the flaws in the euro. *Financial Times.*
Rohrlich, P. E. (1987). Economic culture and foreign policy: The cognitive analysis of economic policy making. *International Organization, 41*(1), 61–93.
Samuelson, R. J. (2015, January 7). Europe's unending crisis. *Washington Post.* http://www.washingtonpost.com/opinions/robert-samuelson-europes-unending-crisis/2015/01/07/7bdd0650-9688-11e4-927a-4fa2638cd1b0_story.html
Sanders, P. J. (2015, February 12). 5 reasons arming Ukraine won't work. *National Interest.* http://nationalinterest.org/feature/5-reasons-arming-ukraine-won%E2%80%99t-work-12234
Sanderson, R., & Segreti, G. (2014, August 7). Renzi's economic strategy questioned as GDP shrinks. *Financial Times.*
Schäuble, W. (2012, May 17). Speech at the occasion of the Karls Prize Award, Aachen. http://www.karlspreis.de/preistraeger/2012/rede_von_dr_wolfgang_schaeuble.html
Schäuble, W. (2014a, March 27). *Strategies for European recovery.* College of Europe, Bruges. http://www.bundesfinanzministerium.de/Content/EN/Reden/2014/2014-03-27-bruges.html
Schäuble, W. (2014b, May 27). *Die Lage in Europa: Welche Governance braucht die Europäische Union?* Hertie School of Governance, Berlin. http://www.bundesfinanzministerium.de/Content/DE/Reden/2014/2014-05-27-rede-hertie-school.html?view=render
Schäuble, W. (2014c, December 12). Das europäische Modell mit wirtschaftlicher Stärke untermauern. *Frankfurter Allgemeine Zeitung.*
Schäuble, W., & Lamers, K. (1994, September 1). Überlegungen zur europäischen Politik. Position paper of the CDU/CSU Parlamentarian Group, Bonn. Reprinted in *Blätter für Deutsche und Internationale Politik*, Vol. 39, No. 1, October 1994, pp. 271–280.
Schild, J. (2013). Germany, France, and the management of the Euro crisis. *German Politics and Society, 31*(1), 24–47.
Schmemann, S. (2015, February 11). United against Putin, divided on how to stop him. *International New York Times.*
Schmitt, E. (2015, March 16). Leading role for France as Africa battles back. *International New York Times.*
Schwarzer, D. (2012, Juli–September). La gouvernance èconomique en Europe au point de vue franco-allemenand. *Allemagne aujordhui*, No. 201.
Schwarzer, D., & Land, K.-O. (2012, October 2). The myth of German hegemony. Why Berlin can't save Europe alone. *Foreign Affairs.* http://www.foreignaffairs.com/articles/138162/daniela-schwarzer-and-kai-olaf-lang/the-myth-of-german-hegemony
Sierakowski, S. (2014, August 23/24). NATO's second class members. *International New York Times.*
Smale, A. (2014, August 20). Obama sidelined, Merkel takes lead in the Ukrainian crisis. *International New York Times.*
Smale, A. (2015, February 9). On Ukraine, two different lessons from the Cold War. *International New York Times.*
Smale, A., & Alderman, L. (2014, September 22). Growing imbalance between Germany and France strains their relationship. *New York Times.*
Snyder, T. (2015, March 16). Russlands neokoloniales Projekt. *Frankfurter Allgemeine Zeitung.*
Speck, U. (2012, April). *Why Germany is not becoming Europe's hegemon* (Policy Brief No. 126). Madrid: Fride. http://fride.org/download/PB_126_Germany_not_becoming_Europe_hegemon.pdf
Stark, J. (2015, February 12). German prudence is not to blame for the eurozone ills. *Financial Times.*
Steinmeier, F.-W. (2015, March 12). Save our trans-Atlantic order. *International New York Times.*
Stephens, P. (2013, September 12). The audacity of stealth – Merkel's plan for the euro. *Financial Times.*

Stephens, P. (2014a, May 30). A diminished France could spell the end of Europe. *Financial Times*.

Stephens, P. (2014b, May 10). German angst is leading Europe back to Yalta. *Financial Times*.

Stephens, P. (2014c, November 7). After 25 years Germany needs a foreign policy. *Financial Times*.

Stephens, P. (2015a, February 13). Guns are only half an answer for Ukraine. *Financial Times*.

Stephens, P. (2015b, February 6). Ukraine is only part of Putin's game plan. *Financial Times*.

Stokes, B., & Bell, J. (2013, May 13). *The new sick man of Europe: The European Union*. Washington, DC, Pew Research Center. http://www.pewglobal.org/files/2013/05/Pew-Research-Center-Global-Attitudes-Project-European-Union-Report-FINAL-FOR-PRINT-May-13-2013.pdf

Stokes, B., & Oates, R. (2014, May 12). *A fragile rebound for EU image on European Parliament elections*. Washington, DC, Pew Research Center. http://www.pewglobal.org/files/2014/05/2014-05-12_Pew-Global-Attitudes-European-Union.pdf

Taylor, P. (2014, June 10). Latest risk for the euro: Bitter politics. *International New York Times*.

Taylor, P. (2015, February 3). Greece rocks the E.U.'s centrist pact. *International New York Times*.

Techau, J. (2013a, June 18). *Why Germany won't be America's new geopolitical partner*. Carnegie Europe, Brussels. http://carnegieeurope.eu/strategiceurope/?fa=52126

Techau, J. (2013b, September 20). Chancellor Merkel's double vision. *New York Times*.

The Economist. (2013a, May 4). A tandem in trouble. *The Economist*. http://www.economist.com/news/europe/21577100-european-union-fretting-over-widening-gulf-between-two-partners-have-always

The Economist. (2013b, June 29). The occasional leader. *The Economist*. http://www.economist.com/news/europe/21580174-do-not-expect-germany-play-bigger-or-more-strategic-role-any-time-soon-occasional-leader

The Economist. (2013c, September 14). One woman to rule them all. *The Economist*. http://www.economist.com/news/leaders/21586343-german-voters-should-re-elect-angela-merkel-their-chancellorand-europes-leader-one-woman

The Economist. (2014a, October 15). The pendulum swings to the pit. *The Economist*. http://economist.com/node/21627625

The Economist. (2014b, October 25). The pendulum swings to the pit. *The Economist*.

The Economist. (2014c, May 26). The Eurosceptic union. *The Economist*. http://www.economist.com/blogs/charlemagne/2014/05/european-elections-0

The Economist. (2015a, January 17). The era of Syriza. *The Economist*. http://www.economist.com/node/21639524/

The Economist. (2015b, January 26). Greece turns, Europe wobbles. *The Economist*. http://www.economist.com/node/21640746

The Economist. (2015c, February 28). A lurch onto the world stage. *The Economist*. http://www.economist.com/node/21645223

The Federal Chancellor. (2015a, March 30). Speech by Federal Chancellor Dr Angela Merkel at the University of Helsinki on "European Security and the Conflict in Ukraine", Helsinki. http://www.bundeskanzlerin.de/Content/EN/Reden/2015/2015-03-30-merkel-helsinki_en.html

The Federal Chancellor. (2015b, February 7). Speech by Federal Chancellor Angela Merkel on the occasion of the 51st Munich Security Conference, Munich. http://www.bundeskanzlerin.de/Content/EN/Reden/2015/2015-02-07-merkel-sicherheitskonferenz_en.html

The White House. (2015, February 9). Remarks by President Obama and Chancellor Merkel in Joint Press Conference, Washington, DC. http://www.whitehouse.gov/the-press-office/2015/02/09/remarks-president-obama-and-chancellor-merkel-joint-press-conference

Thurau, J. (2013, April 22). Merkel: 'Streben nach Hegemonie ist mir fremd'. *Deutsche Welle*. http://www.dw.de/merkel-streben-nach-hegemonie-ist-mir-fremd/a-16762690

U.S. Diplomatic Mission in Germany. (1989, May 31). Remarks by President George Bush to the Citizens of Mainz, Mainz. http://usa.usembassy.de/etexts/ga6-890531.htm

Védrine, H. (2000). *L'hyperpuissance americaine*. Paris: Fondation Jean Jaurès.

Wagstyl, S. (2014, August 6). German diplomacy: Dominant by default. *Financial Times.*

Wanner, M., & Bulmahn, T. (2013, August). *Sicherheits- und verteidigungspolitisches Meinungsklima in der Bundesrepublik Deutschland. Ergebnisse einer Bevölkerungsumfrage 2012.* Potsdam: Zentrum für Militärgeschichte und Sozialwissenschaften der Bundeswehr. http://www.mgfa-potsdam.de/html/einsatzunterstuetzung/downloads/sicherheitspolitik.pdf?PHPSESSID=92bb8

Wergin, C. (2014, May 6). Why Germans love Russia. *New York Times.*

Winkler, H. A. (2006). *Germany: The long road west. Volume I: 1789–1933.* Oxford: Oxford University Press.

Winkler, H. A. (2007). *Germany: The Long Road West. Volume II: 1933–1990.* Oxford: Oxford University Press.

Winkler, H. A. (2014, July 18). Ein ziemlich deutscher Pazifismus. *Süddeutsche Zeitung.*

Witte, G. (2015, January 25). Greeks emphatically reject austerity, elect Syriza in a historic vote. *Washington Post.* http://www.washingtonpost.com/world/greeks-expected-to-elect-leftist-syriza-party-in-sunday-vote/2015/01/25/6e273dea-a246-11e4-91fc-7dff95a14458_story.html

Wolf, M. (2010, March 10). Germany's eurozone crisis nightmare. *Financial Times.*

Wolf, M. (2014a, March 12). The spectre of Eurozone deflation. *Financial Times.*

Wolf, M. (2014b, April 10). Only the ignorant live in fear of hyperinflation. *Financial Times.*

Wolf, M. (2014c, May 14). Time for Draghi to open the sluice. *Financial Times.*

Wolf, M. (2015a, February 18). Unbalanced hopes for the world economy. *Financial Times.*

Wolf, M. (2015b, January 28). Greek debt and a default of statesmanship. *Financial Times.*

World Economic Forum. (2014, January 24). *Global economic outlook 2014.* Davos. http://www.weforum.org/sessions/summary/global-economic-outlook-2014

Yardley, J., & Alderman, L. (2015, January 26). Greeks vote in austerity foes, a major shift. *New York Times.*

Chapter 6
"Merkelism" and the "New Normal"

What are we left with after more than 5 years of step-by-step euro crisis management? If there was ever logic to Merkel's cautious step-by-step policy, it has been exhausted. Persistent stagnation is the the price of her muddling through the crisis policy and this has become "the new, dismal normal" (Portes and Weil 2014; Krugman 2014a; Münchau 2014a)[1] where the German prescription of austerity, regardless of the economic circumstances, coupled with structural changes threatens to turn the euro area misery belt into a long-term malaise of meagre growth, staggering joblessness, towering public debt and damaging deflation. If prolonged cyclical stagnation becomes the new, dismal normal, the political risk that one or two countries decide to leave the monetary union increases over the next critical years.[2]

Merkel does indeed see a certain amount of accommodation and compromise as necessary to preserve the monetary union as she demonstrated at the near-breakup of the euro in summer 2012. But her tactical skills may become her strategic liability. Merkel's temporizing step-by-step approach to prevent a disintegration of the currency union cannot work indefinitely. Time and again, the ECB has stood up while governments and parliaments dithered. "The standard pattern has been to do the right thing between 6 and 18 months too late, the delay generally originating in Frankfurt and Berlin."[3] It was Mario Draghi's pledge "to do whatever it takes" that has managed to quiet financial markets by making it clear that the ECB would not allow the euro zone to unravel. His "Bazooka" prevented a catastrophic collapse in summer 2012 and provided euro member countries some breathing space to address the structural problems laid open by the crisis. But his highly contested OMT program has not averted further deterioration of the peripheral economies and

[1] ibid, Why economics failed, New York Times, May 3, 2014

[2] That sinking feeling (again), *The Economist*, August 30, 2014 [http://www.economist.com/node/21614137/].

[3] ECB's Mario Draghi and his misguided malcontents, *Financial Times*, October 3, 2014.

F.-J. Meiers, *Germany's Role in the Euro Crisis*,
DOI 10.1007/978-3-319-20514-4_6

their slow slide to insolvency. The Eurozone economy looks like a patient with a chronic illness. The fundamental crisis of the euro area has not been resolved, and another year of Merkel's preferred step-by-step policy could revive these risks in a more virulent form in the coming years.

The sovereign debt crisis revealed the fatal flaws of Germany's ordoliberal economic model based on predictability and certainty. Germany's intellectual starting point is "national resources for national problems".[4] The certainties of the export-driven ordoliberal model that underpinned its postwar success cannot be carried over to the larger and more diverse euro area economy. Ordoliberalism emphasizes national responsibility at the expense of the financial and economic consequences of interconnected economies. German policymakers have to understand the connection between interdependence and collective action. The ECB was established in the tradition of the Bundesbank. But there is a fundamental difference between both institutions sharing the same mandate to guarantee price stability. "The ECB is not responsible for just one country, but 19. The instruments that is has to fulfill this mandate are different. That is... the message that some in Germany must understand," Mr. Draghi pointed out.[5] Christine Lagarde put the message to Berlin this way. The architects of the IMF and the World Bank looked beyond the deceptive lure of unvarnished sovereignty. They "were determined to set a new course—based on mutual trust and co-operation, on the principle that peace and prosperity flow from the font of co-operation, on the belief that the broad global interest trumps narrow self-interest" (Lagarde 2014; Stephens 2014). For a globally networked country, markets and economies are inextricably linked by an ever thickening thread of economic and financial transactions. Interdependence cannot be wished away; rising turbulence in the euro area and beyond may yet exact a toll on Germany. The reality of complex interdependence cuts both ways: Germany cannot succeed without Europe and vice versa! The imperative of collective action means that Europe's central power must share responsibility for post-crisis economic adjustment. German decision makers need to embrace

The central question is: how does Germany's behaviour determine the stability and success of the Eurozone economy as a whole from which it benefits so much and for which it bears large responsibilities? (Wolf 2014c) The German decision makers need to embrace an "all for one, one for all" mindset or what Christine Lagarde called the "new multilateralism." It is far better "to welcome the Three Musketeers than the Four Horsemen of the Apocalypse" (King 2014; International Monetary Fund 2015). The three largest economies—Germany, France and Italy—hold the answer to overcome their deep divisions over austerity versus growth and take concerted action to revive the Eurozone's moribund economy and help the

[4] Mujtaba Rahman, director for Europe at the Eurasian Group, quoted by James Kanter, Germany a hurdle to EU unity on banks, *International Herald Tribune*, July 11, 2013.

[5] European Central Bank, Interview with Mario Draghi with Die Zeit on December 17, 2014, published on January 15, 2015 [https://ecb.europa.eu.press/inter/date/2015/html/sp150115.en.html].

euro area escaping a continuous slide into Japanization (Enderlein and Pisani-Ferry 2014; Kaletsky 2014; Rehn and Arthuis 2014).

German decision-makers show a profound uneasiness to get along on economic and fiscal issues in an imperfect, unpredictable and unstable world who still "assume a natural equilibrium of a future that is predictable." They have to recognize "the new economic thinking" that a highly unpredictable world economy can only be managed "with fairly broad and flexible tolerance ranges for indicators such as inflation, government borrowing or unemployment, instead of the precise inflation targets of the pre-crisis period" (Kaletsky 2013; Bremmer and Roubini 2013). Extraordinary times call for extraordinary measures that run counter to the certainties of Germany's rigid, rule-based ordoliberal economic model. As Mario Draghi succinctly put it, "In exceptional times, regaining stability sometimes requires exceptional measures. We cannot always look to the past for answers."[6] It may take "a witches' brew" (Greetham 2014) of "monetary, fiscal and structural measures at the union level and at the national level", Mr. Draghi said. He believes that there is "scope for a greater role of fiscal policy alongside monetary policy." The Eurozone needs a "more growth-friendly composition of fiscal policies" to promote "aggregate demand" provided governments engage in "necessary structural reforms".[7]

And Berlin must accept the economic logic of sequencing monetary, fiscal and structural changes rightly. What matters is the order in which governments and central banks implement monetary, fiscal and structural accommodation. "It's about how you adjust to a change in circumstances", Angel Guerría, the Secretary-General of the OECD, pointed out.[8] Structural reforms are critical, but do little to promote aggregate demand in the medium-term as Germany experienced in the first decade of the 2000s after the introduction of Chancellor Schröder's Agenda 2010.[9] Deep cuts in public spending should not be front-loaded because

---

[6] European Central Bank, *Introductory statement by Mario Draghi to the press conference (with Q&A)*, Frankfurt am Main, September 6, 2012 [http://www.ecb.europa.eu/press/pressconf/2012/html/is120906.en.html].

[7] European Central Bank, *Speech by Mario Draghi at Symposium in Jackson Hole*, op. cit.; James Kanter, European Finance Ministers Support Investment Program, *New York Times*, September 15, 2014; European Central Bank, *Keynote speech by Benoît Cœuré, Member of the Executive Board of the ECB, Economic conference, Latvijas Banka*, Riga, October 17, 2014 [https://www.ecb.europa.eu/press/key/date/2014/html/sp141017.en.html]; Organization for Economic Cooperation and Development, *Interim Economic Assessment*, op. cit., p. 7; ibid., *Economic Outlook, Volume 2014/2*, op. cit., pp. 10, 15, 55–63; International Monetary Fund, World Economic Outlook. Uneven Growth: Short- und Long-Term Factors, Washington, DC, April 14, 2015, p. 48, 50.

[8] Organization for Economic Cooperation and Development, *Remarks by Angel Guerría, Secretary-General, delivered at the Breakfast with Journalists on the occasion of the Economic Outlook*, Paris, November 25, 2014 [http://www.oecd.org/about/secretary-general/breakfast-journalists-economic-outlook-launch.htm]; ibid., *Putting the euro area on a road to recovery*, Presentation of the OECD Economic Outlook by Catherine L. Mann, op. cit.; ibid., *Economic Outlook, Volume 2014/2*, op. cit., pp. 10, 12, 13, 55–63.

[9] Sebastian Dullien, *A German Model for Europe?* op. cit.; ibid., German Reforms as a Blueprint for Europe, op. cit.

they reduce growth in the short-term and may bear fruit only in the long-run. Fiscal adjustments implemented by national governments in an environment of persistent lowflation may even increase the risk of deflationary pressures which will further aggravate the debt problems of the weak euro area member countries (Bini Smaghi 2014).[10] If monetary expansion is contradicted by premature fiscal consolidation, both policies cancel each other out. Structural reforms would have the same effect as not all member countries can become simultaneously more competitive against each other. The complementarity of the three policy instruments is crucial for a higher growth trajectory. What is needed is a multipronged country-specific strategy that balances fostering growth and manage diverse macroeconomic challenges and not a Teutonic one-policy-fits-all policy which applied by each member country at the same time during a severe recession will only needlessly prolong the downturn of the Eurozone economy for years to come. The current economic problems of the euro area resulted from a "negative aggregate demand shock" and not from "exclusively supply side problems", argued ECB Vice-President Vitor Constâncio. Supply side policies "take time to produce effects and there is a short term horizon of 2–3 years where the question is mostly a situation of lack of aggregate demand and Europe needed to increase growth now in order to avoid vicious circles related with the so-called debt-trap," he concluded.[11] Draghi's new policy mix called Draghinomics or New Deal could provide the comprehensive, concerted and coordinated jolt to bring the sluggish Eurozone economy back to life (Thornhill and Jones 2014; Jones 2014; Münchau 2014b; Wolf 2014a, b; Moghadam 2014).[12] The core question is: will the Merkel government sign up to Draghi's three-pillar strategy?

Merkel's response to the euro crisis has been an uncomfortable balancing act between short-term fire-fighting and working on a long-term strategy to set in place the tools and institutions needed to create a more coherent and resilient monetary union. The handling of the banking union underscores that Berlin makes the case against rushing the process. The Merkel government still fails to recognize that a sustainable monetary union requires reforms deeper than those implemented since May 2010. The failure to press ahead "with a more complete institutional set-up" may be contributing to euro area's sustained economic malaise, argued Jean-Claude Juncker in an "analytical note" distributed to EU leaders at their informal summit meeting in Brussels on February 12, 2015 (Spiegel 2015). Making the currency union work requires more than skillful crisis management. A farsighted approach demands a different kind of vision, reforms and political leadership than Germany

[10] Simon Tilford, *How to safe the euro*, op. cit., p. 7; U.S. Department of the Treasury. Office of International Affairs. *Report to Congress on International Economic and Exchange Rate Policies*, op.cit., p. 25.

[11] European Central Bank, *Monetary policy challenges in the euro area*, Speech by ECB Vice-President Vitor Constâncio at the Annual Conference of the Marshall Society, Cambridge, January 31, 2015 [https://www.ecb.europa.eu/press/key/date/2015/html/sp150131_1.en.html].

[12] Editorial, Mario Draghi's vision for eurozone growth, *Financial Times*, September 13/14, 2014

has shown so far. If the euro has become fundamental to the concept of „Europe", [13] then far deeper economic, fiscal and political integration is needed. As Mario Draghi observed, if member countries want "a genuine monetary union,. . .we need to move from a system of rules and guidelines for national economic policy making to a system of further sovereignty sharing within common institutions so as to strengthen our economic policy governance."[14] A more perfect monetary union calls for a full banking union with significant risk-sharing elements, i.e. a Eurozone-wide bank resolution regime and a deposit and guarantee fund and a fiscal union than can absorb idiosyncratic shocks to specific member states by a federal budget, i.e. a mutualization of national debt and a taxpayer-funded backstop (Enderlein and Fritz-Vannahme 2014; Dawson et al. 2015).[15]

Merkel's cautious incremental policy approach illustrates the mismatch between the supranational imperatives of a more perfect monetary union she has pledged to protect and the political reality where the decision making remains national. Her adherence to Schröder's maxim that all vital decisions are made in Berlin shows a creeping lack of political readiness to tackle the most pressing problems still hanging over the Eurozone (Giugliano 2014; Warner 2013; Peet and La Guardia 2014).[16] The Chancellor's sedative style of governing and communicating may well appeal to her domestic audience. However, her inclination to heed opinion polls underlines her (parochial) understanding of how best to use her power: "amassed but unused."[17] Merkel's penchant for a balanced approach has blinded

[13] See Chancellor Merkel's speech to parliament on Mrach 19, 2015 and her press conference with Greek Prime Minister Tsirpas on March 23, 2015. Deutscher Bundestag, *Plenarprotokoll, 18/94*, Berlin, March 19, 2015, p. 8885; Die Bundeskanzlerin, *Pressekonferenz der Bundeskanzlerin und des griechischen Ministerpräsidenten Tsirpas*, Berlin, March 23, 2015 [http://www.bundeskanzlerin.de/Content/DE/Mitschrift/Pressekonferenzen/2015/03/215-03-23-merkel-tsipras.html]; Ralph Bollmann, Scheitert der Euro, scheitert Europa, *Frankfurter Allgemeine Sonntgaszeitung*, March 22, 2015.

[14] European Central Bank, *Introductory Statement to the European Parliament on the ECB Annual Report 2013*, op. cit. See also ibid., *Introductory statement to the press conference (with Q&A) Mario Draghi, President of the ECB, Vítor Constâncio, Vice-President of the ECB*, Barcelona, May 3, 2012 [http://www.ecb.europa.eu/press/pressconf/2012/html/is120503.en.html]; 'We couldn't just sit back and do nothing', Interview with ECB President Mario Draghi, *Spiegel Online*, October 29, 2012 [http://www.spiegel.de/international/europe/spiegel-interview-with-ecb-president-mario-draghi-a-863971-druck.html]; European Central Bank, *Stability and Prosperity in Monetary Union*, Speech by Mario Draghi, at the University of Helsinki, Helsinki, November 27, 2014 [https://www.ecb.europa.eu/press/key/date/2014/html/sp141127_1.en.html]; ibid., *Introductory remarks at the Finnish parliament*, Speech by Mario Draghi, Helsinki, November 27, 2014 [https://www.ecb.europa.eu/press/key/date/2014/html/sp141127.en.html]. See also Mark Dawson, Henrik Enderlein, and Christian Joerges, *Where Do the EU and the EMU Go From Here?* in The Governance Report. Eurozone Crisis, Economic Governance, Institutional Dilemmas, Constitutionalism, Indicators, ed. by Hertie School of Governance, Oxford: Oxford University Press 2015, pp. 121–126.

[15] Marcel Fratzscher, *Die Deutschland-Illusion*, op. cit., pp. 211–212, 220–232

[16] Fratzscher, M., *Die Deutschland-Illusion*, op. cit., pp. 207–211, 220–232

[17] Sedating not leading, *The Economist*, October 25, 2014 [http://www.economist.com/node/21625790/comments]; Philip Stephens, The stand-off that may sink the euro, *Financial Times*, January 30, 2015; ibid., Europe faces more than a Greek tragedy, *Financial Times*, April 10, 2015.

her into assuming that "finding a compromise is more important than making a choice" (Privitera 2015). Given the scale and advanced stage of the euro crisis, her signature style step-by-step policy approach has reached its limits.

Far greater ambitions mean the acceptance Draghi's grand bargain and the imperative of much deeper, economic, fiscal and monetary integration. The unprecedented economic, fiscal and political challenges facing the Eurozone can only be met if all decision-makers and European institutions act together by taking a comprehensive policy approach that spans fiscal, monetary and structural dimensions. The German government has to walk a fine line between domestic demands that the rules of the Stability and Growth Pact apply equally to all euro member countries and the need not to sow additional seeds of doubt in Germany's commitment to the long-term stability of the euro area and to avoid undermining the grand bargain with France on which the durability of the monetary union critically depends (Münchau 2014c; Rachman 2014; Wolf 2013).[18]

Mr. Draghi's speech at Jackson Hole made explicitly clear: the Eurozone economy is in a mess so grave that "doing too little" is no longer the answer. This may well be a last chance to save the euro economy from another full-scale recession and a deflationary downswing which feed each other in a vicious circle. The stakes for the currency union are high, Mr. Draghi pointed out. "Given the very high costs if the cohesion of the union is threatened, all countries should have an interest in achieving this."[19] Berlin cannot ignore the enormous dangers that come with inaction! If Chancellor Merkel sticks to the categorical imperatives of the ordoliberal recipe as a "mystic panacea" at a time of sluggish growth, towering unemployment, staggering public debt and a too prolonged period of lowflation, she not only unmasks her sober, problem-solving "Merkel method" as hollow words, but she also confirms Albert Einstein's definition of insanity "to keep trying the same thing over and over again and expecting different results" (Meyerson 2014; Luce 2014; Lane 2014; Krugman 2014b).[20] Berlin's unchanged message to its euro area partners: stay the course of fiscal rigour and structural reforms even if your economy remains slumped in a protracted recession makes a Thelma & Louise style plunge into the abyss of a prolonged cyclical stagnation inevitable—call it the German vision of (euro) brinkmanship. Or as Stanley Hoffmann once put it: "The hell of good intentions" (Hoffmann 1977).

Merkel's political career has been built on caution—weighing all options before acting, step-by-step. If the past is the guide to the future, the Chancellor will take action only if the very existence of the monetary union is at stake. "...we are there when there's a need," Wolfgang Schäuble said (Jones and Giles 2014). Responding effectively to a prolonged cyclical stagnation however, requires resolute action by

---

See also Dirk Kurbjuweit, *Alternativlos. Merkel, die Deutschen und das Ende der Republik*, München: Carl Hanser Verlag 2014.

[18] ibid., Courts, voters and the threat of another euro crisis, *Financial Times*, February 11, 2014.

[19] European Central Bank, *Speech by Mario Draghi at Symposium in Jackson Hole*, op. cit.; Benoît Cœuré and Jörg Asmussen, *A three-pillar-strategy for the Euro*, op. cit.

[20] Europe's unbalanced answer to weak growth, *Financial Times*, November 14/15, 2014

national authorities and other European authorities. "The issue now is not diagnosis, it is delivery. It is commitment. And it is timing", Mr. Draghi summed up the urgent need for policy makers to act and act quickly to dispel the spectre of stagnation haunting the euro area economy.[21] Political decision makers have to move beyond "status quo policies" which have not restored "strong, sustainable and balanced growth" but "become recipes for a deeper slump" and a drive "into a deflationary trap".[22] More than ever, the euro area badly needs strong political leadership to respond effectively and decisively to drawn-out depression conditions by adopting all levers of economic policy—monetary, fiscal and structural—to find ways to recover lost output and productivity!

Leadership in foreign policy demands an understanding of the interwoven nature of national interests and those of others and promoting these intertwined interests by common actions and common institutions. It also requires making a choice in extraordinary times. Reconciling the external imperatives of deeper integration and a growth-boosting economic policy in a highly intertwined monetary union with the internal constraints imposed by a deep-seated culture of stability and crucial domestic veto players is the true challenge for Chancellor Merkel's analytical step-by-step policy approach. Instead of pursuing self-centred and self-interested national policy, the Merkel government needs to explain to domestic veto players why a more integrated and solidary acting Europe is in the Berlin Republic's best interest. In short, the decisions taken by Berlin in the next critical months and years will determine whether the euro area economy can be pulled out of its protracted stagnation and whether the monetary union can be put on a sound and sustainable footing. Big choices loom.

References

Bini Smaghi, L. (2014, October 11–12). The eurozone's low inflation problem. *Financial Times*.

Bremmer, I., & Roubini, N. (2013, June 17). The new abnormal. *International Investor*. http://www.institutionalinvestor.com/Article/3218470/Ian-Bremmer-and-Nouriel-Roubini-Unveil-the-New-Abnormal.html#.UycP24WkYug

Dawson, M., Enderlein, H., & Joerges, C. (2015). *Where do the EU and the EMU go from here?* In Hertie School of Governance (Eds.), *The governance report. Eurozone crisis, economic governance, institutional dilemmas, constitutionalism, indicators*. Oxford: Oxford University Press.

Enderlein, H., & Fritz-Vannahme, J. (2014). *Repair and prepare: Strengthening Europe's economies after the crisis*. Gütersloh and Berlin: Bertelsmann Stiftung & Jacques Delors Institut—Berlin. https://www.bertelsmann-stiftung.de/fileadmin/files/user_upload/Pilot_Study_Repair_and_Prepare.pdf

[21] European Central Bank, *Recovery and Reform in the euro area*, Opening remarks by Mario Draghi, Brookings Institution, op. cit.

[22] U.S. Department of the Treasury, Remarks of Secretary Jacob J. Lew at the World Affairs Council of Seattle on *Building a Stronger Global Economy*, op. cit.; Paul Krugman, Apologizing to Japan, *New York Times*, October 31, 2014; ibid., Much too responsible, *New York Times*, January 23, 2015.

Enderlein, H., & Pisani-Ferry, J. (2014, November 27). *Reforms, investment and growth: An agenda for France, Germany and Europe*, Berlin. http://www.bmwi.de/BMWi/Redaktion/PDF/Publikationen/empfehlung-enderlein-pisani-ferry,property=pdf,bereich=bmwi2012,sprache=de,rwb=true.pdf

Giugliano, F. (2014, July 7). Unhappy union: How the euro crisis – and Europe – Can be fixed. *Financial Times*.

Greetham, T. (2014, August 21). Time to dust off old euro crisis strategies. *Financial Times*.

Hoffmann, S. (1977–1978, Winter). The hell of good intentions. *Foreign Policy, 29*, 3–26.

International Monetary Fund. (2015, January 15). *Three "Rosetta Moments" for the Global Economy in 2015* by Christine Lagarde, Managing Director, Washington, D.C. http://www.imf.org/external/np/speeches/2015/011515.htm (See also Wolf, M., *The shifts and the Shocks*, op.cit., p. 326).

Jones, C. (2014, September 3). Eurozone: Draghi's new deal. *Financial Times*.

Jones, C., & Giles, C. (2014, October 14). Germany's woes centre attention at IMF meetings. *Financial Times*.

Kaletsky, A. (2013, April 5). A new era of imperfect solutions. *International Herald Tribune*.

Kaletsky, A. (2014, August 29). Will Merkel help save Europe? *International New York Times*.

King, S. (2014, September 12). To survive, the eurozone must embrace an "all for one, one for all" mindset. *Financial Times*.

Krugman, P. (2014a, March 21). The timidity trap. *New York Times*.

Krugman, P. (2014b, December 1). Being bad Europeans. *New York Times*.

Lagarde, C. (2014, February 3). *A new multilateralism for the 21st century: The Richard Dimbleby Lecture*, London. http://www.imf.org/external/np/speeches/2014/020314.htm

Lane. (2014, November 12). From Germany, an economic Berlin Wall. *Washington Post*. http://www.washingtonpost.com/opinions/charles-lane-from-germany-an-economic-berlin-wall/2014/11/12/e8d8deb4-6a8c-11e4-a31c-77759fc1eacc_story.html

Luce, E. (2014, October 6). Blinded EU can learn from one-eyed US. *Financial Times*.

Meyerson, H. (2014, October 15). Economically, Germany is a threat to itself. *Washington Post*.

Moghadam, R. (2014, October 11–12). To keep its union together, Europe has to break its economic taboos. *Financial Times*.

Münchau, W. (2014a, April 28). Confidence is a poor measure of economic health. *Financial Times*.

Münchau, W. (2014b, September 8). What Mario Draghi must do next to fix Europe's economy. *Financial Times*.

Münchau, W. (2014c, September 29). Germany's eurosceptics sow the seeds of turmoil. *Financial Times*.

Peet, J., & La Guardia, A. (2014). *Unhappy union: How the euro crisis – and Europe – can be fixed*. London: Profile Books Ltd.

Portes, R., & Weil, P. (2014, August 21). Draghi has to do, as well as say, whatever it takes. *Financial Times*.

Privitera, A. (2015, January 13). *What kind of QE?* Washington, DC: American Institute for Contemporary German Studies. http://www.aicgs.org/issue/what-kind-of-qe/

Rachman, G. (2014, October 21). Borders and budgets could lay Europe low. *Financial Times*.

Rehn, O., & Arthuis, J. (2014, October 30). Largest economies must fix the Eurozone. *Financial Times*.

Spiegel, P. (2015, February 13). Juncker revives Eurozone integration proposals. *Financial Times*.

Stephens, P. (2014, February 13). Yelen, tapering and a moribund G20. *Financial Times*.

Thornhill, J., & Jones, C. (2014, September 8). Economists hail birth of Draghinomics. *Financial Times*.

Warner, J. (2013, August 24). Is Europe still in crisis? *The Telegraph*. http://www.telegraph.co.uk/finance/financialcrisis/10263089/Is-Europe-still-in-crisis.html

Wolf, M. (2013, November 12). Why Draghi was right to cut rates. *Financial Times*.

Wolf, M. (2014a, September 10). Europe has to do whatever it takes. *Financial Times*.

Wolf, M. (2014b, October 22). Reform alone is no solution for the eurozone. *Financial Times*.

Wolf, M. (2014c, December 10). Europe's lonely and reluctant hegemon. *Financial Times*.

MIX
Papier aus verantwortungsvollen Quellen
Paper from responsible sources
FSC® C105338

If you have any concerns about our products,
you can contact us on
ProductSafety@springernature.com

In case Publisher is established outside the EU,
the EU authorized representative is:
Springer Nature Customer Service Center GmbH
Europaplatz 3, 69115 Heidelberg, Germany

Printed by Libri Plureos GmbH
in Hamburg, Germany